THE UNIVERSITY OF CHICAGO

AREAL INTERACTION IN INDIA:
Commodity Flows
of the Bengal-Bihar
Industrial Area.

DEPARTMENT OF GEOGRAPHY

RESEARCH PAPER NO. 110

By

WALLACE E. REED

Duke University

1967
Research Papers
1101 E. 58th Street
Chicago, Illinois 60637

Library of Congress Catalog Card Number: 66-29234

ACKNOWLEDGEMENTS

"India a land of unity and diversity." Unity and diversity is certainly reflected in the wonderful friends and diverse organizations who have encouraged this study of Indian commodity flows. Each shares the author's deepest gratitude and each holds a separate and special place in his life.

My warmest thanks go to the three professors and friends who have seen me through my student life: Professor Harold Mayer who opened the world of planning and geography to me and gave direction to my early steps; Professor Norton Ginsburg who introduced me to South Asia and guided me through its many grandeurs and bustees; and particularly Professor Brian Berry who showed me the way through India's teeming railway yards. Special thanks go also to Professor Chauncy Harris for his many ideas and suggestions. Working with the faculty and fellow students of the University of Chicago's Geography Department has been a rare honor and privilege.

In the Indian Phase of my research, no one was more helpful and encouraging than Dr. Leslie P. Green, Director of the Institute of Public Administration, New York, Calcutta Studies Program. Special thanks go also to my Indian colleagues in this program, Dr. Ranajit Dhar and Mr. P. N. Sinha, and to all of my other friends associated with the IPA group. Friends in the Calcutta Metropolitan Planning Organization and its Ford Foundation advisory team were all helpful in this study, and I am especially grateful to each.

I wish also to thank my colleagues in the Economics and Sociology Departments at Duke University for their advice and encouragement. Chats with Professor H. H. Winsborough were particularly stimulating and useful.

In addition to the friendship and help of individuals, financial support for this study was generously provided through the University of Chicago South Asian Studies Program and Department of Geography Fellowships, an Institute of Public Administration, New York, Calcutta Studies Program Fellowship, and National Defense Foreign

Language Fellowships under Title VI of the National Defense Education Act. Ample computing facilities were provided by the computer centers of the University of Chicago and Duke University.

Of course my deepest gratitude and affection goes to my parents, Elzie and Sue Reed, who have seen me through it all, to my sturdy and loving wife, Kathy, who shared and suffered, and to Lynn and Jim who kindly slept during the later phases of writing.

Although I can only say thanks, to each and all is owed more than I can ever express.

Wallace E. Reed
Duke University
Durham, North Carolina
July, 1967

TABLE OF CONTENTS

Page

ACKNOWLEDGEMENTS   iii

LIST OF TABLES   vii

LIST OF ILLUSTRATIONS   x

Chapter

I.   INDIAN ECONOMIC REGIONALIZATION AND THE BENGAL-BIHAR
     INDUSTRIAL AREA   1

     Economic Regions
     Indian Economic Regions
     Commodity Flows and Indian Regional Analysis

II. THE STUDY AREA AND DATA   11

     The Eastern India Industrial Region
     The Bengal-Bihar Industrial Area
     The Data

III. ROLES AND EXCHANGES OF THE BENGAL-BIHAR INDUSTRIAL
     AREA   26

     Economic Regions and Exchange Patterns
     Roles and Exchange Patterns of the Bengal-Bihar
         Industrial Area

IV. STATION EXCHANGES AND THE ROLES OF OTHER SPECIALIZED
     AREAS   61

     Individual Station Exchanges and Locational Effects
     Roles of Other Specialized Areas with Respect to the
         to the Study Area

V.   THE BENGAL-BIHAR INDUSTRIAL AREA IN THE INDIAN NATIONAL
     ECONOMY   96

     The Indian and United States Economies: Comparison
         of Spatial Organization
     Relative Location, Specialization, and Exchange
     The Bengal-Bihar Industrial Area and the Spatial
         Structure of the Indian Economy

v

Page

Chapter

VI.   BENGAL-BIHAR INDUSTRIAL AREA EXCHANGES, SUPPLY,
      DEMAND AND DISTANCE EFFECTS   145

      Outflows
      Inflows
      Explaining Additional Variation in Study-Area
          Exchange
      Summary

VII. BENGAL-BIHAR INDUSTRIAL AREA TRADE AND AREAL
      INTERACTION IN INDIA   197

      Planning and Bengal-Bihar Industrial Area
          Exchanges

SELECTED BIBLIOGRAPHY   204

LIST OF TABLES

Table   Page

1. Indian Economic Regions (1959 Trade Blocks)   6

2. Study-Area Station Groups   17

3. Commodity Groups   22

4. Percentage by Commodity of Total Inflows from All of India to Study-
   Area Stations   32

5. Percentage by Commodity of Total Outflows to All of India from
   Study-Area Stations   34

6. Percentage of Total Inflows to Study-Area Stations from Regions
   of India   55

7. Percentage of Total Outflows from Study-Area Stations to Regions
   of India   55

8. Percentage of Total Inflows of Selected Commodities by Area   58

9. Percentage of Total Outflows of Selected Commodities by Area   59

10. Flows by Commodity to Study-Area Stations from the City of Calcutta
    as a Percentage of Total Flows from All of India to Study-Area
    Stations   76

11. Flows by Commodity to Study-Area Stations from the Calcutta
    Metropolitan Area as a Percentage of Total Flows from All of
    India to Study-Area Stations   78

12. Flows by Commodity from Study-Area Stations to the City of Calcutta
    as a Percentage of Total Flows to All of India from Study-Area
    Stations   80

13. Flows by Commodity from Study-Area Stations to the Calcutta
    Metropolitan Area as a Percentage of Total Flows to All of
    India from Study-Area Stations   82

14. Flows by Commodity to Study-Area Stations from the Five Surrounding
    Districts as a Percentage of Total Flows from All of India to Study-
    Area Stations   84

15. Flows by Commodity to Study-Area Stations from the Five Surrounding
    Districts as a Percentage of Total Flows to All of India from Study-
    Area Stations   86

LIST OF TABLES--<u>Continued</u>

Table   Page

16. Flows by Commodity to Study-Area Stations from the Calcutta Region
     as a Percentage of Total Flows from All of India to Study-Area
     Stations   88

17. Flows by Commodity from Study-Area Stations to the Calcutta Region
     as a Percentage of Total Flows to All of India from the Study-Area . . 90

18. Flows by Commodity to Study-Area Stations from Outside Calcutta
     and the Calcutta Region as a Percentage of Total Flows from All
     of India to Study-Area Stations   92

19. Flows by Commodity from Study-Area Stations to Points Outside Calcutta
     and the Calcutta Region as a Percentage of Total Flows to All of India
     from Study-Area Stations   94

20. Relation of Total Outflows to Urban Population and Distance   147

21. Relation of Selected Outflows to Urban Population and Other Selected
     Demand Variables   149

22. Simple Correlation of Outflows with Selected Demand and Distance
     Variables   149

23. Relation of Selected Outflows to Distance   150

24. Relation of Selected Outflows to Combined Demand and Distance Effects. .   152

25. The Potential Model for Selected Outflows   152

26. Variation in the Volume of Selected Commodity Outflows to the Calcutta
     Economic Region and to the Rest of India   153

27. Relation of Selected Outflows to Combined Demand and Distance Effect
     for the Calcutta Economic Region and the Rest of India   154

28. Relation of Total Inflows to Urban Population and Distance   158

29. Simple Correlation of Inflows, Supply and Distance   159

30. Relation of Selected Inflows to Selected Supply Variables   160

31. Relation of Selected Inflows to Distance   162

32. Relation of Selected Inflows to Combined Supply and Distance Effects . .   164

33. The Potential Model for Selected Inflows   165

34. Variation in the Volume of Selected Inflows from the Calcutta Economic
     Region and the Rest of India   166

35. Relation of Selected Inflows to Combined Supply and Distance Effects
     for the Calcutta Economic Region and the Rest of India   167

36. Simple Correlation of Distance with Intervening Opportunity Measures . .   173

37. Relation of Selected Outflows to Combined Demand and Intervening
     Opportunity Effects   174

38. Relation of Selected Inflows to Combined Supply and Intervening
     Opportunity Effects   175

Table   Page

39. Correlation of Selected Study-Area Flows, Demand, Supply,
     Intervening Opportunity and Competition Variables 177

40. Relation of Selected Outflows to Combined Demand, Distance,
     Competition and Redistribution Effects 185

41. Correlation of Selected Study-Area Flows and Supply, Demand,
     Distance, Competition, Redistribution and Concentration
     Variables 188

42. Relation of Selected Inflows to Combined Supply, Distance, Competition
     and Concentration Effects 189

43. The Expanded Potential Model for Selected Outflows 191

44. The Expanded Potential Model for Selected Inflows 192

LIST OF ILLUSTRATIONS

Figure   Page

1.   Indian Economic Regions (Based on 1959 Trade Blocks)   5

2.   The Bengal-Bihar Industrial Area in Eastern India: Resources . . .   12

3.   The Bengal-Bihar Industrial Area in Eastern India: Transport and
           Industry   14

4.   The Bengal-Bihar Industrial Area   15

5.   Calcutta Region Districts   36

6.   Bengal-Bihar Industrial Area: Inflows of Non-metallic Minerals
           (% of Total Non-metallic Minerals Inflows)   37

7.   Bengal-Bihar Industrial Area: Inflows of Other Mineral Ores
           (% of Total Other Mineral Ores Inflows)   37

8.   Bengal-Bihar Industrial Area: Inflows of Firebricks (% of Total
           Firebricks Inflows)   38

9.   Bengal-Bihar Industrial Area: Inflows of Lime and Limestone
           (% of Total Lime and Limestone Inflows)   38

10.   Bengal-Bihar Industrial Area: Inflows of Iron, Steel, Cast Iron
           (% of Total Iron, Steel, Cast Iron Inflows)   40

11.   Bengal-Bihar Industrial Area: Inflows of Non-Ferrous Metals
           (% of Total Non-Ferrous Metals Inflows)   40

12.   Bengal-Bihar Industrial Area: Inflows of Machinery (% of Total
           Machinery Inflows)   41

13.   Bengal-Bihar Industrial Area: Inflows of Electrical and Telephone
           Goods (% of Total Electrical and Telephone Goods Inflows)   41

14.   Bengal-Bihar Industrial Area: Inflows of Chemicals and Explosives
           (% of Total Chemicals and Explosives Inflows)   42

15.   Bengal-Bihar Industrial Area: Inflows of Wood Manufactures
           (% of Total Wood Manufactures Inflows)   42

16.   Bengal-Bihar Industrial Area: Inflows of Wheat (% of Total
           Wheat Inflows)   44

17.   Bengal-Bihar Industrial Area: Inflows of Gram (% of Total
           Gram Inflows)   44

Figure   Page

18.   Bengal-Bihar Industrial Areas: Inflows of Cement (% of Total
       Cement Inflows)   45

19.   Bengal-Bihar Industrial Area: Inflows of Wood and Timber, Raw
       (% of Total Wood and Timber, Raw Inflows)   45

20.   Bengal-Bihar Industrial Area: Inflows of Non-Wood Building
       Material (% of Total Non-Wood Building Material Inflows)   46

21.   Bengal-Bihar Industrial Area: Outflows of Coal and Coke
       (% of Total Coal and Coke Outflows)   46

22.   Bengal-Bihar Industrial Area: Outflows of Iron, Steel, Cast Iron
       (% of Total Iron, Steel, Cast Iron Outflows).   50

23.   Bengal-Bihar Industrial Area: Outflows of Non-Ferrous Metals
       (% of Total Non-Ferrous Metals Outflows)   50

24.   Bengal-Bihar Industrial Area: Outflows of Firebricks (% of Total
       Firebrick Outflows)   51

25.   Bengal-Bihar Industrial Area: Outflows of Chemicals and
       Explosives (% of Total Chemicals and Explosives Outflows) . . .   51

26.   Bengal-Bihar Industrial Area: Outflows of Wood Manufactures
       (% of Total Wood Manufactures Outflows)   52

27.   Bengal-Bihar Industrial Area: Outflows of Machinery (% of Total
       Machinery Outflows)   52

28.   Bengal-Bihar Industrial Area: Outflows of Electrical and Telephone
       Goods (% of Total Electrical and Telephone Goods Outflows) . . .   53

29.   Bengal-Bihar Industrial Area: Total Inflows   56

30.   Bengal-Bihar Industrial Area: Total Outflows   56

31.   Raniganj: Inflows of Rice Not in Husk (% of Total Rice Not in Husk
       Inflows to Raniganj)   63

32.   Ranchi: Inflows of Rice Not in Husk (% of Total Rice Not in Husk
       Inflows to Ranchi)   63

33.   Asansol: Inflows of Wheat (% of Total Wheat Inflows to Asansol) . .   64

34.   Dhanbad: Inflows of Wheat (% of Total Wheat Inflows to Dhanbad) . .   64

35.   Asansol: Outflows of Coal and Coke (% of Total Coal and Coke
       Outflows from Asansol)   65

36.   Dhanbad: Outflows of Coal and Coke (% of Total Coal and Coke
       Outflows from Dhanbad)   65

37.   Adra: Outflows of Coal and Coke (% of Total Coal and Coke Outflows
       from Adra)   66

38.   Raniganj: Inflows of Cement (% of Total Cement Inflows to Raniganj).   66

39.   Kharagpur: Inflows of Cement (% of Total Cement Inflows to
       Kharagpur)   67

Figure   Page

40. Durgapur: Outflows of Iron, Steel, Cast Iron (% of Total Iron, Steel, Cast Iron Outflows from Durgapur)   67

41. Burnpur: Outflows of Iron, Steel, Cast Iron (% of Total Iron, Steel, Cast Iron Outflows from Burnpur)   68

42. Jamshedpur: Outflows of Iron, Steel, Cast Iron (% of Total Iron, Steel, Cast Iron Outflows from Jamshedpur)   68

43. Indian Limestone Production Potential with Study-Area Inflows of Limestone   103

44. Indian Iron Ore Production Potential with Study-Area Inflows of Other Mineral Ores   104

45. Indian Electrical Machinery Employment Potential with Study-Area Outflows of Iron, Steel, Scrap Iron   105

46. Indian Other Machinery Employment Potential with Study-Area Outflows of Iron, Steel, Scrap Iron   106

47. Indian Manufacturing Employment Potential with Study-Area Outflows of Iron, Steel, Scrap Iron   107

48. Indian Urban Population Potential with Study-Area Outflows of Iron, Steel, Scrap Iron   108

49. Indian Population Potential with Study-Area Outflows of Iron, Steel, Scrap Iron   109

50. Indian Per Capita Income Potential with Study-Area Outflows of Iron, Steel, Scrap Iron   110

51. Indian Coal Production Potential with Study-Area Outflows of Coal and Coke   111

52. Indian Other Machinery Employment Potential with Study-Area Outflows of Coal and Coke   112

53. Indian Manufacturing Employment Potential with Study-Area Outflows of Coal and Coke   113

54. Indian Urban Population Potential with Study-Area Outflows of Coal and Coke   114

55. Indian Population Potential with Study-Area Outflows of Coal and Coke .   115

56. Indian Other Machinery Employment Potential with Study-Area Inflows of Iron, Steel, Scrap Iron   116

57. Indian Manufacturing Employment Potential with Study-Area Inflows of Iron, Steel, Scrap Iron   117

58. Indian Other Machinery Employment Potential with Study-Area Inflows of Machinery   118

59. Indian Non-Ferrous Metals Employment Potential with Study-Area Inflows of Machinery   119

Figure   Page

60. Indian Manufacturing Employment Potential with Study-Area
     Inflows of Machinery   120

61. Indian Urban Population Potential with Study-Area Inflows of
     Machinery   121

62. Indian Electrical Machinery Employment Potential with Study-Area
     Inflows of Electrical and Telephone Goods   122

63. Indian Chemical Employment Potential with Study-Area Inflows of
     Chemicals and Explosives   123

64. Indian Other Machinery Employment Potential with Study-Area
     Outflows of Machinery   124

65. Indian Manufacturing Employment Potential with Study-Area
     Outflows of Machinery   125

66. Indian Urban Population Potential with Study-Area Outflows of
     Machinery   126

67. Indian Electrical Machinery Employment Potential with Study-Area
     Outflows of Electrical and Telephone Goods   127

68. Indian Other Machinery Employment Potential with Study-Area Out-
     Outflows of Electrical and Telephone Goods   128

69. Indian Manufacturing Employment Potential with Study-Area
     Outflows of Electrical and Telephone Goods   129

70. Indian Chemical Employment Potential with Study-Area Outflows
     of Chemicals and Explosives   130

71. Indian Manufacturing Employment Potential with Study-Area
     Outflows of Chemicals and Explosives   131

72. Indian Wheat Production Potential with Study-Area Inflows of Wheat .   132

73. Indian Gram Production Potential with Study-Area Inflows of Gram,
     Pulses   133

74. Indian Cement Employment Potential with Study-Area Inflows of
     Cement   134

75. Indian Urban Population Potential with Study-Area Total Inflows . . .   135

76. Indian Manufacturing Employment Potential with Study-Area
     Total Inflows   136

77. Indian Urban Population Potential with Study-Area Total Outflows . .   137

78. Indian Manufacturing Employment Potential with Study-Area
     Total Outflows   138

CHAPTER I

INDIAN ECONOMIC REGIONALIZATION AND THE

BENGAL-BIHAR INDUSTRIAL AREA

Among regional analysts and planners, a general view of the structure of the
Indian economy and planning objectives for it has emerged. This view is most clearly
expressed in a recent essay by Friedmann and Alonso.

> . . . the fundamental goal of most transitional societies is their economic and
> social integration in space. Large underdeveloped nations, such as Indonesia and
> India, generally find that their regional elements are insufficiently interrelated,
> that they are nations composed of regional "islands." The struggle is to achieve
> a common ethos and a closely interdependent national economic system. Such
> countries look upon their development as a process leading to the progressive
> internal integration of their national territories. [1]

The purpose of this study is to put some empirical flesh on this general view of the
regional structure of India's economy by examining in detail the spatial interaction of
the Bengal-Bihar Industrial Area with the rest of India. Such an examination provides
a basis for evaluating both this view and planning objectives stemming from it.

Economic Regions

Following Adam Smith's argument, within an economic system any area may
have a relative or comparative cost advantage in the production of certain goods and
services. [2] Therefore it is able to deliver such goods and services to other areas of the
system at a cost lower than they themselves would incur in producing them. Each area

---

[1] John Friedmann and William Alonso, Regional Development and Planning: A
Reader (Cambridge: M. I. T. Press, 1964), p. 4.

[2] Adam Smith, The Wealth of Nations (New York: The Modern Library, 1937),
Book IV, Chapters II and III.

1

specializes in the types of production in which it enjoys a comparative advantage and ex-changes its specialties with other complementary areas of the system.[1] Through trade each area receives a full range of goods and services from the system at the lowest possible cost.

An area's comparative advantage is achieved by minimizing two sets of costs associated with its production and consumption activities. One set involves factors af-fecting the area's costs of production. Such costs are constrained mainly by the region's resource endowment and the skills of its population. The second set relates to an area's exchange costs and is a function of its location relative to other complementary and competing areas of the system. Since the costs of exchange are in large part transpor-tation costs, costs which increase with distance, an area's comparative advantage at any point would be inversely related to the distance separating the area from that point. To minimize its exchange costs, an area would be expected to exchange most heavily with those complementary areas nearest to it.[2]

Constrained by local production costs and the relationship between exchange costs and distance, various areas of an economic system would be expected to specialize and cluster in such a way that complementary exchange of their specialties would incur the lowest total production and exchange costs, yet would provide the widest possible range of goods and services within the cluster. Such clusters of complementary areas with a high proportion of intra-cluster exchange may be termed "economic regions." Such eco-nomic regions might not produce the full range of goods and services they demanded and, to satisfy the full range of their needs, would engage in interregional trade with comple-mentary areas in other regions. These regions linked by interregional trade could be called a "system" of economic regions. Such systems of economic regions may be con-ceived of at any areal scale and the types of specialized activities and degree of intra- and interregional integration within such systems may be inferred from the type and rela-tive magnitude of their exchanges.

According to metropolitan dominance theory, by performing administrative, fi-nancial, assembly, processing and marketing functions for surrounding rural and urban

---

[1] Edward L. Ullman, <u>American Commodity Flow, A Geographical Interpretation of Rail and Water Traffic Based on Principles of Spatial Interchange</u> (Seattle: University of Washington Press, 1957), pp. 20-27.

[2] Walter Isard, <u>Location and Space Economy</u> (Cambridge: M. I. T. Press, 1956), pp. 1-9, develops a similar argument.

areas, cities dominate the economic and social conditions of surrounding regions.[1] Cities mediate many of the flows of goods and services exchanged within an economy. Economic regions based on urban dominance relationships and systems of such regions may thus be identified from patterns of exchange between an economy's cities and the areas surrounding them. To establish the context of this study of regional exchange patterns of the Bengal-Bihar Industrial Area, it will be useful first to examine the extent to which analyses of the spatial structure of the Indian economy have identified economic regions and systems of such regions in India.

Indian Economic Regions

Numerous studies of exchange patterns within the Indian economy have been undertaken. The majority of these studies have focused on highly nodal city-hinterland exchange patterns such as those of Banaras[2] and Calcutta;[3] on the supply and marketing exchanges of specific industries such as iron and steel[4] or agriculture;[5] or on commodity exchanges within specific states such as Madras[6] and Mysore.[7] Although information on the exchange patterns of various cities and major industrial and agricultural activities had been available, no one had attempted to define a system of economic regions for all of India based on the exchange patterns of various activities in such regions.

Recently, a group of geographers and economists has been concerned with

---

[1] Basic references to metropolitan dominance theory and regional urban organization are Donald J. Bogue, The Structure of the Metropolitan Community (Ann Arbor: The University of Michigan Press, 1949); Rupert B. Vance and Sara Smith, "Metropolitan Dominance and Integration," in Rupert B. Vance and Nicholas J. Demerath, eds., The Urban South (Chapel Hill: The University of North Carolina Press, 1954); Otis D. Duncan et al., Metropolis and Region (Baltimore: The Johns Hopkins Press, 1960); and Amos H. Hawley, Human Ecology (New York: The Ronald Press, 1950).

[2] R. L. Singh, Banaras: A Study in Urban Geography (Banaras: Nand Kishore & Bros., 1955).

[3] N. R. Kar, "Economic Character of Metropolitan Sphere of Influence of Calcutta," Geographical Review of India, Vol. XXV, No. 2 (June, 1963).

[4] John E. Brush, "The Iron and Steel Industry of India," Geographical Review, XLII, 1 (1952), 37-55.

[5] India (Republic) Directorate of Economics and Statistics, Indian Agricultural Atlas (2d ed.; New Delhi: Directorate of Economics and Statistics, 1958).

[6] National Council of Applied Economic Research, Economic Atlas of Madras State (New Delhi: National Council of Applied Economic Research, 1962).

[7] Indian Statistical Institute, Mysore State, ed. A. T. A. Learmonth (and L. S. Bhat) (Indian Statistical Series No. 13 and 16) (New York: Asia Publishing House, 1961-62).

defining and analyzing such a system of Indian economic regions. Ranajit Dhar has developed an interregional, intersectoral input-output matrix indicating the proportions of exchange between the sectors and regions with which he was concerned.[1] Beginning with a matrix of commodity exchanges and a matrix of the location and concentration of various economic activities in India, Brian Berry proposed a set of Indian economic regions based on interstate and intermetropolitan exchange.[2]

Berry's analysis of the locational pattern of Indian economic activities and their interstate exchanges by rail confirms the hypothesis that India's space economy is composed of a system of four economic regions Figure 1, Table 1 . Agriculture is the predominant economic activity in each of these regions as in the whole of India, and each region includes nearly a full range of agricultural production. Local industrial activities are oriented to local raw materials and markets and the interregional trade integrating the four regions consists primarily of the most specialized agricultural, mineral, and industrial commodities of each region.

Each regional economy is dominated by the major metropolis of the region (Calcutta, Bombay, Madras, and Delhi). These metropolitan nodes perform the functions of collection, processing, and storage of regional and extra-regional products and the distribution of such products back to the region or to other regions. Studies of foreign, coastal, and inland rail commodity flows associated with the three major ports, acting

---

[1] Ranajit Dhar, Robert Venning, and Brian J. L. Berry, "Interregional Intersectoral Relations of the Indian Economy," Essays on Commodity Flows and the Spatial Structure of the Indian Economy, ed. Brian J. L. Berry (Chicago: Department of Geography, University of Chicago, Research Paper No. 111, 1966), pp. 257-324.

[2] This system of Indian economic regions is based on factor analysis of the exchanges of sixty-three commodities by rail between thirty-six trade blocks of India as reported in the India (Republic), Department of Commercial Intelligence and Statistics, Accounts Relating to the Inland (Rail and Water-Borne) Trade of India for Twelve Months ending March, 1960 (Calcutta: Government of India Press, 1961). These regions represent groupings of trade blocks with similar patterns of shipment or receipt for the various commodities, Table 1, Figure 1. Each region contains nearly a full range of agricultural production, and the intraregional exchange of the aggregated sixty-three commodities exceeds interregional exchange. Within this system, interregional exchange consists primarily of the specialized industrial or agricultural products of the various regions. Further factor analysis of levels of population, employment, and production in these same trade blocks confirmed that the pattern of difference in the physical organization of the Indian economy conformed closely to its pattern of commodity exchanges. The trade blocks employed in this study consist of the States of the Indian Union as they were prior to the reorganization of the Indian States under the States Reorganization Act of 1956 plus the major port cities and Goa. The full findings of this study are published in Brian J. L. Berry, et al. "Commodity Flow Patterns," Essays on Commodity Flows and the Spatial Structure of the Indian Economy, ed. Brian J. L. Berry (Chicago: Department of Geography, University of Chicago, Research Paper No. 111, 1966), pp. 5-188.

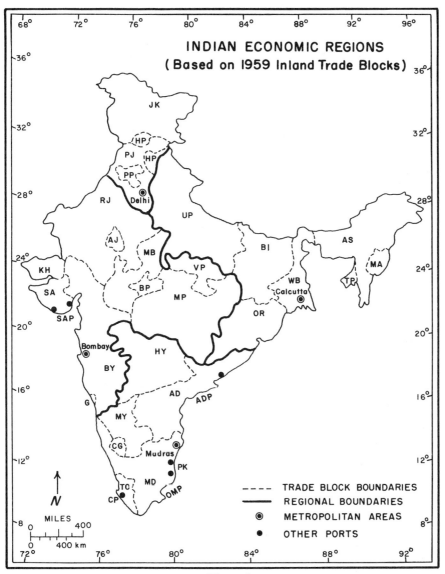

Figure 1

TABLE 1

INDIAN ECONOMIC REGIONS (1959 TRADE BLOCKS)

CALCUTTA REGION

C   - Calcutta
AS - Assam
MA - Manipur
TR - Tripura
WB - West Bengal (excld. Calcutta)
OR - Orissa
BI   - Bihar
UP - Uttar Pradesh

BOMBAY REGION

B   - Bombay Port
BY - Bombay (excld. Bombay Port)
MP - Madhya Pradesh
MB - Madhya Bharat
BP - Bhopal
VP - Vindhya Pradesh
RJ   - Rajasthan
AJ   - Ajmer
KU - Kutch
SA - Saurashtra (excld. Ports)
SAP - Saurashtra Ports
G   - Goa

MADRAS REGION

M   - Madras
AD   - Andhra (excld. Ports)
ADP - Andhra Ports
HY   - Hyderabad
MD   - Madras (excld. Ports)
OMP - Other Madras Ports
PK   - Pondicherry and Karikal
MY - Mysore
CG - Coorg
TC   - Travancore-Cochin (excld. Cochin Port)
CP   - Cochin Port

DELHI REGION

D   - Delhi
PJ   - Punjab
PP   - Patiala and PESPU
JK   - Jammu and Kashmir
HP   - Himichal Pradesh

as collectors and distributors, exhibit distinctive port-hinterland relationships.[1] Within their larger economic regions, these major ports have established import and export hinterlands for the specialized import and export commodities of the region.

Although much of India's inland commodity exchange focuses upon metropolitan areas, a considerable volume of direct intra- and interregional exchange of bulky raw and semi-finished goods takes place between highly specialized, non-metropolitan production areas in each region. These patterns of linkage between the specialized metropolitan and non-metropolitan areas of Indian economic regions are similar to those identified by the authors of Metropolis and Region for the highly integrated United States economy.[2]

---

[1] Studies of commodity flows associated with the port of Calcutta and Madras include: David B. Longbrake, "The Regional and Interregional Relations of the Port of Madras" (unpublished Master's dissertation, Department of Geography, University of Chicago, 1964) and Brian J. L. Berry and Wallace E. Reed, "Calcutta's External Relations" (unpublished report to the Calcutta Metropolitan Planning Organization, Department of Geography, University of Chicago, May, 1962).

[2] Duncan et al., op. cit.

Looking specifically at the characteristics of Indian cities, Qazi Ahmad's classi-fication of Indian cities casts further light on the wide range of functions and interlink-ages of major urban areas of the Indian economic system.[1] He provides evidence that Indian cities over 100,000 population tend to have lognormal size distribution. This group of cities thus displays rank-size regularity and "one can safely presume that Indian cities . . . are organized in a system comprising interacting, interdependent parts."[2] In his analysis, measures of distance to nearest neighbor, number of radiat-ing rail routes, proportion of in-migrants from urban as well as rural areas, occupa-tional structure, and generalized accessibility to segments of India's population provide further evidence of the interrelationship of the cities of this system. Such measures indicate that the cities of the system vary in their functions within the system and in their degree of accessibility; but lacking appropriate intercity exchange data, Ahmad's analysis does not deal with the actual types, degrees, direction, and regional groupings of interrelationships between the cities of the Indian system.

This group of studies reflects the progress which has been made in identifying and analyzing the spatial structure and integration of the Indian economic system. Co-efficients of exchange between various sectors of Indian economic activity have been analyzed; the spatial distribution and grouping of these activities into relatively inte-grated economic regions within a system of Indian economic regions have been identified; and the roles played by specialized urban areas within this system have been pointed out. However, the roles played by other types of specialized areas within the Indian economic system have yet to be analyzed.

Analysis of commodity flows between specialized sub-state areas in India has been precluded because commodity flow data used in these studies were published only on a state basis. Further, the sixty-three commodities treated in the Berry study do not include many of the manufactured goods important in exchanges between India's newly developing production complexes and cities. Ahmad in his study measures the general-ized accessibility of various urban places to India's nationwide distribution of population and employment characteristics through use of the potential model. He then relates the size and functions of Indian cities to these measures of accessibility to the Indian eco-nomic system. However, no research has been undertaken relating the patterns of re-gional or sub-state area commodity flows to their relative accessibility to the national system summarized by potential measures. This study attempts to fill certain gaps

[1]Qazi Ahmad, Indian Cities: Characteristics and Correlates (Chicago: Depart-ment of Geography, University of Chicago, Research Paper No. 102, 1965).

[2]Ibid., p. 8.

in these earlier studies of state and metropolitan linkages in India by analyzing the commodity flow patterns for one of India's sub-state, non-metropolitan areas specialized in
mining and industrial activity, the Bengal-Bihar Industrial Area.

Commodity Flows and Indian Regional Analysis

The Bengal-Bihar Industrial Area has been referred to in a number of studies as
a highly specialized industrial and mining area engaged in both traditional agricultural
and modern industrial commodity exchange. [1] Its exchanges can provide a great deal of
information on the roles and linkages of specialized sub-state areas with other areas
and regions of the Indian economy. Examination of flows of commodities treated in the
Berry study and of flows of other specialized industrial goods are used to indicate the
study area's linkages with India's traditionally agricultural and emerging industrial
areas.

Rodgers' study of the port of Genova indicates many of the ways in which commodity flows may be used to analyze the roles and degree of integration of a specialized
area with the rest of an economic system. [2] In his study of commodity flows associated
with the port, Rodgers examined commodity types to identify the specialized activities
of Genova and its hinterland. Using a specific percentage of total flows to and from the
port as his measure, he determined the areal extent of the hinterland, the port's degree
of integration or association with various specialized areas in the hinterland, and its
competitive position within its hinterland vis-à-vis all other ports and regions of Italy.
Similarly, this study's conclusions about the complementary roles played by the Bengal-
Bihar Industrial Area and its degree of integration with other specialized areas and
regions of the Indian economic system are based upon an examination of the types of
commodities exchanged by the study area and the proportion of total flows of various
commodities exchanged with other areas of the system.

In order to evaluate the degree of study-area integration with other areas of the
Indian economic system, a model has been developed concerning the proportion of local,
intra- and interregional exchanges expected between variously specialized and located
areas. Weber, Hoover, and Isard have demonstrated that the weight and value of various commodities which an area may exchange are related to transport costs and the

---

[1] L. S. Bhat, "Aspects of Regional Planning in India," Geographers and the
Tropics: Liverpool Essays, ed. Robert W. Steel and Robert M. Prothero (London:
Longmans, Green, 1964), p. 316; and Oskar H. K. Spate, India and Pakistan: A Re-
gional Geography (New York: E. P. Dutton, 1957), p. 287.

[2] Allan L. Rodgers, "The Port of Genova: External and Internal Relations," Annals of the Association of American Geographers, XLVII (December, 1958), 319-51.

distance over which they can be economically transported. [1] Once the territorial extent
of a market has been determined, relative accessibility to the market from any point
within it may be measured using the potential model. Harris has shown that relative
accessibility to the total market influences the location of industrial activity in its attempt to minimize transport costs to the market. [2] Pred has developed a set of expectations based on Weber and Harris concerning the length and volume of various types of
manufacturing flows from different locations relative to a national market. [3] The model
developed in this study expands Pred's analysis and argues that exchange costs and accessibility of the activities to the total supplies and markets within an economic system
give rise to a set of proportions of local, intraregional, and interregional exchange in
which an area would be expected to engage.

Harris has shown that an area's accessibility to various markets will influence
its mix of industries. [4] Pred has indicated that this same accessibility will influence the
scale of industries in an area. [5] This study examines the impact upon the specialization
of study-area industries and upon the observed length and volume of its commodity flows
resulting from its location and relative accessibility to the total pattern of market and
supply areas throughout India.

The potential model used in estimating the relative accessibility of an area to a
total market assumes that the attractive market force at a point is related directly to
some measure of the concentration of demand at that point and inversely related to some
measure of the distance which must be overcome in reaching the point. [6] Thus Isard
hypothesizes that the volume of goods flowing from any given point i to any other point j
should be directly proportionate to the demand for such goods at j and inversely

---

[1] Alfred Weber, "Über den Standort der Industrien," Alfred Weber: Theory of
the Location of Industries, translated by Carl J. Friedrich (Chicago: University of
Chicago Press, 1929); Edgar M. Hoover, The Location of Economic Activity (New York:
McGraw Hill, 1948); and Isard, Location and Space Economy.

[2] Chauncy D. Harris, "The Market as a Factor in the Location of Industry in the
United States," Annals of the Association of American Geographers, XLIV (December,
1954), 315-48.

[3] Allan Pred, "Toward a Typology of Manufacturing Flows," The Geographical
Review, LIV (January, 1964), 65-73.

[4] Harris, op. cit.   [5] Pred, op. cit.

[6] Harris, op. cit. , and Gerald A. P. Carrothers, "Historical Review of the Gravity and Potential Concepts in Human Interactance," Journal of the American Institute of
Planners, XXII, No. 2 (1956), 94-102.

proportionate to the costs of overcoming the intervening distance between points i and j.[1] However, Stouffer and Ullman argue that opportunities for i to interact with points intervening between it and j and opportunities for j to interact with points competing with i as in the case of distance will reduce the effect upon i of demand at j.[2] This study examines the adequacy in accounting for variation in the volume of Bengal-Bihar Industrial Area exchanges of the potential model and two models incorporating variables related to intervening opportunity and competition.

Chapter II reviews the characteristics of the Bengal-Bihar Industrial Area and the data used in this study. Chapter III compares the intra- and interregional patterns of the study area's major commodity exchanges with a set of patterns hypothesized for such an area. Chapter IV examines the effect of location within the study area upon the flow patterns of individual stations. Complementary relationships between the study area, its region, and other specialized areas throughout India are also noted. The effect upon study-area specialization and pattern of exchanges because of its location relative to the Indian national market is examined in Chapter V, and Chapter VI presents an analysis of regularity in the pattern of study area commodity flows related to measures of demand and competition in areas complementary to the study area.

[1]Walter Isard, Methods of Regional Analysis: An Introduction to Regional Science (Cambridge: MIT Press, 1960), pp. 49-499.

[2]Samuel A. Stouffer, "Intervening Opportunities and Competing Migrants," Journal of Regional Science, II, No. 1 (Spring, 1960), 1-26; and Ullman, op. cit.

CHAPTER II

THE STUDY AREA AND DATA

The Eastern India Industrial Region

Even at the present stage of development this region, (the North-eastern Plateau) particularly the Choto Nagpur plateau, stands out as the "core" area of industrial development, unlike the scattered and isolated industries in other parts of India.[1]

This country on the Bihar-Bengal-Orissa border is really the only zone of primary heavy industry in the sub-continent, a concentration obviously due to the comparable concentration of resources, facilitating linked development, but hampering distribution by the long rail haul necessary to any markets but those of Hooghlyside. . . . Around Jamshedpur and Asansol-Burnpur cluster ancillary and associated industries: refractories, tubes and wires, heavy chemicals and so on.[2]

The area immediately to the west of Calcutta lying partially in the states of West Bengal, Bihar, Orissa, and Madhya Pradesh contains India's richest mineral deposits and its greatest concentration of metallurgical industries Figure 2 . A number of studies of India's regional economic organization have identified this Eastern India Industrial Region as one of India's specialized industrial areas, and planning schemes have designated it as a locus for extensive investment in mining, industrial, and urban development.

In 1962 the Eastern India Industrial Region produced 88 per cent of India's coal.[3] Rich deposits of iron ore, bauxite, manganese, other ferro-alloys, limestone, dolomite, fire clays, glass sands, and other metallic and non-metallic minerals feed its local

---

[1]Bhat, op. cit. , p. 316.   [2]Spate, op. cit. , p. 287.

[3]Indian Bureau of Mines, Nagpur, Mineral Economics Division, Indian Minerals Yearbook 1962 (Delhi: Government of India Press, 1965), table 184, "Output of Coal from Different Coalfields, 1961 and 1962," pp. 242-3.

11

12

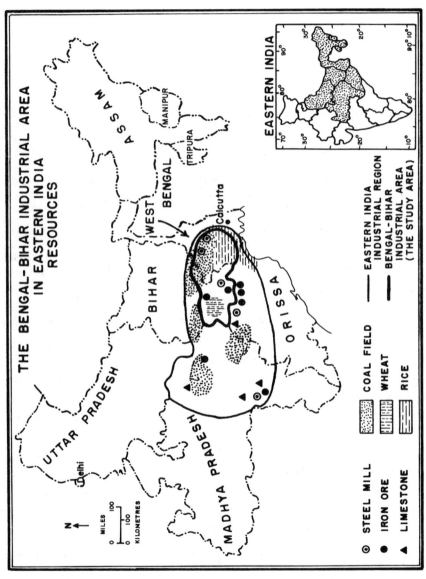

Figure 2

industries.[1] The area contains five of India's six iron-and-steel complexes and produced approximately 96 per cent of India's iron and steel in 1962-63.[2] Other industries include aluminum reduction, heavy machinery, chemical and electrical industries, and numerous small ancillary industries.[3] The area is served by a dense transportation network including India's Eastern and Southeastern Railways, by the Grand Trunk Road, and by other transcontinental routes to Calcutta, Delhi, Bombay, and Madras, Figures 2 and 3 .

The area's forests contribute ancillary support to major local industries and provide the basis for numerous small scale wood manufacturing industries. Although rich in minerals and forest products, this area's rough terrain rules out much of it as a source of agricultural surplus. Although the Midnapore area of West Bengal, the coastal plain of Orissa, the Ranchi area of Bihar, and parts of eastern Madhya Pradesh produce marketable surpluses of rice or wheat, much of this surplus is consumed by the Calcutta metropolitan area. Food grains in considerable quantity are shipped into the area to supply its non-agricultural population.

The Bengal-Bihar Industrial Area

The historic core of the Eastern Indian Industrial Region has been the Bengal-Bihar Industrial Area, the group of coal mining, industrial, and service centers bounded on the east by Durgapur and Kharagpur in the state of West Bengal and on the west by Dhanbad, Ranchi, and Jamshedpur in the state of Bihar, Figures 3 and 4 . The rapidly growing industrial, urban, and export market of Calcutta immediately to its east has long provided a stimulus to the area's industrial development, and India's first major mining and metallurgical development took place within the Bengal-Bihar Industrial Area.

---

[1] For a review of the area's physical, agricultural, mineral, and industrial characteristics see: Spate, op. cit. , and National Council of Applied Economic Research, Techno-Economic Survey of Bihar, Vol. I (Bombay: Asia Publishing House, 1960), National Council of Applied Economic Research, Techno-Economic Survey of West Bengal (New Delhi: National Council of Applied Economic Research, 1962); National Council of Applied Economic Research, Techno-Economic Survey of Orissa (New Delhi: National Council of Applied Economic Research, 1962); and National Council of Applied Economic Research, Techno-Economic Survey of Madhya Pradesh (New York: Asia Publishing House, 1960).

[2] Hindustan Steel Limited, Statistical Division, Statistics for Iron and Steel Industry in India 1964 (Ranchi: Hindustan Steel Limited, 1964), Table 4.1, p. 3.

[3] A discussion of the types and symbiotic relations of ancillary industries in the Asansol-Durgapur area is contained in: John MacDougall, Ancillary Industries in Asansol-Durgapur: A Preliminary Study (New York: Asia Publishing House for The Institute of Public Administration, 1964).

14

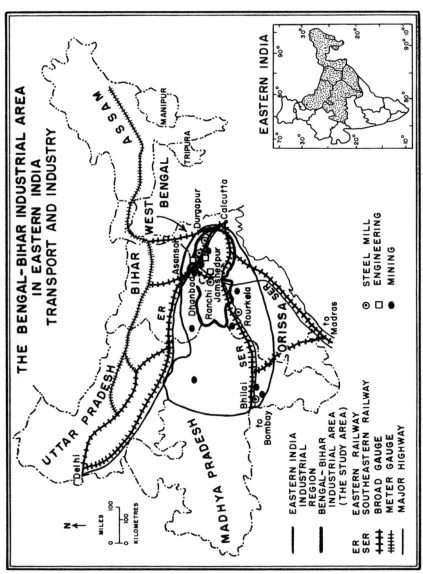

THE BENGAL-BIHAR INDUSTRIAL AREA
IN EASTERN INDIA
TRANSPORT AND INDUSTRY

EASTERN INDIA

STEEL MILL
ENGINEERING
MINING

EASTERN INDIA
INDUSTRIAL
REGION

BENGAL-BIHAR
INDUSTRIAL AREA
(THE STUDY AREA)

ER   EASTERN RAILWAY
SER SOUTHEASTERN RAILWAY
BROAD GAUGE
METER GAUGE
MAJOR HIGHWAY

Figure 3

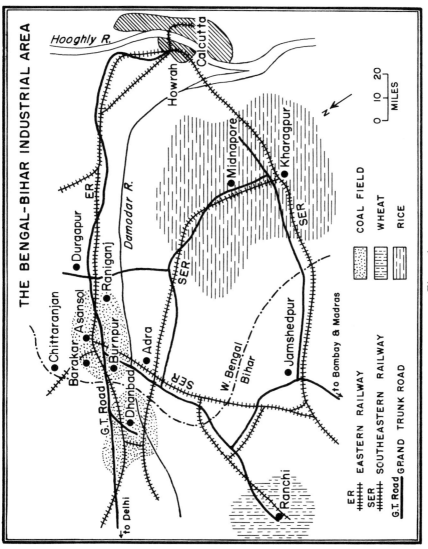

THE BENGAL-BIHAR INDUSTRIAL AREA

Hooghly R.

Calcutta
Howrah

Kharagpur
Midnapore

Damodar R.

Durgapur
Raniganj
Asansol
Chittaranjan
Barakar
Burnpur
Adra
Dhanbad
G.T. Road

ER
SER
SER

W. Bengal
Bihar

Jamshedpur

to Bombay & Madras

to Delhi

Ranchi

0 10 20
MILES

N

COAL FIELD

WHEAT

RICE

ER   EASTERN RAILWAY
SER   SOUTHEASTERN RAILWAY
G.T. Road GRAND TRUNK ROAD

Figure 4

In it are located the rich Raniganj and Jharia coal fields, some of India's richest deposits of iron ore, limestone, manganese, mica, china clay, fire clay, and glass sands, the Damodar river with power and transport development, and the Midnapore rice surplus area. Nearly all the metallic and non-metallic minerals necessary to support its metallurgical industries are found within one hundred miles of this core. The core area contains India's three largest iron-and-steel complexes which produced approximately 80 per cent of the nation's 1962-63 iron and steel. In addition, it contains most of the other industries of the larger Eastern India Industrial Region and the most developed transport network in India.[1]

Outside the Bengal-Bihar Industrial Area, intensive development of iron-and-steel, engineering, and mining activities in the Orissa and Madhya Pradesh portion of the Eastern India Industrial Area is of recent origin. Most of the new plants and expansion projects in these two states have been in operation only since the early 1960's. Within the larger industrial region of Eastern India, this core area is growing most rapidly both in size and diversity of production. As it continues to develop, its linkages with the rest of the Indian economy will continue to dominate the flow pattern of the larger industrial region. Knowledge of flow patterns for existing industries in this core will be useful in anticipating future patterns for these industries and in predicting patterns for similar industries developing throughout the larger area.

Inputs and Outputs of Major Industrial Activities

This study is concerned with the roles which Bengal-Bihar Industrial Area mining and industrial activities play in the Indian economy as indicated by the patterns of commodity flows associated with these activities. To keep data collection and analysis problems manageable, only the major urban and industrial places of the study area were surveyed. Table 2 indicates the major industries of the area and the railway stations serving them. The study area encompasses a large area of varied physical and population characteristics straddling the West Bengal-Bihar border. Throughout the area, industries with similar exchange patterns have tended to cluster at varying distances from each other. To simplify the analysis and provide information on variation in exchange patterns due to variation in production and location within the study area, stations have been grouped both on the basis of close areal proximity and similarity in local production. Table 2 indicates these groupings and Figure 3 their location within the study area.

The northern group of stations from Durgapur through Dhanbad are served by the Eastern Railway and the Grand Trunk Road. The Damodar Valley Corporation canal to

---

[1]See footnotes 1 and 2, p. 13, and Figures 2 and 3.

TABLE 2

STUDY-AREA STATION GROUPS

Station Group	Stations	Major Local Industries
1. Durgapur	Durgapur	(Hindustan Steel, Ltd.), steel works, iron, steel, scrap, rolled steel, fabricated structures, machinery, coke, coal chemicals
2. Raniganj	Raniganj	Paper, glass, railway equipment, machinery, ceramics, firebricks, oil mills, coal
3. Asansol	Asansol J. K. Nagar	Coal, railway equipment and rolling stock, aluminum and aluminum products, bicycles, drugs
4. Burnpur	Burnpur Sitarampur Scob siding Palasdiha siding	(Indian Iron and Steel Co., Ltd.), steel plants, iron, steel, scrap, rolled steel, fabricated structures, machinery, coke, coal chemicals, rice mills
5. Barakar	Barakar Kalubathan Kumardhubi Mugma Kulti	Rolled steel, castings, machinery, glass, firebricks
6. Chittaranjan	Chittaranjan Rupnarayanpur	Railway locomotives, railway equipment, aluminum, electrical wires and equipment, ceramics and firebricks.
7. Dhanbad	Dhanbad Jharia Lodna	Coal, coke, firebricks, castings, flour mill
8. Ranchi	Ranchi	Wire and cables, electric power, oxygen and other gases, machinery, bauxite, chrome, oil and flour mills, lac, wood, wheat and dry grains
9. Jamshedpur	Jamshedpur	(Tata Iron and Steel Co.), steel works, iron, steel, scrap, rolled steel, fabricated structures, pipes and tubing, tinplate, castings, coke, chemicals, locomotives, trucks, engines, concrete pipe, oxygen, firebricks, lumber, limestone, ores, fertilizers
10. Kharagpur	Kharagpur Midnapore	Railway repair shops, machinery, college, rice mills, agricultural products, electric power
11. Adra	Adra	Coal mining

Calcutta was not in operation at the time of this study. Nearly all the industries in this area are first- or second-stage resource users. Major iron and steel production associated with these stations is oriented to the use of locally available coals and refractories of the Raniganj and Jharia coal fields. Iron ore, fluxes, and alloys are brought in from outside the area. The large concentration of metal-using industries in this area receives much of its input of iron and steel from local production. Little or no food grains or other agricultural products are grown in the area. The stations surveyed act as central places mainly for manufacturing and mining populations in their immediate vicinities.

Durgapur is the site of the Hindustan Steel Ltd. Durgapur Steel Works, an integrated iron, steel, chemical, and machinery complex operated by the Government of India. Major inputs of this plant include coal, limestone and other fluxes, iron ore, alloy ores, machinery and equipment, food stuffs, and other consumer goods for plant employees. The major output of this plant includes iron and steel, rolled steel, fabricated steel structures, coal mining and other machinery, coke, and coal chemicals.

The stations of the Raniganj grouping are Raniganj and Andal, serving part of the Raniganj coal field of West Bengal. A paper mill, glass works, railway equipment plant, and ceramic and refractory plants are located within the vicinity of these stations. Inputs to these factories include wood, local clays, glass sands, coal, machinery, food, and other consumer goods for the local manufacturing and mining population. The main output of the area includes paper, glass, ceramics, firebricks, railway equipment, and other machinery.

The Asansol group of stations include Asansol and J. K. Nagar. Coal from the Raniganj coal field is recorded by the railways as being booked through Asansol. Besides its coal shipments, the area produces railway equipment and rolling stock, aluminum and aluminum products, drugs, and bicycles. Inputs to the area are mainly alumina and other non-ferrous metal and mineral products, machinery, food, and other consumer products for both the local manufacturing and mining populations.

The Burnpur group of stations, Burnpur, Sitarampur, Scob, and Palasdiha sidings, serve the Indian Iron and Steel Company's iron and steel complex producing iron, steel, fabricated structures, rolled steel, machinery, coke, coal chemicals, and oxygen and other gases. Inputs of this area include coal, iron and alloy ores, limestone and other fluxes, machinery and equipment, foodstuffs, and other consumer goods for the local manufacturing population.

The Barakar station grouping, Barakar, Kalubathan, Mugma, Kumardhubi, and Kulti, serves steel rerolling, coasting, machinery, glass, and refractory plants. Inputs to the area include machinery, iron, steel and non-ferrous metals, coal, local clays and sand, consumer goods, and foods for the local manufacturing population.

The Chittaranjan station grouping includes the stations of Chittaranjan and Rupnarayanpur. The industries served by this group include a large engineering works producing railway locomotives and other equipment, foundries, an aluminum smelter, an aluminum fabrication plant, an electrical equipment plant manufacturing wires and cables, and ceramic and firebrick works. Inputs to the area include coal, alumina and other minerals, machinery, iron, steel and non-ferrous metals, local clays, and consumer goods for the local manufacturing population.

The stations of the Dhanbad grouping include Dhanbad, Jharia, and Lodna. The area is located in the Jharia coal field of Bihar, and coal of the area is recorded as shipped through Dhanbad station. Other industries of the area include coal washeries, coke ovens, chemical plants, firebrick works, foundries, and machinery plants. Inputs to the area include iron and steel, local clays, coal, food, and other consumer goods for the manufacturing and mining population.

The Ranchi, Jamshedpur, Kharagpur-Midnapore, and Adra areas are served by the Southeastern Railway. Their road connections to Calcutta and Delhi are much poorer than the groups of stations along the Grand Trunk Road. The major industries of these station groups are again first- and second-stage resource users. Jamshedpur's iron and steel production draws locally on the rich mineral deposits of Singhbhum and adjacent Bihar and Orissa districts and brings in coal from fields to the north. Metal-using industries in Jamshedpur, Ranchi, and Kharagpur draw inputs mainly from local core-area iron and steel production. The districts surrounding each of these southern station groups produce considerably more agricultural goods than do Burdwan and Dhanbad districts containing the northern station groups. Local forests and agriculture give rise to wood manufacture and grain shipping from Ranchi and Midnapore. Adra distributes coals from the Southern Raniganj coal field. Each of the stations of the southern group serves as a central place for the surrounding rural population of their districts as well as for local manufacturing employment.

The Ranchi area is located in an agricultural and forest area of Bihar's Choto Nagpur Plateau southwest of the Jharia coal fields. Within the vicinity of Ranchi are rich bauxite and other mineral deposits. At the time of this study, the Indian government's Heavy Machine Building Plant was under construction near Ranchi. Other industries in the area include machinery, wire and cable manufacture, cement products, manufacture of oxygen and other gases, electric power, and local oil and flour mills. In addition, the area produces lac, wheat, and other grains. Inputs to the area include iron and steel, machinery, non-ferrous metals, coal, and consumer goods for the local population. The area acts as distributor for surrounding districts of Bihar.

Jamshedpur is the site of the Tata Iron and Steel Company steel works and numerous other heavy machinery industries. These industries produce iron, steel, pipes and tubing, castings, tinplate and boxes, trucks, railway equipment, other machinery, coke, coal chemicals, concrete pipes, firebricks, lumber, and fertilizer. Limestone and metallic and non-metallic ores are mined in the vicinity, and local agriculture produces small surpluses of food grains. Inputs of the area include coal, ores, limestone and fluxes, machinery, ferrous and non-ferrous metals, chemicals, firebricks, food, and consumer products for the local urban and industrial population. Jamshedpur acts as a central place for Singhbhum district and parts of nearby Orissa.

The Midnapore area includes the stations of Midnapore and Kharagpur. The area serves the agriculturally rich Midnapore district. Local industries include rice, wood, other agricultural production, food processing, railway workshops, machinery, and an engineering college. Inputs include metals, coal, machinery, and consumer goods for the local college and urban population.

Adra is a booking station for coal produced in the southern part of the Raniganj coal field. The station serves as a central place for the local population. However, no large industries other than mining are associated with it.

The Data

For analyzing the study area's patterns of commodity exchanges with a system of Indian regions and the national market, the basic data consist of the origins, or destinations, and tonnages of all goods shipped or received by rail in the twenty-three study-area stations listed in Table 2 during three months of 1962--April, July and October.[1] Flows during these months provided the best representation of the range of movement associated with the study area during the post harvest, monsoon, and early harvest seasons respectively. It was not possible to obtain comparable monthly data for the Indian cool season, November through February, the rice harvesting season within the study area. Checks of data which could be made indicated that during this cool period the seasonal variation in study area flows consisted of increased outflows of coal from the Asansol, Dhanbad, and Adra areas and rice from the Kharagpur-Midnapore area. However, since the distribution patterns from these stations for the increased amounts of coal and rice did not vary from the patterns for the other three months, it was concluded that the three month sample

---

[1] These data were compiled from station records by the staff of the Institute of Public Administration, New York, Calcutta Studies Program, through the permission and very kind cooperation of the Indian Government, Ministry of Railways and the staff of the Eastern and Southeastern Railways. Less than wagon lots, "smalls," were not included.

was representative of study-area goods movement.

To simplify the analysis, study-area exchanges with individual stations of origin or destination were aggregated by district for the five states surrounding the Bengal-Bihar Industrial Area and by state elsewhere. Analysis of study-area exchange patterns with sub-state areas are thus confined to the Calcutta region and Madhya Pradesh. Except for Bombay and Punjab,[1] the state areas used in this study are the states of the Indian Union according to the 1956 States Reorganization Act and not the trade blocks of the 1959 Accounts;[2] however, an idea of the volume and direction of study-area exchanges with these trade blocks can be gained from the figures in Chapter III. States of the Calcutta region did not change under the reorganization, and the study area's exchanges with them may be compared with interstate exchanges in the Accounts.[3] Study-area exchanges with Calcutta and Delhi were recorded separately. The area's exchanges with Bombay, Madras, Hyderabad, and other major metropolitan areas were not recorded separately from the surrounding states. Patterns of West Bengal and Bihar exchanges with these metropolitan areas and industrial employment figures for metropolitan areas and non-metropolitan districts imply however that exchanges of many specialized goods would most likely be associated only with these metropolitan areas.[4]

To examine the range of study-area commodity exchanges with the Indian economy and to gain some idea of the pattern of movement of machinery, chemicals, and flows of other manufactures not recorded in the Accounts,[5] movements of all commodities associated with study-area stations were enumerated. Table 3 indicates the commodities which were important in trade associated with the study area's industrial and urban activities. Because of small quantities, many of the categories broken down in the Accounts[6] have been grouped in this study whereas items which the area exchanged in large volume such as wheat, coal and coke, wood and timber, machinery, and chemicals

---

[1] Due to the small volume, study-area exchanges with Gujarat have been combined with those of Maharashtra and called "Bombay" exchanges. Similarly, exchanges with Himichal Pradesh and Jammu and Kashmir have been combined with Punjab and called "Punjab" exchanges.

[2] India (Republic), Department of Commercial Intelligence and Statistics, op. cit.

[3] Ibid.

[4] India (Republic), Ministry of Labor and Employment, Labor Bureau, Large Scale Establishments in India, List of Registered Factories, 1958 (Simla: Government of India Press, 1961).

[5] India (Republic), Department of Commercial Intelligence and Statistics, op. cit.

[6] Ibid.

TABLE 3

COMMODITY GROUPS

Group	Commodities
1. Other Food	Livestock,* Dried Fruit,* Ghee,* Other Milk Products, Soft and Alcoholic Drinks, Confectionary, Potatoes, Other Vegetables
2. Wheat*	
3. Wheat Flour*	
4. Rice in Husk*	
5. Rice not in Husk*	
6. Other Grains	Maize,* Jowar,* Bajra,* Other Millets,* Others*
7. Gram,* Pulses*	
8. Sugar	Sugar,* Khandsari,* Gur,* Molasses*
9. Tea*	
10. Coffee*	
11. Groundnut Seed*	
12. Rape and Mustard Seed*	
13. Other Seeds	Castor,* Cotton,* Linseed,* Til*
14. Salt*	
15. Groundnut Oil*	
16. Other Vegetable Oil	Castor,* Coconut,* Others*
17. Tobacco Products	
18. Tobacco Raw*	
19. Other Agricultural Products	Dyes and Tans, Myrobalans,* Bones,* Lac and Shellac,* Raw Rubber,* Oilcakes*
20. Hides* and Skins* Raw	
21. Leather Manufactures	Hides and Skins Tanned and Leather,* Other Leather Manufactures
22. Straw	
23. Raw Jute	Loose* and Pucca Bales*
24. Other Raw Fibre	Indian and Foreign Cotton and Cotton Waste,* Wool,* Hemp Indian and Other Fibres*
25. Cement*	

*Commodity category in India (Republic), Department of Commercial Intelligence and Statistics, <u>Accounts Relating to the Inland (Rail and Water-Borne) Trade of India</u> (Calcutta: Government of India Press, 1956–date).

TABLE 3--Continued

Group	Commodities
26. Firebricks	
27. Lime and Limestone*	
28. Other Mineral Ores	Iron Ore, Manganese Ore,* Bauxite, Ferrous Silica, Other Metallic Minerals
29. Non-Metallic Minerals	Silica, Clay, Mica
30. Coal and Coke*	
31. Iron, Steel, Cast Iron	Iron and Steel Bars, Sheets, Girders, and Other Commercial Forms of Iron and Steel,* Cast Iron, Pig Iron
32. Scrap Iron	
33. Non-Ferrous Metals	Aluminum, Copper, Tin
34. Machinery and Transport Machinery	Non-Electrical Heavy and Light Machinery, Rail and Road Vehicles, Bicycles
35. Electrical & Telephone Goods	Electrical Machinery and Equipment, Wires
36. Chemicals and Explosives	Heavy and Light Chemicals, Explosives
37. Medicine and Cosmetics	Medicines, Cosmetics, Stationery
38. Paper and Paper Products	
39. Glass*	
40. Kerosene*	
41. Other Petroleum Fuels	Gasoline, Diesel, Lubricants, Fuel Oils, Asphalt, Tar
42. Rubber Manufactures	
43. Wood Manufactures	
44. Wood and Timber, Raw	Teak,* Other Timber, Lumber
45. Gunnies, Jute Products*	
46. Other Textile Products	Indian and Foreign Cotton Twist and Yarn,* Cotton Piece Goods,* Wool Goods, Coir Products, Other Textiles
47. Non-Wood Building Materials	Bricks,* Tiles,* Cement Products, Sand, Rock and Gravel, Other Non-Wood Building Materials

have been singled out for separate study.

The study's primary flow data are in volume units. The assignment of value units to mixed commodities such as machinery or chemicals would have been very difficult; however, the relative value of different commodities could be estimated. The mixed commodities used in this study combine goods similar in value per unit of weight. Individual commodity flow figures indicate the percentage of total study-area exchanges of that commodity exchanged with various points of origin or destination. Inferences concerning the influence of relative volume and value on study-area flow patterns were drawn through comparison of figures for commodities of different relative value.

Unfortunately, information concerning total 1962-63 flows of study-area stations could not be obtained. Further, data on the total flows of the various points of origin and destination and of the West Bengal and Bihar trade blocks were not available for the three sample months. Also, for earlier time periods, flow data were not available either for the study area or for points of origin and destination. Therefore, direct analysis of stability in the volume and pattern of study-area flows was not possible; nor was such analysis possible either of the exact relation of study-area flows to flows of the West Bengal and Bihar trade blocks or of its competitive position in the trade of points of origin and destination. However, a large proportion of the coal, iron and steel, limestone, and certain other commodity exchanges of the West Bengal and Bihar trade blocks recorded in the Accounts[1] originated or terminated within the study area. Temporal and areal stability in study-area flows of these commodities was inferred from stability in West Bengal and Bihar exchanges for such commodities. For study-area commodity flows not covered by the Accounts[2] and for flows covered but not constituting a large proportion of the shipments or receipts of the West Bengal and Bihar trade blocks, no information is available with which to check stability in the pattern of such flows.

During the period of study, allocation of domestic iron and steel, coal, cement, petroleum, and foreign imports among various Indian users was controlled by government-administered priority systems. To subsidize industrial development in areas remote from India's steel mills, the delivered price of many grades of steel was to be the same throughout India by government regulation. Since Independence in 1947, the location and establishment of industries and projects using controlled and uncontrolled items has been influenced by government licensing procedures and policies. The aim of many

[1] Ibid.

[2] Ibid.

of these policies is to reduce congestion in the Calcutta area by discouraging the establishment of new industrial activities in or near the Calcutta area including the study area. At various times the distribution of food products such as domestic rice and imported wheat is regulated by the government for reasons of transport efficiency or famine prevention. In analyzing the pattern and regularity of study-area flows, an attempt has been made to take into account the influence of government controls.

A high proportion of Indian goods movements, especially bulky commodities and goods shipped distances over 150 miles, move by rail because of high costs of long distance road movement and the inadequacy of roads to handle large volumes of freight. Checks of road movement in the study area indicate considerable trucking movement within the area and between it and the Calcutta metropolitan area; however, relatively few truck movements were found between the study area and areas to the west and south. [1] This pattern of trucking movement is to be expected on the basis of the higher quality road network linking the study area to Calcutta. Due to the relative speed and safety of trucking, there is a management preference for truck shipment of specialized machinery, chemicals, and other high value goods. In addition, lack of rail cars and other bottlenecks in rail transportation in the study area at the time of this survey led the Indian government to establish a policy of sending coal by road within a 150 mile radius of West Bengal and Bihar collieries. Thus certain commodities, including all foodstuffs, coal, petroleum products, wood and building materials, machinery, electrical goods, chemicals, medicines, paper, glass, rubber, textiles, and some grades of steel, would tend to move more frequently by truck and heavy minerals and firebricks would move mainly by rail. Intra-study-area movements by rail are not assumed to represent the full range of commodities or the total volume of movement, but, for movements farther to the west and south, it is assumed that rail is the primary carrier.

---

[1] During the spring of 1963, a three-day check of the weight and type of goods moved by truck on all the main roads linking the study area with the rest of India was carried out by the staff of the Institute of Public Administration, New York, Calcutta Program. Information on trucking movements in the Jamshedpur area was secured from road tax records.

CHAPTER III

ROLES AND EXCHANGES OF THE BENGAL-BIHAR

INDUSTRIAL AREA

Economic Regions and Exchange Patterns

Within a system of economic regions the commodity flows associated with areas
of specialized production and consumption may involve three types of exchange: local
intra-area, intraregional, or interregional exchange. A major concern of this study is
with the roles played by the Bengal-Bihar Industrial Area and with the proportions of its
commodity flows in each of these three types of exchange within the system of Indian economic regions described in Chapter I. [1]

Pred has enumerated a set of principles influencing the proportions of manufacturing flows in each of these three types of exchange. He argues that the length and volume (proportions) of an industry's commodity shipments are related to the type and scale
of the industry and to its relative accessibility to the national market for its goods. [2] Expanding on this set of principles, it can be argued that the proportion of local, intra- and
interregional exchange engaged in by a specialized area or region will be related to the
diversity and scale economies of both its specialized production and consumption activities. These proportions are further related to the area's relative exchange costs which
are in part a function of its production costs and value per unit of weight in its mix of
commodities and in part a function of its location relative to other areas of the economic
system. For any specialized area or region of a system, a set of expectations can be
developed concerning the proportion of its total or individual commodity exchanges to be
found in each of these three types of exchange. Such a set of expectations has been

---

[1] Chapter I, footnote 2, page 4, and Table 1 and Figure 1.

[2] Pred, op. cit.

developed for the Bengal-Bihar Industrial Area in this study.

Expected Exchange Patterns of the Bengal-Bihar Industrial Area

The location of a region within an economic system affects its accessibility to and its costs of exchange with other regions of the system. A centrally located region with a high degree of proximity to other regions of the system and lower exchange costs would be expected to specialize in goods demanded throughout the system and engage in a higher proportion of interregional receipts and shipments than if it were more peripherally located. Similarly, the accessibility of a specialized area to complementary areas within or outside its region would affect its proportion of intra- and interregional exchanges. A location in the center of a region such as that occupied by the study area would be expected to encourage a high proportion of intraregional trade. The study area's location off center with respect to India as a whole would be expected to further decrease its propensity toward interregional trade.

The difference between a commodity's production costs and its market price is the maximum amount which can be spent on its transportation, thus limiting the distance over which it can be moved to the market. Since the costs of transporting commodities are a function of their weight or bulk, the distance over which an area will exchange goods is generally determined by the production costs, market value, and weight of the commodities it exchanges.[1] An area specializing in mining and metallurgy such as the study area would have a high proportion of heavy, low value commodities in its exchange mix, with little of the commodity's value available for transportation costs. Such an area would be expected to engage in a large proportion of short distance, local, or intraregional exchanges.[2]

Recent trade theory literature recognizes two distinct patterns of international and interregional commodity exchange based on different stages of production.[3] The first pattern relates to the exchange of raw materials and finished goods between differently specialized areas. In stating the theory of comparative advantage, Smith, Ricardo,

---

[1] Isard, Location and Space Economy.

[2] Pred, op. cit.

[3] Richard N. Cooper, "Growth and Trade: Some Hypotheses About Long-Term Trends," Journal of Economic History, XXIV, No. 4 (Dec. 1964), 609-628; Raymond Vernon, "International Investment and International Trade in the Product Cycle," Quarterly Journal of Economics, LXXX, No. 2 (May 1966), 190-207; M. V. Posner, "International Trade and Technical Change," Oxford Economic Papers, XIII (Oct. 1961), 323-341; and Staffan B. Linder, An Essay on Trade and Transformation (New York: John Wiley and Almquist and Wiksell, 1961).

and other classical economists argued that trade arose from the demand of manufacturing for raw materials and foodstuffs and the demand of extractive industries for manufactured goods.[1] "Land-using" goods were exchanged for "labor-using" goods. Thus American and later Indian cotton was exchanged for British textiles. Within the framework of this argument, the exchange of similar goods between similarly specialized areas would not be expected.

However, a great proliferation of types and qualities of manufactured goods and greatly expanded world trade in "labor-using" goods has been associated with the expansion of manufacturing and service activities in the last half century. Most of this trade occurs among countries specializing in similar "labor-using" activities.[2] This second pattern, the exchange of similar goods between similarly specialized areas, has been related to: economies of scale at various locations; rates of technologic advance which have given various areas short-term monopoly advantages in various types of manufacture; mobility of capital; and to manufacturing trends toward fabrication of goods in multiple stages at various locations, assembly of multiple components produced at various locations, and minute product differentiation.[3] Since the underlying principles appear to be generally applicable, both these patterns of exchange might be expected in exchanges at any areal scale, local, regional, or interregional.

Thus an area's specialization can relate it to complementary areas both similarly and dissimilarly specialized. The number and location of areas with which it exchanges will be a function of the diversity of its specialization. An area specializing in one activity or in non-complementary activities would not be likely to engage in much local exchange, increasing the probability of intra- or interregional trade. An area whose specialization included several stages of goods fabrication and the assembly of components produced by local ancillary industries might be expected to engage in considerable local as well as extra-local trade. Exchanges of specialized activities, such as iron ore mining, which are complementary with a small number of other activities would likely evidence a high proportion of short distance local or intraregional exchanges. On the other hand, exchanges of activities such as steel and machinery production which are complementary with a large number of other activities should evidence a larger proportion of interregional trade since some of these activities would most likely be located outside the

---

[1] Smith, op. cit.; David Ricardo, "On Foreign Trade," International Trade Theory: Hume to Ohlin, ed. W. R. Allen (New York: Random House, 1965), pp. 62-67.

[2] Cooper, op. cit.

[3] Ibid. and Murphy, op. cit.

region. Exchanges of raw materials, foods, and goods in early stages of fabrication would be expected between differently specialized areas, while exchanges of goods at later stages of fabrication would be expected between similarly specialized areas as well.

An area such as the Bengal-Bihar Industrial Area with complementary coal mining, iron, steel, and machinery production would be expected to engage in extensive local along with intra- and interregional exchange. Its raw material exchanges would be expected primarily with local and intraregional areas of dissimilar mining specialization. Its metals and machinery exchanges would be expected primarily with areas specializing in similar manufacturing activities, mainly local and regional, but with some areas located outside the region.

Different economies of scale are associated with each stage in production and transport of various goods. In the production of basic steel, only a large-scale plant can economically reduce the ore and other raw materials. Further, in many cases only a large-scale demand for raw materials make their mining and transportation economically justified. Once produced, the steel from the large plant may be used in various quantities by a large number of specialized activities located throughout an economic system. An area such as the Bengal-Bihar Industrial Area, engaged in iron-and-steel manufacture and aluminum reduction, would be expected to have large volume inflows of raw materials from a small number of sources, reducing the probability of interregional exchange. On the other hand, inflows of machinery and other manufactures to the area might be expected in small volume from numerous sources in similarly specialized areas increasing the probability of interregional exchange. Likewise steel and machinery produced in the study area would be expected to flow to a wide range of complementary areas, many of which might be located outside the region.

Based on its central location within the region and proximity to the industrial Calcutta metropolitan area, its wide diversification in manufacture, its specialization in heavy raw material reduction, and its deficit in the production of food and consumer goods, the Bengal-Bihar Industrial Area would be expected to have a high proportion of intraregional and local exchanges. The area's interregional exchanges should stem from its scale of mining and diversity of metallurgical and machinery production filling demands throughout the Indian economy. How do study-area proportions of local, intra- and interregional exchanges compare with this set of expectations; and how can variation from the expected be explained within the Indian context?

Roles and Exchange Patterns of the Bengal-Bihar Industrial Area

Major Commodities Exchanged

What are the primary roles which the Bengal-Bihar Industrial Area plays with respect to the Indian economy? Five major groups of commodities are identified in the mix of commodities which the study area exchanged by rail, Tables 4 and 5. Approximately 60 per cent of the study area's inflows were raw materials, limestone, other mineral ores, non-metallic minerals, and firebricks, indicating the area's role as a first-stage processor of raw materials into ferrous and non-ferrous metals. Another 20 per cent of its inflows consisted of iron and steel, other metals, and machinery, indicating the area's role as a manufacturing complex producing a wide range of machinery. Sixteen per cent of the study area's inflows were food grains, cement, wood and non-wood building materials, indicating the area's food deficit and the large amount of construction underway in the area. Coal accounted for 70 per cent of the area's outflows by weight, indicating its role as a major coal-mining area. With 22 per cent of its outflows consisting of iron and steel, the study area's role as a major steel producer is clear, and its role as a major manufacturing complex is indicated by sizable outflows of machinery and other manufactures.

Associated with each of the five major commodity groups exchanged by the study area is a pattern of local, intra- and interregional exchanges and a set of complementary areas for which the study area performs its various roles. The specialized areas and regions singled out in this study include: the five local districts in which the study area is located; the city and port of Calcutta; the Calcutta metropolitan area including the districts of Calcutta, 24 Parganas, and Howrah; the Calcutta region defined as the states of Assam, West Bengal excluding the District of Calcutta, Orissa, Bihar, and Uttar Pradesh; and the rest of India.[1] Since the study area's exchange patterns are the aggregate of these individual commodity exchange patterns, it will be useful to examine them separately.

Raw Material Receipts

Raw materials for steel were the area's largest volume of inflows. As expected, these raw materials came in large quantities to large-scale plants in the study area from relatively few sources. Due to their low value per unit of weight, these goods

---

[1] An extensive analysis of inter-industry and inter-urban exchange, both by rail and truck, within the study area and the prospects for further industrial and urban development in the area has been undertaken by the Institute of Public Administration, New York, Calcutta Studies Program, under the direction of Leslie P. Green.

were transported only short distances to the study area and thus show primarily intra-regional patterns of receipts. In its role as processor of raw materials into steel, the study area is most closely linked with the rich deposits of minerals within the study area and immediately adjacent to it in southern Bihar and northern Orissa. Almost no comple-mentarity exists between the Calcutta metropolitan area and the study area in this role since the metropolitan area has no local deposits and imports only limited quantities of raw materials.

Figures 6-9 indicate the highly intraregional pattern of inflows for non-metallic minerals, other minerals, firebricks, and limestone.[1] Ninety-seven per cent of the other mineral ores, 80 per cent of the non-metallic minerals, and 98 per cent of the firebricks were from intraregional sources, located mainly in northern Orissa, southern Bihar, and within the study area. Firebricks are produced in large quantities within the study area itself from local deposits of fire clay associated with the northern station groups or in northern Orissa. Apparent cross-hauling of firebrick may be due to prod-uct differentiation. Except for limestone, raw material receipts of the various study area stations were generally from the nearest available source. Seventy-five per cent of the area's receipts of limestone were from outside the region, which would not be ex-pected as intraregional sources of limestone are available in Bihar. This limestone, however, came from points adjacent to the regional boundary in Madhya Pradesh. Mine ownership, quality of limestone, or government regulation may account for the apparent deviation from the expectation that raw materials will flow from the nearest available source.

Metals and Manufactures Receipts

The next largest volume of study-area receipts were iron, steel, non-ferrous metals, chemicals, and machinery to be processed by local industry into later stages of manufactured goods. With a high demand for such goods in India, these valuable,

---

[1] The flow figures of this study indicate for the study area and various stations by commodity the percentage of the station's total exchange of a given commodity with vari-ous areas of India. The areas identified include the states of the Calcutta Region as de-fined in Table 1, Chapter I, the Calcutta and Delhi metropolitan areas, and other states of the Indian Union according to the 1956 States Reorganization Act. Due to the small volume, study-area exchanges with Gujarat have been combined with those of Maharash-tra and called "Bombay" exchanges. Similarly, exchanges with Himachal Pradesh and Jammu and Kashmir have been combined with Punjab and called "Punjab" exchanges. Flow lines outside the Calcutta Region indicate only the existence and strength of a link, those within the region, except for Assam, indicate approximately the location of the dis-trict with which the flow was exchanged. Figure 5 indicates the districts of the Calcutta Region.

TABLE 4

PERCENTAGE BY COMMODITY OF TOTAL INFLOWS FROM ALL OF INDIA TO STUDY-AREA STATIONS

Commodities	Durga-pur	Rani-ganj	Asan-sol	Burn-pur	Bara-kar	Chitta-ranjan	Dhan-bad	Ranchi	Jamshed-pur	Khar-agpur	Adra	Study-Area Total
1. Other foods	-*	4.8	4.9	.1	.2	.1	10.6	.6	.8	6.6		1.0
2. Wheat		1.4	44.1	.1	1.1	1.0	23.5	5.5	28.7	5.9		6.9
3. Wheat flour			–	–	.1	–	.8	.1	.4	2.0		.2
4. Rice in husk	–	.1	–		.4	10.2	1.4	1.5	.1	4.1		.4
5. Rice not in husk	–	.8	.2	.1	.7		4.2	1.3	.7	1.5		.4
6. Other grains		.1	–		–		.3	–		–		–
7. Gram, pulses	–	6.6	3.0	.2	1.2	.1	5.0	1.6	1.0	6.3		1.0
8. Sugar		6.0	4.3	.2	1.4	.3	5.4	.1	.7	3.5		.8
9. Tea	–	.1	–		–		–	–	–			–
10. Coffee							–					–
11. Groundnut seed		–					.1					–
12. Rape & mustard seed		7.4	–	.3	.3		2.8	.3	.3	4.6		.6
13. Other seeds		–	–				.1	–	–			–
14. Salt	–	.5					.3	2.3	.3	2.4		.3
15. Groundnut oil		.1	–		.1	–	.1	.4	.4	.7		.1
16. Other vegetable oil		.2			.1	–	.4	.3	.5	1.6		.2
17. Tobacco products	–	.6	–		–		.3	–		.1		–
18. Tobacco raw	–	.3	.2		.1		.3	.1		.1		–
19. Other agri. products	–	.5			.2	.5	.7	.1	.3	.4		.1
20. Hides & skins, raw	–	.3					.6	–	–	.1		–
21. Leather manufactures	.1				–	–	1.6	–				.1
22. Straw		2.5			.1		1.6	.3	.6			.2
23. Raw jute		–			–		–					–
24. Other raw fibre	–	.1			–		.4	–	.2	3.4		.2
25. Cement	1.3	2.3	1.3	.5	.9	1.0	1.2	10.5	1.0	12.1		1.9

												Total
26. Firebricks	2.7	—	.1	3.8	3.6	1.6	.1	.1	5.5	1.1	—	2.9
27. Lime & limestone	24.8	11.5	.7	45.9	.3	.5	.9	.9	1.5	—	—	19.6
28. Other mineral ores	65.3	.3	5.8	3.4	8.3	1.2	1.2	.6	6.7	.1	—	31.8
29. Non-metallic minerals	.9	10.2	.5	7.8	25.9	1.8	.6	.8	12.7	—	—	5.8
30. Coal & coke	—	—	—	—	.1	—	.2	.6	.6	—	—	.1
31. Iron, steel, cast iron	1.9	2.2	19.0	30.8	43.0	46.0	7.4	14.8	17.7	3.3	—	13.2
32. Scrap iron	.3	.2	.4	—	.4	.3	.6	—	—	—	—	.2
33. Non-ferrous metals	.3	.8	5.9	.2	—	8.3	—	.1	1.2	.2	—	.6
34. Machinery	.1	.1	.5	1.2	.4	3.7	.9	8.7	3.2	1.9	—	1.3
35. Elec. & tel. goods	.1	2.2	1.1	.1	.1	3.0	.7	.9	.2	.4	—	.3
36. Chemicals, explosives	.7	1.8	1.4	3.6	.6	2.7	13.4	2.1	5.8	1.5	—	2.4
37. Medicine, cosmetics	—	.1	.1	—	.1	.2	.4	.1	.1	—	—	.1
38. Paper & paper products	—	2.1	.2	—	—	—	.1	.3	—	.1	—	.1
39. Glass	—	—	—	—	—	.2	—	1.5	—	—	—	—
40. Kerosene	—	.4	—	.1	.1	—	1.0	1.4	.2	—	—	.3
41. Other petroleum fuels	.1	.3	2.3	.5	.3	7.1	1.8	1.1	3.8	6.4	—	1.6
42. Rubber manufactures	—	.2	.3	—	—	1.9	.2	.1	.3	20.8	—	.1
43. Wood manufactures	.1	5.4	.7	—	.6	1.1	1.5	17.7	.6	.8	—	1.2
44. Wood & timber, raw	.1	11.2	1.3	.4	.4	1.9	2.4	.7	.4	2.1	—	.8
45. Gunnies, jute products	.1	—	—	—	—	.2	—	.1	.2	—	—	.1
46. Other textiles	—	.2	.1	.2	.2	1.8	.9	.4	.1	.1	—	.1
47. Non-wood bldg. material	1.2	14.5	.3	.3	8.5	1.5	1.8	.2	1.6	3.4	—	2.1
48. Miscellaneous	—	1.5	1.3	.1	.4	1.8	2.1	3.7	1.6	2.3	—	.7
Percentage of total	100.0	100.0	100.0	100.0	100.0	100.0	100.0	100.0	100.0	100.0	0.0	100.0
Metric tons (100's)	6440	538	434	2106	998	156	327	615	2205	447	0	14271

Source: Data compiled from individual station records for April, July, and October, 1962.

* Dash indicates less than .1 per cent.

TABLE 5

PERCENTAGE BY COMMODITY OF TOTAL OUTFLOWS TO ALL OF INDIA FROM STUDY-AREA STATIONS

Commodities	Durga-pur	Rani-ganj	Asan-sol	Burn-pur	Bara-kar	Chitta-ranjan	Dhan-bad	Ranchi	Jamshed-pur	Khar-agpur	Adra	Study-Area Total
1. Other foods	-*	.1	–	–	–	1.2	–	.9	.1	.3	–	–
2. Wheat	–	–	–	–	.2	–	–	–	.1	–	–	–
3. Wheat flour	–	–	–	–	.3	–	–	–	–	–	–	–
4. Rice in husk	.3	1.0	–	–	–	–	–	–	–	1.0	–	–
5. Rice not in husk	–	–	–	–	–	–	–	–	–	79.2	–	.7
6. Other grains												
7. Gram, pulses	–	.1	–	.2	–	–	–	–	–	.2	–	–
8. Sugar	–	–	–	–	.1	–	–	–	–	–	–	–
9. Tea	–	–	–	–	–	–	–	–	–	–	–	–
10. Coffee												
11. Groundnut seed												
12. Rape & mustard seed	–	–	–	–	–	–	–	–	–	.1	–	–
13. Other seeds	–	–	–	–	–	–	–	–	–	.1	–	–
14. Salt	–	.6	–	–	–	–	–	–	–	.1	–	–
15. Groundnut oil												
16. Other vegetable oil	–	–	–	–	–	–	–	–	–	–	–	–
17. Tobacco products	–	.1	–	–	–	–	–	–	–	–	–	–
18. Tobacco raw	–	.1	–	–	–	–	–	–	–	–	–	–
19. Other agri. products	–	1.7	–	–	–	–	–	–	–	.4	–	–
20. Hides & skins, raw	–	–	–	–	–	.1	–	26.0	–	.2	–	–
21. Leather manufactures	–	–	–	–	–	–	–	–	–	–	–	–
22. Straw	–	–	–	–	–	–	–	–	–	5.3	–	.1
23. Raw jute	–	–	–	–	–	–	–	–	–	–	–	–
24. Other raw fibre	–	–	–	–	–	–	–	–	–	–	–	–
25. Cement	–	–	–	–	–	–	–	–	–	–	–	–

	(28217)	(5120)	(244)	(3158)	(29)	(7632)	(55)	(952)	(1953)	(7190)	(108)	(1773)
26. Firebricks	1.3				.3		2.5	31.5	.6		18.6	1.1
27. Lime & limestone	.2			.3				–	2.0	–	.3	–
28. Other mineral ores	.2		.1				1.7	.1	2.6		4.5	–
29. Non-metallic minerals	.5			1.9	99.1		.1	3.6	2.2	99.8	11.0	.1
30. Coal & coke	70.5	100.0				26.4		–				93.7
31. Iron, steel, cast iron	22.4		1.5	84.6	.1		29.9	47.1	77.4		.1	.6
32. Scrap iron	1.2		.3	2.8			10.9	.1	11.2			
33. Non ferrous metals	.5		–	4.6			8.5		–			.1
34. Machinery	.1		–	.2		1.6	8.8	.1	1.3			.1
35. Elec. & tel. goods	.3		.3	2.2		1.2	20.2	.1	.2			.4
36. Chemicals, explosives	.5		.1	1.4	.3		4.2	.4	1.5		1.9	1.9
37. Medicine, cosmetics	–		–	–		.1			–		–	–
38. Paper & paper products	.1		.1	.1	.1						19.8	
39. Glass	–			.1							.9	
40. Kerosene	–		–			2.7						
41. Other petroleum fuels	–		.1	.1		.5	.2					.2
42. Rubber manufactures	–		–			19.7	.9				1.3	
43. Wood manufactures	.1		.1	.1		3.9	1.1		.4			
44. Wood & timber, raw	–		1.8	–		3.1	1.5				.9	.1
45. Gunnies, jute products	–		1.3	.1		.3	.7	.1				
46. Other textiles	–		–	–		–	2.5					
47. Non wood bldg. material	.6		4.5	.8		1.4	3.8	7.0	.2		32.0	1.1
48. Miscellaneous	.4		2.8	.3		10.7	1.0	9.1	.1		5.0	.2
Percentage of total	100.0	100.0	100.0	100.0	100.0	100.0	100.0	100.0	100.0	100.0	100.0	100.0
Metric tons (100's)	28217	5120	244	3158	29	7632	55	952	1953	7190	108	1773

Source: Data compiled from individual station records for April, July, and October, 1962.

* Dash indicates less than .1 per cent.

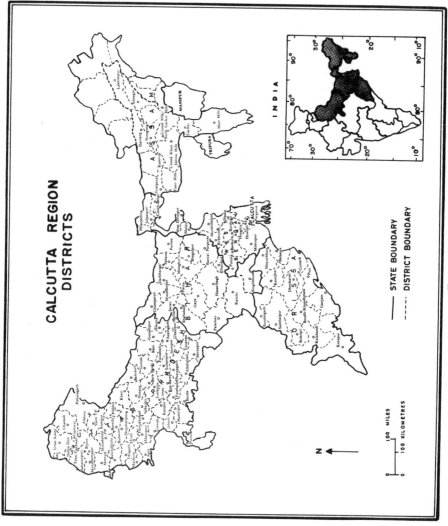

Figure 5

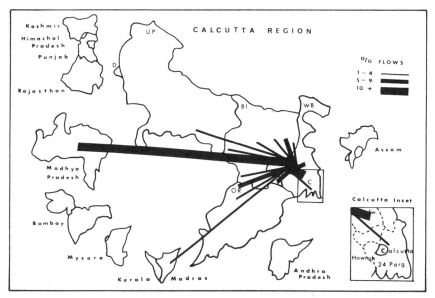

Figure 6. Bengal-Bihar Industrial Area - Inflows of Non-Metallic Minerals
(% of Total Non-Metallic Minerals Inflows)

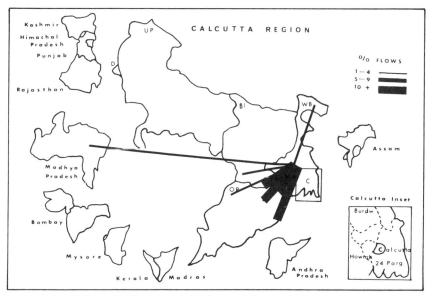

Figure 7. Bengal-Bihar Industrial Area - Inflows of Other Mineral Ores
(% of Total Other Mineral Ores Inflows)

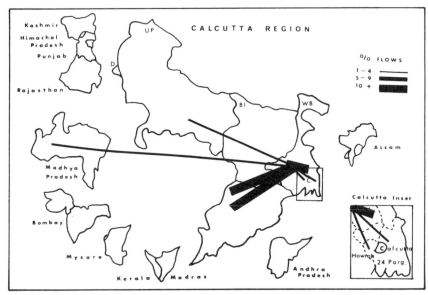

Figure 8. Bengal-Bihar Industrial Area - Inflows of Firebricks
(% of Total Firebricks Inflows)

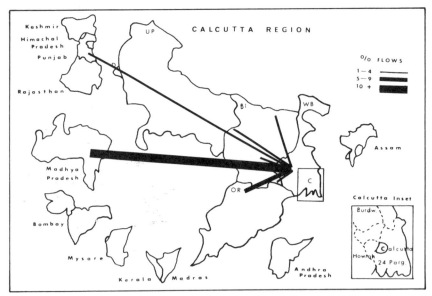

Figure 9. Bengal-Bihar Industrial Area - Inflows of Lime and Limestone
(% of Total Lime and Limestone Inflows)

semi-finished materials might be expected to support considerable transportation costs and come in quantity from all over India. However, the Bengal-Bihar Industrial Area specializes in the production of these metals itself and is located in close proximity to the northern Orissa steel mill and to imported and domestic metals and machinery available in the Calcutta metropolitan area. Inflows of metals and other goods to the study area for further manufacture come mainly from nearby intraregional sources. Only the most valuable commodities, such as machinery and electrical machinery, were received in any quantity from production points outside the region. In its role as producer of machinery and other manufactures, the study area was most closely linked to local exchange and to exchange with the Calcutta metropolitan area.

Figures 10-15 indicate inflows of iron and steel, non-ferrous metals, machinery, electrical machinery, chemicals, and wood manufactures. Ninety-one per cent of the iron and steel, 80 per cent of the non-ferrous metals, 80 per cent of the machinery and transport equipment, 56 per cent of the electrical machinery, 60 per cent of the chemicals, and 90 per cent of the wood manufactures came from intraregional sources. With three of India's largest steel mills and a large aluminum reduction plant located within it, the study area itself is one of India's largest steel and non-ferrous metals producers. Sixty per cent of the area's steel receipts were from within the study area, another 16 per cent came from the steel mill at Rourkela and other steel yards in northern Orissa, and the remainder of intraregional receipts were from imports, re-rolling mills, and steel yards in the Calcutta metropolitan area. The small amount of steel from outside the region came mainly from the steel works at Bhilai in adjacent Madhya Pradesh. Although the Accounts[1] indicate considerable interstate exchange of steel throughout India, local production appeared to satisfy local steel demands in the study area, and little steel was shipped in from other states.

Thirty per cent of the study area's non-ferrous metals receipts were from local exchange within the study area and another 30 per cent came from imports, scraping, and remanufacture in the Calcutta metropolitan area. Smaller intraregional flows came from northern Orissa. Interregional receipts were mainly from adjacent Andhra and from the Delhi and Bombay areas.

Intraregional receipts of machinery, equipment, and electrical machinery were mainly from the Calcutta metropolitan area, constituting 66 per cent and 40 per cent respectively of the area's total receipt of these goods by rail. These proportions indicate Calcutta's specialization as a major machinery center and port, the limited local

---

[1] India (Republic), Department of Commercial Intelligence and Statistics, Accounts, op. cit.

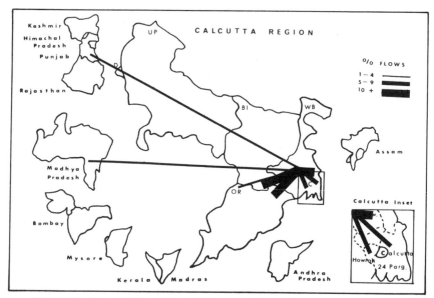

Figure 10. Bengal-Bihar Industrial Area - Inflows of Iron, Steel, Cast Iron
(% of Total Iron, Steel, Cast Iron Inflows)

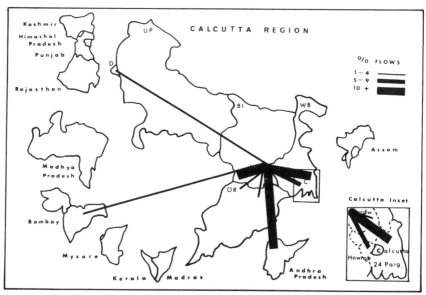

Figure 11. Bengal-Bihar Industrial Area - Inflows of Non-Ferrous Metals
(% of Total Non-Ferrous Metals Inflows)

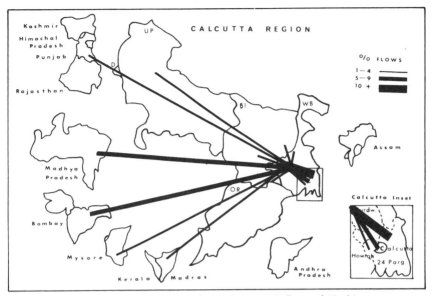

Figure 12. Bengal-Bihar Industrial Area - Inflows of Machinery
(% of Total Machinery Inflows)

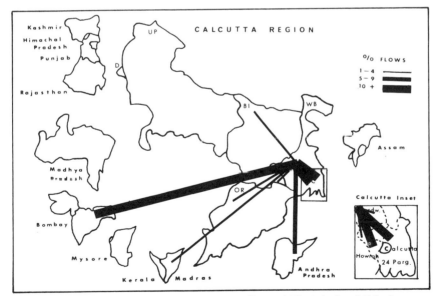

Figure 13. Bengal-Bihar Industrial Area - Inflows of Electrical and Telephone
Goods (% of Total Electrical and Telephone Goods Inflows)

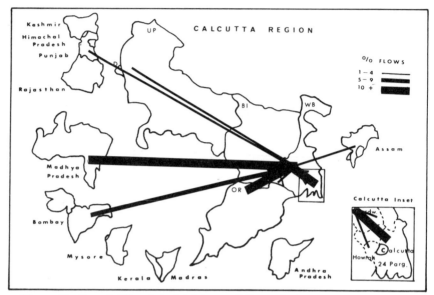

Figure 14. Bengal-Bihar Industrial Area - Inflows of Chemicals and Explosives
(% of Total Chemicals and Explosives Inflows)

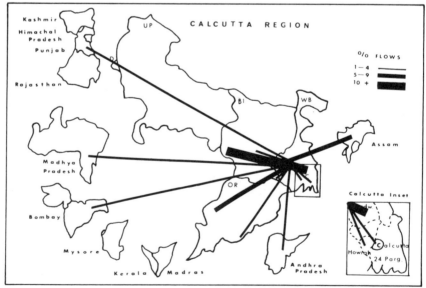

Figure 15. Bengal-Bihar Industrial Area - Inflows of Wood Manufactures
(% of Total Wood Manufactures Inflows)

exchange of machinery by rail within the study area itself, and the lack of major metal-working industries in the Calcutta region outside of the study area and the Calcutta metropolitan area. As expected, machinery and electrical goods produced in a wide range of areas throughout the rest of India were received in considerable quantities by the study area. Electrical goods came mainly from western and southern India. Other machinery came from the upper Ganges Valley as well as from western and southern sources. The Bombay and Madras areas are prominent in these flows.

Intraregional receipts of chemicals were mainly from sources in northern Orissa, the study area itself, and the Calcutta metropolitan area. Interregional shipments came mainly from Madhya Pradesh and the Bombay area. Chemicals were received in large volumes from only a few sources, reflecting limited chemical production throughout India.

The study area's receipts of wood manufactures came mainly from intraregional sources. Bihar and Orissa originated the greatest amounts of wood products; the study area exchanged extensively within itself; and Assam sent small amounts of specialized wood products. Interregional receipts of wood products were very limited, coming mainly from nearby Andhra and Madhya Pradesh.

Food and Construction Material Receipts

Small amounts of food and construction materials were received by rail in the area. As expected, the bulk of the low value construction goods moved short distances to the study area from intraregional sources. Interregional receipts of these consumer and construction goods were mainly from specialized grain and forest areas located near the region's boundaries. Except for imported food and petroleum products, the Calcutta metropolitan area sent almost no other consumer or heavy construction goods by rail to the study area. In its receipts of food the area was most closely linked to Calcutta and the Ganges Valley.

Figures 16-20 indicate the receipt patterns of wheat, gram, cement, raw wood, and non-wood building materials. Ninety per cent of the wheat, 99 per cent of the cement, 97 per cent of the non-wood building materials, and 75 per cent of the raw wood came from intraregional sources. Nearly 82 per cent of the study area's receipts of wheat came from imports through the Calcutta port although small amounts came from surplus growing areas in Punjab and Andhra. Gram came mainly from specialized areas of Uttar Pradesh, Punjab, and Rajasthan in the upper Ganges Valley. Rice came by truck from the Calcutta area and surrounding areas of West Bengal, Orissa, and Bihar. Like the raw minerals discussed earlier, heavy, lower value cement, wood, and non-wood

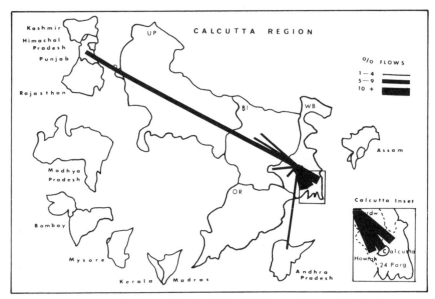

Figure 16. Bengal-Bihar Industrial Area - Inflows of Wheat
(% of Total Wheat Inflows)

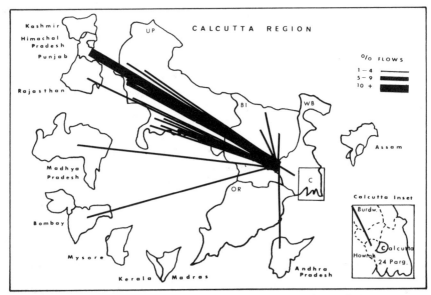

Figure 17. Bengal-Bihar Industrial Area - Inflows of Gram
(% of Total Gram Inflows)

45

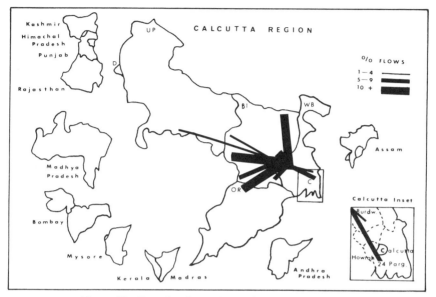

Figure 18. Bengal-Bihar Industrial Area - Inflows of Cement
(% of Total Cement Inflows)

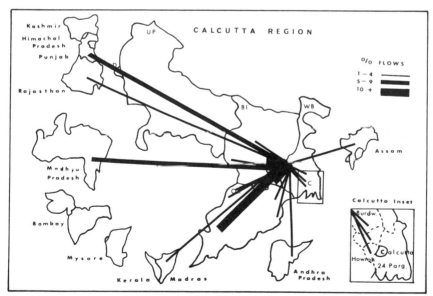

Figure 19. Bengal-Bihar Industrial Area - Inflows of Wood and Timber, Raw
(% of Total Wood and Timber, Raw Inflows)

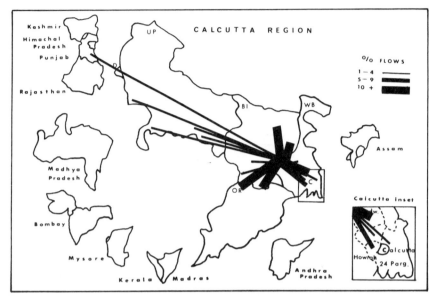

Figure 20. Bengal-Bihar Industrial Area - Inflows of Non-Wood Building
Material (% of Total Non-Wood Building Material Inflows)

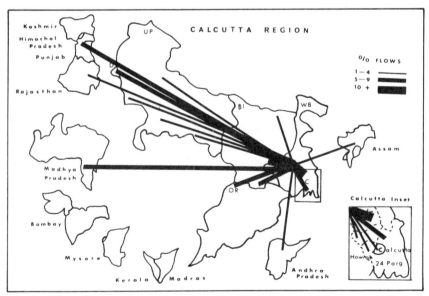

Figure 21. Bengal-Bihar Industrial Area - Outflows of Coal and Coke
(% of Total Coal and Coke Outflows)

building materials were able to stand only limited transport costs and came almost entirely from local and nearby intraregional sources. Twenty-five per cent of the cement received in the study area came from sources within the area itself; 70 per cent came from other areas of Bihar, with another 15 per cent from northern Orissa. Only 10 per cent of raw wood receipts came from within the study area, however, with 50 per cent coming from adjacent areas of Bihar and northern Orissa and small amounts from the rest of the region. Adjacent Madhya Pradesh, Punjab, and Andhra sent various types of wood in interregional trade. Nearly 30 per cent of the area's non-wood building materials were received from local production, the remainder from nearby areas of Bihar, northern Orissa, and small amounts from the Calcutta metropolitan area.

Coal Shipments

Coal constituted by far the largest volume of study-area outflows. As India's major industrial fuel, coal was distributed to numerous customers. Figure 21 indicates the pattern of study-area coal distribution. Nearly 75 per cent of the shipments went to the region with 40 per cent going to the study area itself, 10 per cent to the Calcutta metropolitan area, and 14 per cent to Uttar Pradesh. This pattern is clearly intraregional, oriented to the local area and Ganges Valley and conforms to the hypothesis of short hauls for heavy raw materials and fuels. Since the area's coals include India's finest metallurgical and higher grade coals on which the equipment in many of the older industries throughout India depends, more interregional flows might have been expected. In fact, although not reflected in rail statistics, considerable coal was shipped by water from Calcutta to the older industrial areas along the coasts of India.[1]

Part of the explanation of the highly interregional pattern of coal movement may be found in governmental regulation. Allotment of receipt priorities among coal consumers and the allotment of rail cars to move coal were under government regulation. To avoid rail bottlenecks, coal mines in Bihar, Madhya Pradesh, and Andhra to the study area's south were programmed to ship coal to the central, western, and southern Indian markets. Coal from the study area flowing to Andhra, Orissa, and Madhya Pradesh generally represented specialized metallurgical and higher grade coals not produced outside the study area and which could bear the price of transport. Due to shortages of rail cars, much coal was shipped by truck within a 150-mile radius of the study area's mines. The proportion of coal moving by rail within the study area and moving to the Calcutta

---

[1] India (Republic), Department of Commercial Intelligence and Statistics, Statistics of the Coasting Trade of India for Twelve Months ending March, 1962 (Calcutta: Government of India Press, 1962).

metropolitan area for local consumption or for coastal export would be much higher if trucking movements were accounted for. Due to the economies of coal transport and to governmental regulation, the study area was highly intraregionally oriented in its coal producing role.

Iron and Steel Shipments

Iron and steel shipments were the study area's next largest category of outflow. With India's largest concentration of metal-using industries located in the Calcutta metropolitan area and within the study area itself, the area was most strongly linked to local and intraregional markets. As expected, its main markets for steel outside the Calcutta region were found in the major industrial states.

Figure 22 indicates the pattern of outflow for iron and steel. Under government regulation at the time of this study, shipments of steel from the original producers and regulated steel yards were delivered at a uniform price throughout India. Purchasers near the mill bore part of the transport costs of those further away. In addition, receipts of steel by various consumers were allocated on an industry priority basis by the government. Under these conditions, one would expect a nationwide pattern of outflows of steel from the study area. However, over 60 per cent of iron and steel outflows went to intraregional destinations. Thirty-four per cent of these outflows went to the Calcutta metropolitan area, 12 per cent to the local study area, 6 per cent to Uttar Pradesh, 4 per cent to Orissa, and another 3 per cent to other areas of Bihar and Assam. This pattern clearly indicated the study area's role as supplier of metals to the concentration of machinery and metal-working industries in the Calcutta metropolitan area. Twenty per cent of the iron and steel shipped went to the machinery industries of Howrah and another 14 per cent to the rest of the metropolitan area. Many of the machinery industries of the study area are integrated on site with its large steel mills, and steel shipped within the plant for later fabrication is not recorded in the rail statistics. The quantity of local steel exchange was smaller than expected, reflecting interplant movement and movement of steel within the area by truck. Distribution of steel to other parts of the Calcutta region reflected the location of urban and industrial activities throughout the region.

Of the 40 per cent iron and steel shipments outside the region, the largest volume went to the Bombay area, followed by the Punjab and Rajasthan areas. Under the government's pricing policies and with numerous industries and construction sites throughout India using steel, the interregional pattern reflected the concentration of industries by state. The two steel mills at Rourkela and Bhalai near India's western and southern markets did not appear to act as intervening opportunities in the distribution of steel to these areas from the study area. This is to be expected since India's individual steel plants were not designed, and under government regulation not programmed, to produce or stock all grades of steel. The five steel mills in the Eastern Indian Industrial Region must all distribute nationally to provide the required product mix to the economy.

Shipments of Manufactures

Although obscured in the total outflow patterns by the large volume of coal and steel, the non-ferrous metals, chemicals, machinery, and other manufactures of the study area present a variety of intra- and interregional distribution patterns. Figures 23-28 indicate the pattern of non-ferrous metals, firebricks, chemicals, wood manufactures, machinery, and electrical machinery. For lower value materials such as non-ferrous metals, chemicals, firebricks, and wood manufactures, the patterns are highly intraregional, while for high value machinery and electrical machinery, distribution is much more interregional.

In its role as producer of heavy semi-finished manufactures, the study area was most closely linked with the nearby concentration of Calcutta and local study-area industry, displaying a highly intraregional pattern of distribution for these goods. In its role of finished machinery producer, however, the local area and the Calcutta metropolitan area provided only a limited market for the study area's output, and the area was most closely linked with interregional markets, mainly the Bombay, Punjab and Rajasthan areas of western and northwestern India. For both its heavier and its lighter manufactures, the concentration of complementary industry rather than distance appeared to have the greatest influence on study-area outflows of these goods.

Ninety per cent of the non-ferrous metals shipped from the study-area production and scraping went intraregionally, 60 per cent in local exchange, 12 per cent to northern Orissa, and 10 per cent to Calcutta. Interregional shipments went only to the Punjab and Madras areas. Eighty per cent of the study area's firebrick shipments went intraregionally, 60 per cent to the steel mills of the study area and northern Orissa and 12 per cent to Calcutta area industry. Interregional shipments of firebricks went to the steel mill at Bhilai in Madhya Pradesh and to the Bombay and Madras areas. Over 90 per cent of the study area's chemical shipments went to intraregional users, 30 per cent to the study area, 20 per cent to northern Orissa steel mills, and 20 per cent to the Calcutta metropolitan area. Small quantities went to the rest of the region and to adjacent Punjab. Of the wood manufactures shipped by rail, 85 per cent went into intraregional movement,

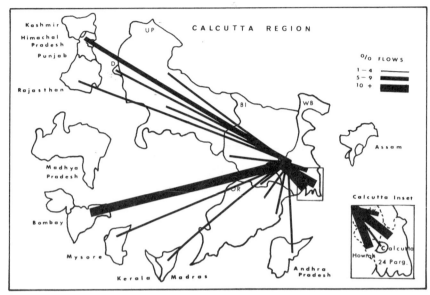

Figure 22. Bengal-Bihar Industrial Area - Outflows of Iron, Steel, Cast Iron
(% of Total Iron, Steel, Cast Iron Outflows)

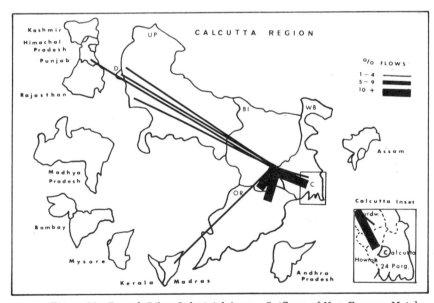

Figure 23. Bengal-Bihar Industrial Area - Outflows of Non-Ferrous Metals
(% of Total Non-Ferrous Metals Outflows)

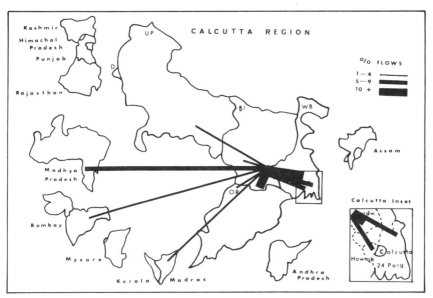

Figure 24. Bengal-Bihar Industrial Area - Outflows of Firebricks
(% of Total Firebricks Outflows)

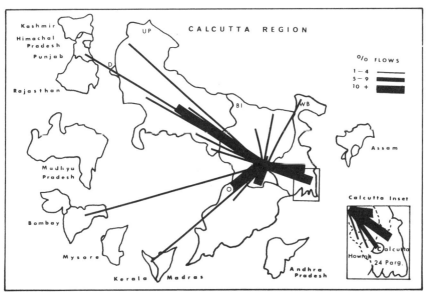

Figure 25. Bengal-Bihar Industrial Area - Outflows of Chemicals and
Explosives (% of Total Chemicals and Explosives Outflows)

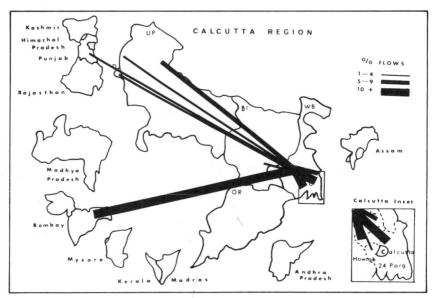

Figure 26. Bengal-Bihar Industrial Area - Outflows of Wood Manufactures
(% of Total Wood Manufactures Outflows)

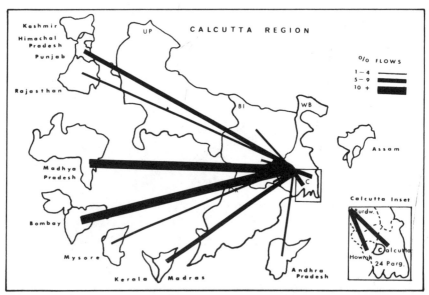

Figure 27. Bengal-Bihar Industrial Area - Outflows of Machinery
(% of Total Machinery Outflows)

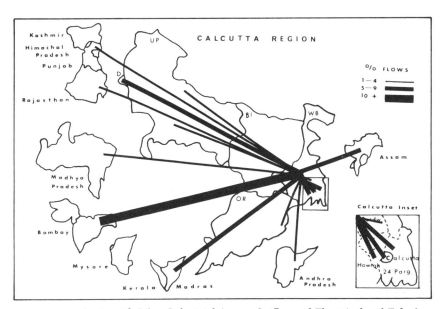

Figure 28: Bengal-Bihar Industrial Area - Outflows of Electrical and Telephone Goods (% of Total Electrical and Telephone Goods Outflows)

60 per cent of these to the Calcutta metropolitan area. Twelve per cent went to the Bombay area outside the region. In its production of these heavier materials, the study area played a major role as local and metropolitan area supplier.

Machinery and electrical machinery presented quite a different picture. Only 35 per cent and 44 per cent respectively of the study area's distribution went to intraregional destinations. Ten per cent of the machinery went to the study area itself, 15 per cent to the Calcutta metropolitan area, and small amounts to Bihar, Orissa, and Uttar Pradesh. Electrical machinery went in small amounts to the local area, 25 per cent to the Calcutta metropolitan area, 5 per cent to Assam (most likely to a construction site), and in smaller amounts throughout Uttar Pradesh and Orissa. If trucking movements were accounted for, local and metropolitan proportions would be much higher. Like steel which was distributed to a wide range of industries throughout India, interregional shipments of machinery went to a wide range of points. Electrical goods, however, went primarily to the Bombay area with small amounts to Punjab, Delhi, and Madras.

Aggregate Study-Area Exchange Patterns

The sum of these major commodity flow patterns gives rise to the study area's pattern of local, intra- and interregional exchange. The proportions of study-area and station-group exchanges with the city and metropolitan area of Calcutta, the five local districts of the study area, the Calcutta Region, and the rest of India are given in Tables 6 and 7 and the patterns indicated in Figures 29 and 30. The importance of various specialized areas as sources of supply or markets for study-area activities may be inferred from these proportions.

As expected, the greatest proportion of study-area rail exchange was intraregional. The study area's higher percentage of inflows from the Calcutta region than outflows to it indicated the study area's considerable dependence upon nearby sources for raw materials and upon extra-regional markets for many of its goods. Within its region, the study area depended upon the five local districts and the Calcutta metropolitan area more for markets than for supplies. However, the opposite was true with respect to its trade with the city and the port of Calcutta.

Also as expected, two distinct patterns of exchange were discernible between similarly and dissimilarly specialized areas. Receipts of raw materials for study-area industries tied it to other specialized mining areas within the Calcutta region. Producing little food itself, receipts of wheat tied the study area closely with the port of Calcutta. Its other food receipts tied the study area to specialized production areas throughout the Calcutta region. Shipments of coal from mines within the area tied it closely to industrial activities locally, in the Calcutta metropolitan area, and throughout the Calcutta region. Little coal was sent to other coal mining areas of the region. On the other hand, metals and machinery were exchanged mainly with other local industries of the study area, with industries of the Calcutta metropolitan area, and with other industrial areas throughout the region and rest of India specializing in similar lines of metal working and machinery manufacturing.

The proportions of exchange given in Tables 6 and 7 are in line with expectations for such an area given its diversity of specialization, its central location within the Calcutta region, and the existence of trucking within it and between the study area and the Calcutta metropolitan area. The major components of study-area receipts from the Calcutta metropolitan area--wheat, metals, and machinery--relate to Calcutta's role as manufacturer and urban population center. The large volume of wheat receipts ties the study area most closely to the city of Calcutta and its port. Coal, iron, and steel were the main components of shipments to the metropolitan area from the study area with the largest proportion of these heavy goods going to Howrah industries.

Inflows of heavy limestone and food grains and outflows of heavy steel and coal were the main components of the study area's interregional exchanges. Study-area complementarity with the rest of India is closely related to its mining and industrial roles and

TABLE 6

PERCENTAGE OF TOTAL INFLOWS TO STUDY-AREA STATIONS FROM REGIONS OF INDIA

Regions	Durga-pur	Rani-ganj	Asan-sol	Burn-pur	Bara-kar	Chitta-ranjan	Dhan-bad	Ranchi	Jamshed-pur	Khar-agpur	Adra	Study-Area Total
Calcutta and Its Region	79.8	70.7	95.3	38.8	93.0	91.6	83.4	85.5	89.2	79.5	0.0	76.5
Calcutta Region*	78.8	68.8	44.7	36.9	90.6	53.6	66.8	69.4	50.5	45.1	0.0	65.4
Five Local Districts	19.8	11.1	13.4	19.4	59.1	29.6	11.3	15.6	23.7	8.7	0.0	22.3
Calcutta	1.0	1.9	50.6	1.9	2.4	38.0	16.6	16.1	38.7	34.4	0.0	11.1
Metropolitan Area	1.1	7.2	64.9	2.3	4.8	45.3	32.0	22.9	41.0	47.4	0.0	13.5
Rest of India	19.9	28.6	4.7	60.7	6.3	8.1	16.0	14.5	9.9	18.8	0.0	22.6

TABLE 7

PERCENTAGE OF TOTAL OUTFLOWS FROM STUDY-AREA STATIONS TO REGIONS OF INDIA

Regions	Durga-pur	Rani-ganj	Asan-sol	Burn-pur	Bara-kar	Chitta-ranjan	Dhan-bad	Ranchi	Jamshed-pur	Khar-agpur	Adra	Study-Area Total
Calcutta and Its Region	79.1	90.2	76.3	59.4	83.4	86.1	70.5	81.4	59.4	97.0	77.0	72.8
Calcutta Region*	58.9	76.9	60.1	46.2	78.2	47.3	67.2	50.8	49.2	69.2	72.8	63.3
Five Local Districts	4.1	30.2	15.5	21.0	53.3	27.5	31.6	17.3	16.2	9.8	49.1	27.3
Calcutta	20.2	13.3	16.2	13.2	5.2	38.8	3.3	30.6	10.2	27.8	4.2	9.5
Metropolitan Area	59.9	44.0	19.4	23.0	8.6	51.4	4.1	49.7	25.9	57.8	4.6	16.1
Rest of India	20.7	9.6	23.2	40.4	16.5	13.7	29.1	18.6	39.7	3.0	22.8	26.9

* The Calcutta Region is defined as the states of Assam, West Bengal excluding Calcutta, Orissa, Bihar, and Uttar Pradesh. The Calcutta Metropolitan Area is defined as the West Bengal districts of Calcutta, 24 Parganas, and Howrah. Exchanges of less than .1 per cent were not included sc figures do not add to 100 per cent.

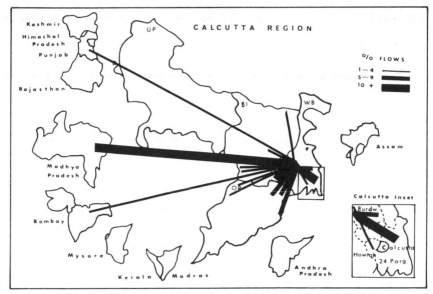

Figure 29. Bengal-Bihar Industrial Area - Total Inflows

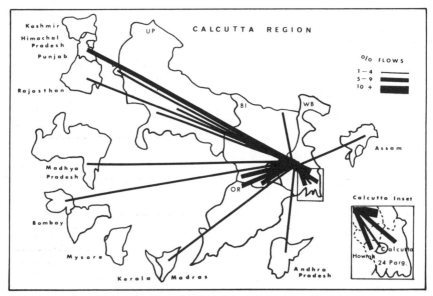

Figure 30. Bengal-Bihar Industrial Area - Total Outflows

to its needs for foodstuffs.

The large volume of heavy minerals and metals exchanged within the five local districts of the study area comprise the bulk of its high proportion of local exchanges indicating complementarity between the various mining and manufacturing specialties of the area. The study area's high proportion of intraregional exchanges reflects its large volume of heavy raw materials, steel and coal exchanged with the Calcutta region. In its basic roles, the study area is highly complementary with its surrounding region. Each of these exchange patterns reflects the area's diversity in specialization, scale of production, and location within a major mining and manufacturing area of India.

Comparison of Study Area with West Bengal, Bihar, and Calcutta Region Exchange Patterns

Another perspective on the high degree of complementarity between the study area and the Calcutta region may be seen by comparing the proportions of local, intra- and interregional exchanges of various goods for the study area, the two surrounding states, and the Calcutta region. For a range of goods, Tables 8 and 9 indicate that study-area exchanges were much more oriented toward intraregional exchange than either the two surrounding states or region. Limestone was the only exception and the conditions influencing its exchange by the study area were noted earlier. Except for wheat receipts, the study area is much less dependent upon the Calcutta metropolitan area than were the two states or the Calcutta region. This may be due in part to trucking movements reducing the importance of study-area rail exchanges with the Calcutta area. Also, the heavy goods which the study area exchanged with Calcutta were mainly coal, steel, and wheat; while in addition, the surrounding states and region exchanged large volumes of other heavy grains increasing their proportions of rail exchanges with Calcutta.

Various factors are involved in the difference between study-area proportions in the different types of exchange and those of the Calcutta region and two states. One factor related to the degree of diversity in the specialization of each of these areas. The less diversified an area, the more likely it is to have a high proportion of its exchanges in but one of the three types of exchange, probably intraregional. Because the study area was much less diversified in its production and consumption than the surrounding states or the region, it would be expected to have a much higher proportion of local or intraregional exchange. Since local flows were recorded for the study area and only interstate flows were reported for the two states and region, the figures for the study area were further biased toward intraregional exchange. And, as noted earlier, the location of a specialized area within its region should result in differences between an area and its region in the proportions of local, intra- and interregional exchanges. The study area

TABLE 8

PERCENTAGE OF TOTAL INFLOWS OF SELECTED
COMMODITIES BY AREA

		All Com-modities	Coal	Steel	Lime-stone[a]	Cement	Wheat	Raw Wood
From Calcutta to:								
Calcutta Region[b]	(1959)	15.1	.3	44.2	.1	.4	57.8	6.8
Bihar	(1959)	14.4	-	47.5	-	8.4	57.7	10.1
W. Bengal	(1959)	23.1	.1	70.0	.1	.7	98.6	10.1
Study Area	(1962)	11.1	-	8.1	-	6.7	70.8	.6
From Rest of Calcutta Region to:								
Calcutta Region	(1959)	33.6	99.1	45.1	74.3	36.9	1.6	61.7
Bihar	(1959)	47.8	100.0	49.1	85.5	86.2	5.6	76.2
W. Bengal	(1959)	57.9	99.8	27.9	75.1	99.0	.5	80.2
Study Area	(1962)	66.3	100.0	82.7	22.9	89.8	22.6	74.3
From Calcutta and Its Region to:								
Calcutta Region	(1959)	48.7	99.4	89.3	74.4	37.3	59.4	68.5
Bihar	(1959)	62.2	100.0	96.6	85.5	94.6	63.3	86.3
W. Bengal	(1959)	81.0	99.9	97.9	75.2	99.7	99.1	90.3
Study Area	(1962)	77.4	100.0	90.8	22.9	96.5	93.4	74.9
From Rest of India to:								
Calcutta Region	(1959)	51.3	.6	10.7	25.6	62.7	40.6	31.5
Bihar	(1959)	37.7	-	3.2	14.3	5.0	36.3	13.5
W. Bengal	(1959)	19.0	-	1.6	24.3	-	.8	9.7
Study Area	(1962)	22.6	0.0	9.2	77.1	3.2	6.6	25.1

a. Data on limestone is for the twelve months ending March, 1961.

b. The Calcutta Region is defined as the states of Assam, W. Bengal excluding the city of Calcutta, Orissa, Bihar, and Uttar Pradesh.

Source: Computed from India (Republic), Department of Commercial Intelligence and Statistics, Accounts Relating to the Inland (Rail and Water-Borne) Trade of India for twelve months ending March, 1960 (Calcutta: Government of India Press, 1961). Study-area data computed from individual station records.

TABLE 9

PERCENTAGE OF TOTAL OUTFLOWS OF SELECTED
COMMODITIES BY AREA

		All Com-modities	Coal	Steel	Lime-[a] stone	Cement	Wheat	Raw Wood
To Calcutta from:								
Calcutta Region[b]	(1959)	14.2	19.9	20.5	1.6	27.4	1.6	25.2
Bihar	(1959)	17.4	7.1	20.8	13.2	25.8	11.4	21.4
W. Bengal	(1959)	16.8	38.3	22.4	22.7	14.1	12.8	46.8
Study Area	(1962)	9.5	8.7	13.6	.5	-	11.8	40.5
To Rest of Calcutta Region from:								
Calcutta Region	(1959)	26.0	41.6	18.0	96.7	68.0	35.0	34.6
Bihar	(1959)	31.1	50.8	15.5	84.2	74.0	86.3	48.5
W. Bengal	(1959)	21.1	30.5	21.6	60.9	67.3	77.7	28.6
Study Area	(1962)	63.6	66.2	48.1	41.9	98.9	88.2	51.3
To Calcutta and Its Region from:								
Calcutta Region	(1959)	40.2	61.5	38.5	98.3	95.4	36.6	59.8
Bihar	(1959)	48.5	57.9	36.3	97.4	99.8	97.7	69.9
W. Bengal	(1959)	37.9	68.8	44.0	83.6	81.4	90.5	75.4
Study Area	(1962)	73.1	74.9	61.7	42.4	98.9	100.0	91.8
To Rest of India from:								
Calcutta Region	(1959)	59.0	38.5	61.5	1.7	4.6	63.0	40.2
Bihar	(1959)	51.6	42.1	63.7	2.4	-	1.8	30.1
W. Bengal	(1959)	61.9	31.2	56.0	16.2	17.8	8.7	24.6
Study Area	(1962)	26.9	25.0	37.7	57.6	1.2	-	8.0

a. Data on limestone is for the twelve months ending March, 1961.

b. The Calcutta Region is defined as the states of Assam, W. Bengal excluding the city of Calcutta, Orissa, Bihar, and Uttar Pradesh.

Source: Computed from India (Republic), Department of Commercial Intelligence and Statistics, Accounts Relating to the Inland (Rail and Water-Borne) Trade of India for twelve months ending March, 1960 (Calcutta: Government of India Press, 1961). Study-area data computed from individual station records.

has clearly taken advantage of its central location within the Calcutta region and engages in extensive intraregional exchange.

CHAPTER IV

STATION EXCHANGES AND THE ROLES OF OTHER

SPECIALIZED AREAS

The major roles played by the Bengal-Bihar Industrial Area within the Indian economy and the commodity exchanges associated with these roles were discussed in Chapter III. Still to be considered are the effects of specialization and location within the study area upon individual station-group flow patterns, and the effect of roles played by India's other specialized areas upon study-area exchange patterns.

Individual Station Exchanges and Locational Effects

In commodity exchange patterns of individual station groups, east-west differences in the proportion of interregional exchanges, exchanges with the eastern and western areas of the Calcutta Region, and exchanges with the Calcutta metropolitan area are discernible. Those stations located in Bihar with greater proximity to Bihar, Uttar Pradesh, and interregional areas engage more extensively in interregional exchanges and in exchanges with the western part of the Calcutta region than do stations in West Bengal. In turn, West Bengal stations with greater proximity to the Calcutta area engage in considerably more trade with the metropolitan area and points in West Bengal, Orissa, and Assam than do Bihar stations. In addition to these east-west differences, there are north-south differences in the proportion of goods sent to north India and the Ganges Valley and to west and south India. Stations located along the Eastern Railway system serving northeastern India tend to trade heavily with north Indian areas. Stations on the Southeastern Railway system tend to trade heavily with central, western and southern Indian areas served by this system, Figures 3 and 4 .

These locational differences in the pattern of individual station groups' commodity exchanges are due in part to governmental regulation and in part to economies of transporting the specialized mix of commodities exchanged. As noted earlier, low value heavy commodities are more sensitive to variations in transport costs than are high value

61

commodities.[1] In general, lower value goods can be shipped economically only short distances. Thus flow patterns of study-area stations exchanging a high proportion of heavy low value goods were most affected by the station's location within the study area. Similarly, with heavier goods comprising the bulk of intraregional exchange, an individual station's intraregional exchange patterns were much more sensitive to its location within the study area than were its patterns of interregional exchange.

The effects of location within the study area are pronounced in the patterns of food receipts for individual stations. This may be ascribed partially to transport costs and partially to government regulation. Government regulation at the time of this study prevented the flow of rice and other food grains across the West Bengal-Bihar state boundary, creating an east-west split in many food receipt patterns. This split was most clear in the rice receipt patterns of Raniganj and Ranchi, Figures 31 and 32 . Wheat receipts in Asansol were mainly from the Calcutta metropolitan area while those in Dhanbad came more from Bihar and the upper Ganges Valley, reflecting government regulation and proximity to competing imported and domestic sources, Figures 33 and 34 .

Under government regulation, coals from the various coal fields were shipped mainly within the rail system serving the field. Figures 35-37 indicate coal shipment patterns from the Asansol, Dhanbad, and Adra booking points. The Eastern Railway serving the lower Ganges Valley funneled Asansol and Dhanbad coal to northern Bihar and Uttar Pradesh within the region and considerable coal to interregional points in adjacent Delhi, Punjab, and Rajasthan. Coal booked from Adra on the Southeastern Railway went mainly to the steel mills located along its route at Jamshedpur in Bihar, Rourkela in Orissa, and outside the region at Bhalai in Madhya Pradesh. Asansol's proximity to Calcutta made it the leading metropolitan area supplier, while Dhanbad's proximity to the lower Ganges Valley encouraged its heavy shipments to this area. Thus a north-south as well as an east-west split occurs for coal distribution from the study-area stations.

Cement allocation was also under government control at the time of this study, and location within the study area affected the pattern of cement receipts of the various stations. Figures 38 and 39 indicate a north-south split in individual station receipts of cement with cement flowing from northern Bihar sources to Raniganj, while Kharagpur received nearly all its cement from southern Bihar and northern Orissa sources.

Variation in the pattern of steel distribution due in part to product specialization and in part to location may be seen in the distribution patterns of the steel mills at Durgapur, Burnpur, and Jamshedpur, Figures 40-42 . Located nearest to Calcutta,

---

[1] Chapter III, pp. 27-28.

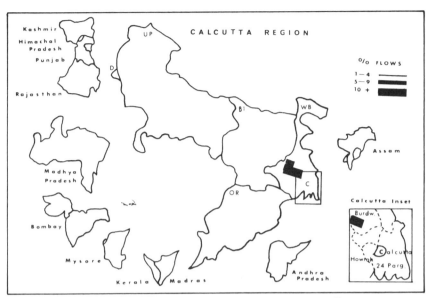

Figure 31. Raniganj – Inflows of Rice Not in Husk (% of Total
Rice Not in Husk Inflows to Raniganj)

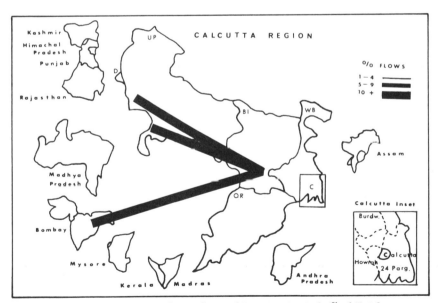

Figure 32. Ranchi – Inflows of Rice Not in Husk (% of Total
Rice Not in Husk Inflows to Ranchi)

64

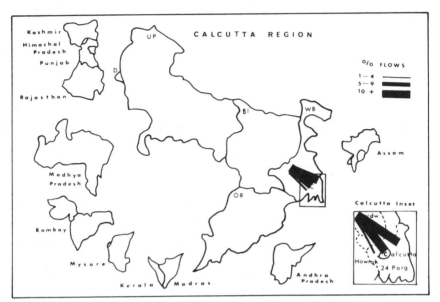

Figure 33.   Asansol - Inflows of Wheat (% of Total
Wheat Inflows to Asansol)

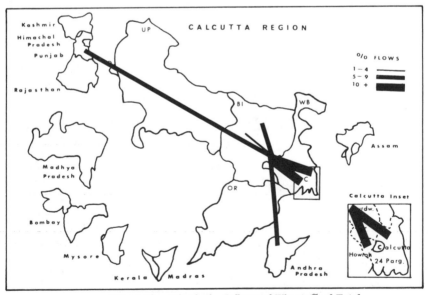

Figure 34.   (Dhanbad - Inflows of Wheat (% of Total
Wheat Inflows to Dhanbad)

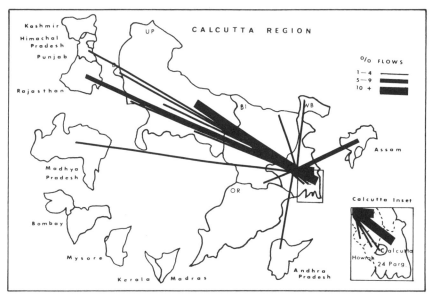

Figure 35.   Asansol – Outflows of Coal and Coke (% of Total
Coal and Coke Outflows from Asansol)

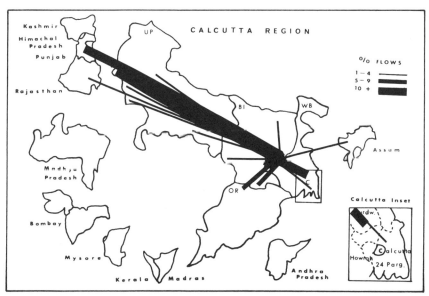

Figure 36.   Dhanbad – Outflows of Coal and Coke (% of Total
Coal and Coke Outflows from Dhanbad)

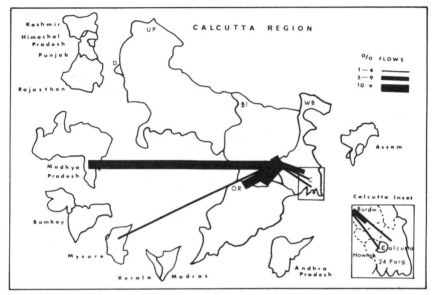

Figure 37.   Adra – Outflows of Coal and Coke (% of Total
Coal and Coke Outflows from Adra)

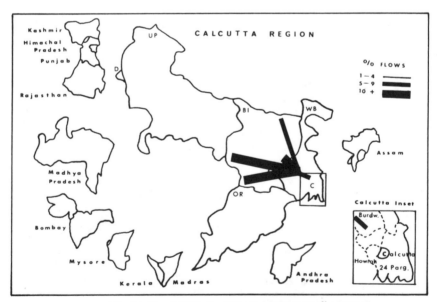

Figure 38.   Raniganj – Inflows of Cement (% of Total
Cement Inflows to Raniganj)

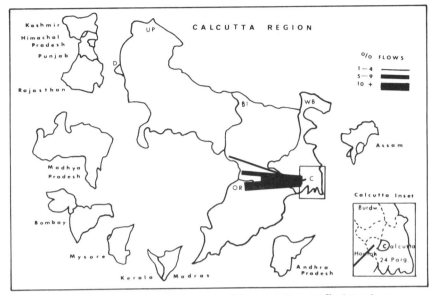

Figure 39. Kharagpur – Inflows of Cement (% of Total
Cement Inflows to Kharagpur)

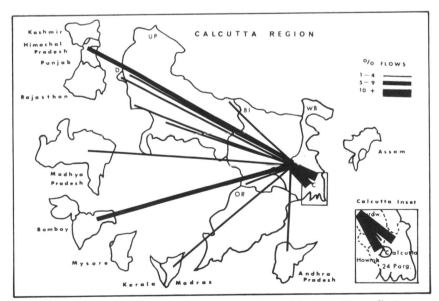

Figure 40. Durgapur – Outflows of Iron, Steel, Cast Iron (% of
Total Iron, Steel, Cast Iron Outflows from Durgapur)

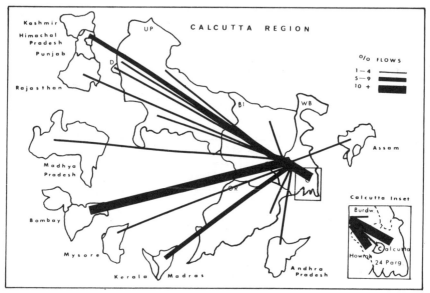

Figure 41.   Burnpur - Outflows of Iron, Steel, Cast Iron (% of
Total Iron, Steel, Cast Iron Outflows from Burnpur)

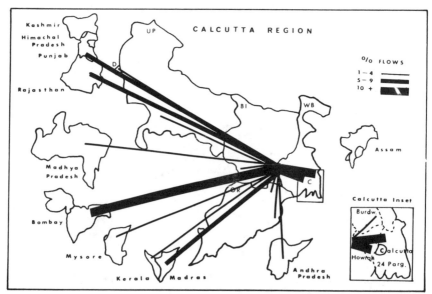

Figure 42.   Jamshedpur - Outflows of Iron, Steel, Cast Iron (% of
Total Iron, Steel, Cast Iron Outflows from Jamshedpur)

Durgapur sent nearly 60 per cent of its outflows of light sections and ingots to the Calcutta area, 20 per cent to the rest of the Calcutta region (mostly to Ganges Valley points), and 20 per cent to the rest of India, mainly the Bombay and Punjab areas. Burnpur and Jamshedpur, producing a wider range of steel products and located further from Calcutta, shipped more extensively throughout the Calcutta region and sent 50 per cent of their iron and steel outside the region to all parts of India, mainly to the Bombay, Punjab, and Rajasthan areas of western and northern India.

An example of the influence of trucking on study-area flow patterns is related to receipts of petroleum products. Petroleum fuels imported through Calcutta were sent mainly by truck to the study area and only Kharagpur, located well off the Grand Trunk Road, received petroleum products in any large quantity by rail.

One would expect location within the study area to have considerable effect on individual station patterns of heavy raw material receipts. However, with a number of stations in both the West Bengal and Bihar segments of the study area engaged in similar iron and steel manufacture, each station had to draw its heavy raw material supplies from the same few available sources. A similar situation existed in the receipts and shipments of machinery and other manufactures. Study-area stations in both states are engaged extensively in their use and manufacture. With the high value per unit of weight of these goods and with an extensive nationwide system for their exchange developed, a station's specialization rather than location within the study area affected most its exchanges of these manufactured goods.

Roles of Other Specialized Areas with Respect to the Study Area

To gain another perspective on the organization of both the Calcutta region and the Indian economic system, it will be useful to consider the roles which other specialized areas of India play in relation to the study area. Evident in this analysis are the patterns of exchange based on complementarity between extractive and manufacturing activities linking areas of dissimilar specialization and those based on complementarity between different stages of manufacturing linking areas of similar specialization. [1]

Due to its manufacturing specialization, the study area acts as a market for specialized agricultural, mining, and industrial areas scattered throughout its region but is most important to Uttar Pradesh, Bihar, and Orissa agriculture; Bihar, Orissa, and West Bengal mining; and Calcutta metropolitan area industry. Interregionally, the study area is most important to Punjab, Rajasthan, and Andhra agriculture; Madhya Pradesh

---

[1] See discussion in Chapter III, pp. 28-30.

minerals; and Bombay, Punjab, and Rajasthan industries.

As a source of supply, the study area's mining and manufacturing specialization makes it most important to industrial areas throughout its region. Its coal is shipped to the Calcutta metropolitan area and to the entire Ganges Valley. As a source of metals and manufactures, the area is again most important to the Calcutta metropolitan area, scattered industry throughout the region, and to the upper Ganges Valley and Bombay areas outside the region. Only its most specialized machinery and metals are sent in any quantity to complementary areas of south India, and the Bengal-Bihar Industrial Area is most closely integrated with north Indian economic activity. Specific exchanges with these other specialized areas will be examined in turn.

As mentioned earlier, Tables 6 and 7 indicate the proportion of each station's total exchange with various specialized areas of the Indian economy. Tables 10-19 found at the end of this chapter are the disaggregation of Tables 6 and 7. For each station, these tables indicate the proportion of that station's total exchanges accounted for by the exchange of individual commodities with the specific area covered by the table. They further indicate the proportion of total goods exchanged with specific states and districts of India. Thus, Table 10 indicates that 41 per cent of all commodities received by rail in Asansol consisted of wheat from the city of Calcutta.

Exchanges with Calcutta and the Calcutta Metropolitan Area

The port of Calcutta's role in importing foreign foodstuffs and petroleum and the manufacturing roles of Calcutta and its metropolitan area in collecting and processing domestic goods for use in later stages of manufacture is evident in the mix of Bengal-Bihar Industrial Area receipts from the Calcutta area. Table 10 reflects the importance of Calcutta's port and manufacturing within the city while Table 11 indicates the importance of the rest of the metropolitan area, especially the Howrah industrial complex, in supplying the study area with machinery and other manufactures. The small additional weight received from the metropolitan area over that from the city reflects the large volume of wheat shipments in the mix of flows from Calcutta.

The study-area stations with the largest proportion of metropolitan area receipts --Asansol, Chittaranjan, Dhanbad, Ranchi, Jamshedpur, and Kharagpur--receive mainly heavy wheat, steel, other metals, machinery, and petroleum from it. The stations receiving the largest quantity of wheat--Asansol, Dhanbad, and Jamshedpur--act as central distributors to local manufacturing and mining populations. Dhanbad and Ranchi show the greatest dependence on the machinery industry of Howrah. The older urban stations of the study area--Raniganj, Asansol, Dhanbad, Ranchi, Jamshedpur, and

Kharagpur--depend on the Calcutta metropolitan area for foods as well as metals and machinery. The industrial stations and new stations--Durgapur, Burnpur, Barakar, and Chittaranjan--received mainly machinery and metals. With all the stations receiving high value goods from the metropolitan area, specialization in wheat distribution seems to affect most an individual station's proportion of receipts from Calcutta.

The roles of the Calcutta metropolitan area as a major industrial area specialized in machinery and other metal manufacturing and as a collector of regional specialties for redistribution is evident in the shipment of heavy raw materials and metals to it from the study area (Tables 12 and 13). Each of the study area's specialized roles link it to the metropolitan area with Asansol sending coal; Durgapur, Burnpur, Chittaranjan, and Jamshedpur sending iron and steel; Durgapur, Chittaranjan, Ranchi, and Jamshedpur sending machinery and other manufactures; and Kharagpur sending rice. All of the study-area stations, except for Barakar, Dhanbad, and Adra sent large quantities of their output to the Calcutta area. These stations located further from the metropolitan area sent their heavy coal and other products to western parts of the Calcutta region. Specialization rather than location within the study area affect most an individual station's pattern of shipment to the Calcutta area. The importance of Howrah's industrial concentration in the consumption of metals and coal is apparent in the differences between shipments to the city of Calcutta and the metropolitan area. Since coal is the only study-area good exported to any extent, the port of Calcutta has little impact on the outflows from the study area.

Exchanges within the Five Local Districts

Each of the study area's major roles leads to internal linkages between the specialized mining and industrial activities of the study area. According to Table 14, the major local receipts from the study area were raw materials, steel, and building materials from local sources, with only limited receipts of machinery and other manufactures. The main shipments from the area to itself, Table 15, were coal, steel, minerals, firebricks, and building materials. Coal receipts were not included in inflow figures but may be inferred from outflows of coal to the study area.

Raw materials and metals were exchanged by all stations within the area; however, rail exchanges within the study area vary considerably, reflecting the specialization of each station, Tables 14 and 15. Barakar had the largest proportion of exchanges within the study area, sending out large quantities of firebricks and exchanging considerable iron and steel with other stations. A large proportion of the outflows to the area were coal from Adra and Dhanbad and firebricks and other minerals from Raniganj. Machinery and other manufactures are exchanged locally mainly by Chittaranjan, Dhanbad, and Ranchi. As noted earlier, this limited machinery exchange reflected the lack of ancillary industries, the integration on site of steel and machinery plants, and local trucking. As one might expect, Tables 14 and 15 indicate that the largest volume of each station's local exchanges tended to be with its local district. The greatest local exchange between districts involved north-south flows of Singhbhum district's minerals, ores, and steel to Burdwan district and Burdwan's coal, other minerals, steel, and machinery to Singhbhum district. Singhbhum and Burdwan coal and machinery exchanges with Dhanbad district were the next largest volume of local exchange.

Exchanges with the Calcutta Region

The effect of the large proportion of heavy commodities exchanged by the study area and the strong complementarity between its specialization and the mining, agricultural, and industrial specialization of other areas throughout the Calcutta region are reflected in the pattern and high proportion of intraregional exchanges in which the study area engages, Tables 16 and 17 . Table 16 indicates that the study-area stations each received nearly a full range of commodities from the Calcutta region, including the five local districts; and that each of the area's roles is associated with this intraregional exchange. Agriculturally specialized areas in the Ganges Valley and the port of Calcutta were the study area's main regional sources of foodstuffs and other consumer goods. The local study area, southern Bihar, and northern Orissa were its main sources of minerals and forest products, while the Calcutta metropolitan area was its main source of industrial goods.

With respect to study-area food receipts, the primary supply areas were the port of Calcutta which sent imported wheat and the rice-surplus areas of West Bengal, Orissa, and northern Bihar which supplied the various study-area stations nearest them. Other consumer goods including grains, pulses, sugar, tobacco, and oilseeds came from agricultural surplus areas in Bihar and Uttar Pradesh. These agricultural goods appeared quite important in the trade of study-area urban centers except for Ranchi and Jamshedpur where tobacco and grains were grown locally. Ranchi received a large proportion of raw fibres from West Bengal. As noted in Chapter III, non-wood building materials, wood, and construction material came mainly from the five local districts. Receipts of cement, firebricks, ores, fluxes, metals, machinery, and chemicals were the largest proportions of intraregional receipts. These materials came mainly from West Bengal, Bihar, and northern Orissa, reflecting the rich mineral deposits, steel mills, and other industries located in these areas.

The largest proportion of study-area receipts came from industrially and mining specialized West Bengal and Bihar. Northern Orissa sent industrial raw materials, steel, and chemicals mainly to the steel stations and the Raniganj and Midnapore areas while coastal Orissa sent small amounts of rice. Trade with Orissa was most important for Durgapur, Jamshedpur, Burnpur, and Midnapore. Agriculturally specialized Uttar Pradesh sent foods and small amounts of machinery and raw materials to nearly all the stations. Trade with Uttar Pradesh was most important for Raniganj and Dhanbad. Agriculturally specialized Assam sent mainly wood products and straw to the study area, with the majority of such shipments to Raniganj and Dhanbad.

The study area's outflows to the Calcutta region reflected the specialization of various receiving areas, Table 17. The coal, steel, other metals, and machinery of the study area went in large volume to the industrially specialized Calcutta metropolitan area and to the study area itself. Steel mills and industries located in Orissa and Uttar Pradesh received small quantities of coal, metals, and machinery. Rice, the area's main food grain, went almost entirely to the Calcutta market.

Except for Ranchi, Adra, and Jamshedpur, the greatest proportion of shipments from study-area stations went to the states in which they are located. Surrounding Bihar and West Bengal received the greatest proportion of study-area shipments. Uttar Pradesh received a considerable volume of coal, metals, and other raw materials; Orissa, less of these goods; and Assam, only small quantities of coal and steel from the study area. These intraregional distribution patterns indicated the limited nature of industrial development in areas of the Calcutta region outside the metropolitan area and the study area itself and the limited degree of complementarity between the study area and these other regional areas.

Exchanges with the Rest of India

In its interregional exchanges, the study area was linked primarily with northern Indian industry and agriculture. The largest interregional inflow to the area was limestone from mineral-rich eastern Madhya Pradesh, Table 18. Other inflows were primarily iron and steel from Madhya Pradesh and the Bombay and upper Ganges Valley areas, and machinery and other manufactured goods again from the Bombay and upper Ganges Valley. Non-metallic minerals came from the Punjab area, and food grains came mainly from the upper Ganges Valley and Andhra. Following Madhya Pradesh, the largest proportion of inflows came from manufacturing and grain surplus areas in the upper Ganges Valley, Delhi, Punjab, and Rajasthan, followed by metals and machinery from the Bombay area and small amounts of food and machinery from southern India,

Madras, Andhra, and Mysore. Each of the stations received metals, machinery, other manufactures, and minerals from outside the region, and the older stations--Raniganj, Dhanbad, Ranchi, and Jamshedpur--received considerable foodstuffs from extra-regional sources.

The study area's outflows to the rest of India reflected its role as coal and steel supplier and went to areas of complementary industrial specialization, mainly in northern and western India, Table 19 . As discussed earlier, coal, including much metallurgical coal, from Asansol was sent throughout India. Dhanbad coal was sent extensively to Delhi and the upper Ganges Valley, while Adra coal went mainly to Madhya Pradesh. Steel from Durgapur was sent to western India, Bombay, Punjab, and Delhi, with lesser amounts to Madhya Pradesh and south to Andhra Pradesh and Madras. Burnpur sent a large proportion of its steel to Bombay and most of the rest of its interregional shipments to western India. Jamshedpur also sent a large proportion of its steel to Bombay and the rest widely throughout western India. Shipments of machinery and chemicals from all the stations went to Bombay and Western India, but show considerable shipments to south India. Asansol coal and Burnpur and Jamshedpur steel were the major shipments to the states of south India. Clearly, areas of north India are most complementary with the specialized production and consumption of the study area.

CHAPTER IV TABLES

Table 10

FLOWS BY COMMODITY TO STUDY-AREA STATIONS FROM THE CITY OF CALCUTTA AS A
PERCENTAGE OF TOTAL FLOWS FROM ALL OF INDIA TO STUDY-AREA STATIONS

Commodities	Durga-pur	Rani-ganj	Asan-sol	Burn-pur	Bara-kar	Chitta-ranjan	Dhan-bad	Ranchi	Jamshed-pur	Khar-agpur	Adra	Study-Area Total
1. Other foods		.7					-*	-	-	-		-
2. Wheat	-		41.1		.4	1.0	12.0	1.0	27.9	2.8		5.9
3. Wheat flour							.5		.1	-		-
4. Rice in husk						10.1		1.5	-			-
5. Rice not in husk							.6		.2	.2		.2
6. Other grains					-				-	.1		-
7. Gram, pulses						-			-	-		-
8. Sugar						-			-	-		-
9. Tea												-
10. Coffee							-					
11. Groundnut seed												
12. Rape & mustard seed					-		-		.2	-		
13. Other seeds							.1		-			
14. Salt									.1	.1		-
15. Groundnut oil		.1						-				-
16. Other vegetable oil					.1			.2	.1	.8		-
17. Tobacco products												-
18. Tobacco raw												
19. Other agric. products					-				-	-		
20. Hides & skins, raw						-						-
21. Leather manufactures												
22. Straw							-	-	-	-		-
23. Raw jute							.1	-	-			-
24. Other raw fibre							-		.1	-		-
25. Cement	.3		-			-	.1	-	.1			.1
26. Firebricks						.5	-		.3			.1
27. Lime & limestone				.3					-			.1

Commodity												
28. Other mineral ores	.4	–		.1	.4				.2	–		–
29. Non-metalic minerals	.1	.1	.5						.2	.2	.1	.1
30. Coal & coke	.3								–	–	–	–
31. Iron, steel, cast iron	–	.3	5.9	.3	.9	14.9	.9	2.8	1.5	1.3	1.5	1.1
32. Scrap iron	.1	–	–			.2		–				–
33. Non-ferrous metals	–					1.8		–	.8	.1		.1
34. Machinery	.1	.1	.1	.1	–	–	–	7.5	2.5	.4	.8	.8
35. Elec. & tel. goods	–	.6	.6			.7	–	.2	.1	.1	.8	.8
36. Chemicals, explosives	.1	.4	.4	.6	.3	.3	.2	.1	.4	.8	.1	.2
37. Medicine, cosmetics		–	–					–				–
38. Paper & paper products								.1				–
39. Glass								–			.1	–
40. Kerosene	.4		.4	.1	.1		1.0	1.3	.2	6.3	.2	.3
41. Other petroleum fuels	.1	2.0	2.0	–	.2	6.1	.9	.6	3.4	20.8	3.4	1.3
42. Rubber manufactures					–							–
43. Wood manufactures	–					.1	.1		.1	.1	.1	–
44. Wood & timber, raw	.1	–	–									–
45. Gunnies, jute products						.9		.1	.1		.1	–
46. Other textiles				–		.9						–
47. Non-wood bldg. material	.6	.1	.1	.1	.1	–	–	–				–
48. Miscellaneous	–	.1	–		.2	.3	.3	.4	.6	.3	.6	.1
Percentage of total	1.0	1.9	50.6	1.9	2.4	38.0	16.6	16.1	38.7	34.4	0.0	11.1
Metric tons (100's)	63	10	222	41	24	59	54	98	252	153	0	980

Source: Data compiled from individual station records for April, July, and October, 1962.

*Dash indicates less than .1 per cent.

TABLE 11

FLOWS BY COMMODITY TO STUDY-AREA STATIONS FROM THE CALCUTTA METROPOLITAN AREA AS A PERCENTAGE OF TOTAL FLOWS FROM ALL OF INDIA TO STUDY-AREA STATIONS[1]

Commodities	Durga-pur	Rani-ganj	Asan-sol	Burn-pur	Bara-kar	Chitta-ranjan	Dhan-bad	Ranchi	Jamshed-pur	Khar-agpur	Adra	Study-Area Total
1. Other foods	-*		.7				6.0	.1				.1
2. Wheat		.3	42.7	.1	1.1	1.0	17.4	4.0	27.9	4.1	-	6.3
3. Wheat flour		-	-				.6	-	.3	1.9		.1
4. Rice in husk	-					10.1		1.5				.2
5. Rice not in husk	-		.1				.6		.2	.7		-
6. Other grains							-	-	-	-		-
7. Gram, pulses		-	.2		-	-	-	-	-	-		-
8. Sugar							-	-	-	.8	-	-
9. Tea	-		-		-	-	-	-	-	.1		-
10. Coffee			-				-			-	-	-
11. Groundnut seed												-
12. Rape & mustard seed			-		-				.2	-	-	-
13. Other seeds							.1	-	-	2.5	-	-
14. Salt	-			-			.1		.1	2.5		.1
15. Groundnut oil		.1	-				-	-	-	-	-	-
16. Other vegetable oil		-	-	-	.1			.2	.1	.8		-
17. Tobacco products		-	-				-	-	-	-		-
18. Tobacco raw		-	-	-								
19. Other agric. products	-	-	-		-	-						-
20. Hides & skins, raw		-	-				-		-			
21. Leather manufactures		-	-		-	-						
22. Straw					-		-	.1	-			
23. Raw jute		-	-		-	-	-		-			-
24. Other raw fibre	-				-	-	.1	-	.2	3.4		.1
25. Cement	.3		-		-	-	.1	-	-	.2		.1
26. Firebricks					.4	.5			.3			.1
27. Lime & limestone				.3	.1		-	-	-			.1

	1	2	3	4	5	6	7	8	9	10	11
28. Other mineral ores	–	–	.1	–	–	–	–	–	.2	–	–
29. Non-metallic minerals	.2	.2	.3	.3	–	.3	–	–	.2	–	.1
30. Coal & coke	1.0	1.0	–	.5	.5	.3	–	.2	–	–	–
31. Iron, steel, cast iron	.4	16.1	16.1	.4	1.7	16.5	2.1	4.4	2.4	2.3	1.8
32. Scrap iron	.1	–	–	–	–	.2	–	–	–	–	–
33. Non-ferrous metals	–	–	.1	.1	–	4.7	.2	–	.9	.2	.2
34. Machinery	.1	–	.2	–	.1	.6	.3	7.7	2.6	.7	.9
35. Elec. & tel. goods	–	–	1.0	–	–	1.3	.4	.5	.2	.3	.2
36. Chemicals, explosives	.1	.1	.4	.6	.4	.4	–	.2	.5	1.0	.3
37. Medicine, cosmetics	–	–	–	–	–	–	.1	–	–	–	–
38. Paper & paper products	–	–	–	–	–	–	–	.1	–	.1	–
39. Glass	–	.4	–	–	–	–	–	.1	–	–	.3
40. Kerosene	.4	.1	2.0	–	.1	.1	1.0	1.3	.2	6.3	1.3
41. Other petroleum fuels	.1	.2	.2	–	.2	6.1	1.0	1.0	3.5	20.8	–
42. Rubber manufactures	.2	–	.2	–	–	1.0	.1	.1	–	–	.1
43. Wood manufactures	–	.1	–	–	–	.1	.2	.3	.3	.1	–
44. Wood & timber, raw	.1	–	.1	–	–	–	–	–	–	–	–
45. Gunnies, jute products	–	–	–	–	–	–	.1	–	.1	–	–
46. Other textiles	–	–	–	–	–	.9	–	–	–	.1	–
47. Non-wood bldg. material	–	4.4	–	.1	.2	1.1	–	–	–	–	.2
48. Miscellaneous	–	–	.1	–	.3	.4	1.5	.7	.7	.8	.2
Percentage of total	1.1	7.2	64.9	2.3	4.8	45.3	32.0	22.9	41.0	47.4	13.5
Metric tons (100's)	70	38	282	48	48	71	104	140	303	212	1319

1. Includes the West Bengal districts of Calcutta, Howrah, and 24 Parganas.

Source: Data compiled from individual station records for April, July, and October, 1962.

*Dash indicates less than .1 per cent.

TABLE 12

FLOWS BY COMMODITY FROM STUDY-AREA STATIONS TO THE CITY OF CALCUTTA AS A
PERCENTAGE OF TOTAL FLOWS TO ALL OF INDIA FROM STUDY-AREA STATIONS

Commodities	Durga-pur	Rani-ganj	Asan-sol	Burn-pur	Bara-kar	Chitta-ranjan	Dhan-bad	Ranchi	Jamshed-pur	Khar-agpur	Adra	Study-Area Total
1. Other foods		-*							-			-
2. Wheat					.1							-
3. Wheat flour	-											-
4. Rice in husk	.2			-						.1		-
5. Rice not in husk										22.3		.2
6. Other grains												
7. Gram, pulses												
8. Sugar												
9. Tea												
10. Coffee												
11. Groundnut seed												
12. Rape & mustard seed												
13. Other seeds												
14. Salt												
15. Groundnut oil												
16. Other vegetable oil												
17. Tobacco products							-					-
18. Tobacco raw												
19. Other agric. products		.1						7.5	-			-
20. Hides & skins, raw						.1	-		-			-
21. Leather manufactures						-	-					-
22. Straw										3.4		
23. Raw jute							-					-
24. Other raw fibre												
25. Cement												
26. Firebricks	.1				2.1	.4						.1
27. Lime & limestone	-				-							-

28. Other mineral ores		.3			.1							–
29. Non-metallic minerals		–		.3	.7							–
30. Coal & coke			16.2	12.6	1.0		3.3				4.2	5.7
31. Iron, steel, cast iron	17.2					13.1	–		9.3			3.1
32. Scrap iron	.1			–		10.9	–		.5			.1
33. Non-ferrous metals						.7			–			
34. Machinery			–	–		1.5			–			
35. Elec. & tel. goods	.4		–			7.0			.1			
36. Chemicals, explosives	1.1		–	–	–	.8			.1	.1		.1
37. Medicine, cosmetics	.7											
38. Paper & paper products		10.2								.1		.1
39. Glass		–										
40. Kerosene												
41. Other petroleum fuels	.1					.2			.1			–
42. Rubber manufactures									–			–
43. Wood manufactures				.1			–	17.8				
44. Wood & timber, raw	.1					.6		.4		.7		–
45. Gunnies, jute products						.2				1.2		–
46. Other textiles								–	–			–
47. Non-wood bldg. material	.8	1.3			.9	2.6	–	–		.1		.1
48. Miscellaneous	.1	.6			.3	.7	–	5.0		–		–
Percentage of total	20.2	13.3	16.2	13.2	5.2	38.8	3.3	30.6	10.2	27.8	4.2	9.5
Metric tons (100's)	358	14	1169	257	49	21	251	9	321	21	214	2688

Source: Data compiled from individual station records for April, July, and October, 1962.
*Dash indicates less than .1 per cent.

TABLE 13

FLOWS BY COMMODITY FROM STUDY-AREA STATIONS TO THE CALCUTTA METROPOLITAN AREA AS A PERCENTAGE OF TOTAL FLOWS TO ALL OF INDIA FROM STUDY-AREA STATIONS[1]

Commodities	Durga-pur	Rani-ganj	Asan-sol	Burn-pur	Bara-kar	Chitta-ranjan	Dhan-bad	Ranchi	Jamshed-pur	Khar-agpur	Adra	Study-Area Total
1. Other foods		-*				—			—	.1		—
2. Wheat					.2							—
3. Wheat flour	—											—
4. Rice in husk	.2			—						.1		.4
5. Rice not in husk			—							48.8		
6. Other grains												—
7. Gram, pulses		—		—	—					.2		—
8. Sugar					—							
9. Tea					—							—
10. Coffee												
11. Groundnut seed												
12. Rape & mustard seed										—		—
13. Other seeds												
14. Salt			—									—
15. Groundnut oil										.1		—
16. Other vegetable oil					—				—			—
17. Tobacco products					—				—			
18. Tobacco raw			—				—					
19. Other agric. products		.1	—					22.5	—	.1		—
20. Hides & skins, raw						.1	—		—	—		—
21. Leather manufactures						—	—		—			—
22. Straw									—	3.9		—
23. Raw jute												—
24. Other raw fibre	—			—	—				—			—
25. Cement				—			—					
26. Firebricks	.4	.2		.4	3.2	.4	—					.2
27. Lime & limestone			—		—		—					—

	1	2	3	4	5	6	7	8	9	10	11	Total
28. Other mineral ores	.4		–	–	.1		–			–		–
29. Non-metallic minerals	.2	.5			.7							–
30. Coal & coke	–	19.4	19.4				3.9	.1		–	4.6	6.8
31. Iron, steel, cast iron	56.1	–	–	21.7	2.8	19.0	.1	22.1		.1		7.7
32. Scrap iron	.4		–	.1	.1	10.9		2.4		.3		.3
33. Non-ferrous metals		–	–	–	–	4.9	–	.4		–		.1
34. Machinery	–	–	–	–	–	1.9	–	.1				–
35. Elec. & tel. goods	.4	–	–	–	–	7.1	.1	.4		–		–
36. Chemicals, explosives	1.1	.7	–	–	.1	.8	.1	.1		.1		.1
37. Medicine, cosmetics	–	–			–		–			–		–
38. Paper & paper products	–	10.2						–		.1		–
39. Glass	–	–								.1		–
40. Kerosene												
41. Other petroleum fuels	.1	–	–	–	–	.2		.1		.1		–
42. Rubber manufactures		–	–	–	–	.9	–	–		–		–
43. Wood manufactures		–	–	.1	–	–	–	–	17.8	–		–
44. Wood & timber, raw	.1	–				.6			.4	1.5		–
45. Gunnies, jute products						.2		.1		1.2		–
46. Other textiles		–	–	–	–	–		–		–		–
47. Non-wood bldg. material	.9	31.3	–	1.1	.3	3.5	.1	–	.3	.4		.3
48. Miscellaneous	.1	.6	–	–	.3	.8	–	–	8.0	.6		–
Percentage of total	61.9	44.0	19.4	23.0	8.6	51.4	4.1	49.7	25.9	57.8	4.6	16.1
Metric tons (100's)	1062	47	1402	447	81	28	309	14	816	94	232	4537

1. Includes the West Bengal districts of Calcutta, Howrah, and 24 Parganas

Source: Data compiled from individual station records for April, July, and October, 1962.

*Dash indicates less than .1 per cent.

TABLE 14

FLOWS BY COMMODITY TO STUDY-AREA STATIONS FROM THE FIVE SURROUNDING DISTRICTS AS A PERCENTAGE OF TOTAL FLOWS FROM ALL OF INDIA TO STUDY-AREA STATIONS[1]

Commodities	Durga-pur	Rani-ganj	Asan-sol	Burn-pur	Bara-kar	Chitta-ranjan	Dhan-bad	Ranchi	Jamshed-pur	Khar-agpur	Adra	Study-Area Total
1. Other foods			.2					-*	-	-		-
2. Wheat						-		.1	-	.1		-
3. Wheat flour						-	.1	.1				-
4. Rice in husk										.3		-
5. Rice not in husk	.3						-	-	-			-
6. Other grains								-				-
7. Gram, pulses			.1			-			-			-
8. Sugar			.1			-	.1	.1		.2		-
9. Tea												
10. Coffee												-
11. Groundnut seed							-					-
12. Rape & mustard seed							-					-
13. Other seeds	-											
14. Salt												-
15. Groundnut oil												-
16. Other vegetable oil							-					-
17. Tobacco products	-	-							-	.1		-
18. Tobacco raw	-	-										-
19. Other agric. products	-	-				.4			-			-
20. Hides & skins, raw	-	-		-				-	-			-
21. Leather manufactures												
22. Straw		.1		-					.4			-
23. Raw jute							-					-
24. Other raw fibre								-				-
25. Cement	.3	1.8	.1	.1	-	.9	.1	.9	.6	3.4		.5
26. Firebricks	.5	.2	.2	1.7	1.4	.6	.1		1.6			.8
27. Lime & limestone	1.7	.2			-	.3			.2	.1		.8

												Total
28.	Other mineral ores	15.5		5.8	1.9	3.4	1.5	.2	.4	3.4	-	8.2
29.	Non-metallic minerals	.7		.2	.4	10.3	18.2	.2	-	3.9	-	2.0
30.	Coal & coke	.3		.2	14.4	.1	1.0	2.9	-	-	-	-
31.	Iron, steel, cast iron	.6		-	-	40.6	2.4	.2	4.1	14.1	.6	7.8
32.	Scrap iron	-		-	-	.4	.6	-	-	-	-	-
33.	Non-ferrous metals	-		5.7	-	-	1.0	-	.3	.1	-	.2
34.	Machinery	.1		-	-	-	-	-	.1	-	.1	-
35.	Elec. & tel. goods	-		-	-	-	.6	-	.3	.3	.3	-
36.	Chemicals, explosives	-		.3	-	-	1.0	6.5	-	-	-	.3
37.	Medicine, cosmetics	-		-	-	-	.2	-	-	-	-	-
38.	Paper & paper products	-		-	-	-	-	-	-	-	-	-
39.	Glass	-		-	-	-	.2	-	-	-	-	-
40.	Kerosene	-		-	-	-	-	-	-	-	-	-
41.	Other petroleum fuels	.4		-	.5	-	-	.3	-	.1	-	.1
42.	Rubber manufactures	-		-	-	-	1.0	-	-	-	-	-
43.	Wood manufactures	-		.3	-	-	-	.2	6.0	-	-	.3
44.	Wood & timber, raw	-		.4	-	-	.1	.3	.1	.1	.3	.1
45.	Gunnies, jute products	-		-	.2	-	.2	-	-	-	-	-
46.	Other textiles	-		-	-	-	.9	-	-	-	-	-
47.	Non-wood bldg. material	.5		-	-	2.6	-	-	.1	.6	3.1	.6
48.	Miscellaneous	-		-	.1	.1	-	.1	2.0	-	.1	.1
	Percentage of station totals, Tables 8-9	19.8	11.1	13.4	19.4	59.1	29.6	11.3	15.6	23.7	8.7	22.3
	Metric tons (100's) accounted for	1271	59	28	412	590	46	37	96	565	39	3178
	By district percentage of station totals, Tables 8-9:											
	Dhanbad	.5	1.5	.4	.1	.8	.9	5.7	1.3	1.0	.3	.7
	Ranchi	.1	5.3	11.8	-	4.4	-	.6	.9	.5	1.1	1.1
	Singhbhum	17.4	1.5	.7	7.5	7.2	17.5	2.8	4.0	18.2	6.5	13.3
	Burdwan	-	2.8	.5	11.9	46.7	11.2	2.2	9.4	3.7	.7	7.1
	Midnapore	-	-	0.0	.1	-	0.0	0.0	0.0	.3	.1	.1

1. Includes the West Bengal districts of Burdwan and Midnapore and the Bihar districts of Dhanbad, Ranchi, and Singhbhum.
Source: Data compiled from individual station records for April, July, and October, 1962.
*Dash indicates less than .1 per cent.

TABLE 15

FLOWS BY COMMODITY FROM STUDY-AREA STATIONS TO THE FIVE SURROUNDING DISTRICTS AS A PERCENTAGE OF TOTAL FLOWS TO ALL OF INDIA FROM STUDY-AREA STATIONS[1]

Commodities	Durga-pur	Rani-ganj	Asan-sol	Burn-pur	Bara-kar	Chitta-ranjan	Dhan-bad	Ranchi	Jamshed-pur	Khar-agpur	Adra	Study-Area Total
1. Other foods	–	–*	–	–	–	1.2		.7	.1			–
2. Wheat					.1				.1			–
3. Wheat flour			–		.2							–
4. Rice in husk				–						.8		–
5. Rice not in husk										.6		–
6. Other grains												
7. Gram, pulses										–		–
8. Sugar	–	–										
9. Tea												
10. Coffee												
11. Groundnut seed												
12. Rape & mustard seed										.1		–
13. Other seeds												
14. Salt												
15. Groundnut oil												
16. Other vegetable oil									–	–		–
17. Tobacco products		–								–		–
18. Tobacco raw							–					
19. Other agric. products		1.0								.2		–
20. Hides & skins, raw						–			–	–		–
21. Leather manufactures												
22. Straw										1.1		–
23. Raw jute	–		–									–
24. Other raw fibre									–			–
25. Cement	–											–
26. Firebricks	.2	12.0		.2	20.6	.4	.1					.7
27. Lime & limestone		.2							.1			–
28. Other mineral ores	–	3.0		1.0						.1		.1

29. Non-metallic minerals	–	10.7	15.5	1.8	.3	–	31.5		.3	.1	.1	.2
30. Coal & coke	3.2	–	–	5.9	27.2	10.7	–	9.7	11.3	–	49.1	21.3
31. Iron, steel, cast iron	.1		–	10.8					.1	.2	.2	2.8
32. Scrap iron									2.9			.8
33. Non-ferrous metals					3.3							.3
34. Machinery			–	–	3.7							–
35. Elec. & tel. goods			–	–	2.5							–
36. Chemicals, explosives	.5		–	1.1	2.7				.3			.2
37. Medicine, cosmetics					–							–
38. Paper & paper products												
39. Glass		–										–
40. Kerosene							2.7			–	–	–
41. Other petroleum fuels	–	–					–					–
42. Rubber manufactures	–	–										–
43. Wood manufactures	–	–		.1								–
44. Wood & timber, raw			–			.5			.2	.1		–
45. Gunnies, jute products		–	–		2.5			3.1				–
46. Other textiles												–
47. Non-wood bldg. material	.2	.4			4.9				.9	4.1	2.0	.3
48. Miscellaneous	–	2.7		.1	.5			1.0				–
Percentage of total	4.1	30.2	15.5	21.0	53.3	27.5	31.6	17.3	16.2	9.8	49.1	27.3
Metric tons (100's)	73	33	1119	407	507	15	2408	5	23	512	2517	7671
District percentage totals												
Dhanbad	.6	–	–	2.6	.8	3.9	12.6	1.5	.7	–	19.5	7.3
Ranchi	1.3	–	–	.7	.3	.8	.4	2.7	1.2	.1	0.0	.4
Singhbhum	.6	2.2	2.3	1.5	13.5	1.0	5.4	.2	11.3	1.5	20.3	7.7
Burdwan	1.1	28.0	13.1	15.6	38.6	21.8	13.2	9.8	2.5	.3	8.8	11.6
Midnapore	.5	–	.1	.6	.1	0.0	–	3.1	.5	7.9	0.0	.3

1. Includes the West Bengal districts of Burdwan and Midnapore and the Bihar districts of Dhanbad, Ranchi, and Singhbhum.

Source: Data compiled from individual station records for April, July, and October, 1962.

*Dash indicates less than .1 per cent.

TABLE 16

FLOWS BY COMMODITY TO STUDY-AREA STATIONS FROM THE CALCUTTA REGION AS A PERCENTAGE OF TOTAL FLOWS FROM ALL OF INDIA TO STUDY-AREA STATIONS[1]

Commodities	Durga-pur	Rani-ganj	Asan-sol	Burn-pur	Bara-kar	Chitta-ranjan	Dhan-bad	Ranchi	Jamshed-pur	Khar-agpur	Adra	Study-Area Total
1. Other foods	-*	3.2	2.9	-	-	-	9.8	.2	.4	1.6	-	.3
2. Wheat	-	.3	3.0	.1	.8	-	7.2	3.7	-	1.6	-	.4
3. Wheat flour		-	-		-	-	.3	.1	.2	1.9		.1
4. Rice in husk	-	.1			.3	-	1.0			3.9		-
5. Rice not in husk	-	.8	.1	.1	.6		3.3	.9	.3	.5		.1
6. Other grains			-				.3					-
7. Gram, pulses	-	4.3	2.4	-	.4	-	3.8	.9	.3	2.8		.1
8. Sugar		5.0	4.3	.1	1.0	.3	5.1	.1	.3	2.9		.6
9. Tea	-	-					-	-		-		-
10. Coffee												-
11. Groundnut seed	-	-					.1					-
12. Rape & mustard seed	-	.2	-		.1		1.7			.1		-
13. Other seeds	-		-	-			-	-				-
14. Salt				-			.1		.3	2.4		.1
15. Groundnut oil						-				.1		-
16. Other vegetable oil	-	-					.1		.2	.2		-
17. Tobacco products	-	.2	-				-		-	.1		-
18. Tobacco raw	-	.1	.1		-		-			-		-
19. Other agric. products	-	.1			.1	.4	.7		.1	.3		-
20. Hides & skins, raw	-	.3	-			-	.5		-	-		-
21. Leather manufactures	-				-	-	1.6	.3				-
22. Straw		2.6			.1		1.5		.4			-
23. Raw jute	-				-			-				-
24. Other raw fibre	-	.1	-	-	-		.3		.1	3.4		.1
25. Cement	1.0	2.3	1.2	.4	.8	.9	1.2	10.5	.8	12.1		1.7
26. Firebricks	2.7	.2	.2	3.7	3.4	.8	.1		5.0			2.7
27. Lime & limestone	7.1	4.2	.1	.2	.1	.5	.2	19.9	.5	.3		4.3

Item											
28. Other mineral ores	64.5	–	5.8	2.9	4.1	–	1.0	1.0	5.1	–	30.8
29. Non-metallic minerals	.8	9.9	.5	.7	24.9	.9	.6	.6	11.3	–	3.9
30. Coal & coke	1.0	–	12.7	26.2	42.0	28.3	5.7	8.4	.6	1.6	.1
31. Iron, steel, cast iron	–	–	.4	–	.4	.1	.5	–	15.2	–	10.8
32. Scrap iron	–	–	5.8	.2	–	6.1	–	–	.3	–	–
33. Non-ferrous metals	–	–	.3	–	.4	3.3	.2	.6	.3	.1	.3
34. Machinery	–	–	.4	.8	–	2.3	.5	.4	.1	1.1	.1
35. Elec. & tel. goods	–	–	.4	–	.2	1.8	.5	.4	–	.3	.1
36. Chemicals, explosives	–	–	–	–	–	.2	9.6	–	4.1	.5	1.0
37. Medicine, cosmetics	–	–	.1	–	–	–	.2	–	–	–	–
38. Paper & paper products	–	1.7	–	–	–	–	.1	–	–	–	–
39. Glass	–	–	–	–	–	–	–	–	–	–	–
40. Kerosene	–	–	.3	.5	–	–	–	–	–	–	–
41. Other petroleum fuels	–	–	.3	–	.5	.9	.5	.4	.2	–	.1
42. Rubber manufactures	–	4.0	.7	.2	–	2.0	.1	.1	.1	–	–
43. Wood manufactures	–	9.1	.6	–	.5	.4	1.3	16.8	.2	.4	.9
44. Wood & timber, raw	–	–	–	.2	.3	.3	2.4	–	.2	1.3	.4
45. Gunnies, jute products	.1	–	.1	–	–	.2	–	.1	.1	–	–
46. Other textiles	–	–	.3	.2	–	.9	.1	–	–	.1	–
47. Non-wood bldg. material	1.1	13.7	.3	–	8.4	.7	1.4	.1	.7	3.2	1.9
48. Miscellaneous	–	1.2	1.1	.1	.2	1.5	1.5	2.7	.6	1.2	.2
Percentage of total	78.8	68.8	44.7	36.9	90.6	53.6	66.8	69.4	50.5	45.1	65.4
Metric tons (100's)	5085	372	193	753	907	84	219	427	1123	203	9401
State percentage totals											
Assam	–	1.8	.1	.3	.1	–	1.3	.4	.8	.3	.2
Bihar	20.9	29.0	18.6	9.2	32.1	20.1	32.1	47.7	23.8	11.4	21.8
Orissa	54.0	11.5	1.1	13.8	.7	11.1	2.6	1.0	15.6	13.5	30.0
Uttar Pradesh	.1	10.4	8.5	.5	3.3	.8	11.7	2.9	3.3	5.6	1.9
West Bengal	3.8	16.1	16.4	13.1	54.4	21.6	19.1	17.4	7.0	14.3	11.5

1. Excludes the city of Calcutta.

Source: Data compiled from individual station records for April, July, and October, 1962.

*Dash indicates less than .1 per cent.

TABLE 17

FLOWS BY COMMODITY FROM STUDY-AREA STATIONS TO THE CALCUTTA REGION AS A PERCENTAGE OF TOTAL FLOWS TO ALL OF INDIA FROM STUDY-AREA STATIONS[1]

Commodities	Durga-pur	Rani-ganj	Asan-sol	Burn-pur	Bara-kar	Chitta-ranjan	Dhan-bad	Ranchi	Jamshed-pur	Khar-agpur	Adra	Study-Area Total
1. Other foods	-*	-	-	-	-	1.2	-	-	.1	.2	-	-
2. Wheat		-	-	-	.2		-	-	.1	-	-	-
3. Wheat flour	.1	-	-	-	.2					.9		-
4. Rice in husk	.1	1.0								.9		-
5. Rice not in husk			-							55.5		.4
6. Other grains												-
7. Gram, pulses		-	-	.1	-				-			-
8. Sugar	-	-	-	-	.1					.2		-
9. Tea					-							-
10. Coffee												
11. Groundnut seed												
12. Rape & mustard seed			-						-	.1		-
13. Other seeds												-
14. Salt		.2								.1		-
15. Groundnut oil									-	.1		-
16. Other vegetable oil			-		-				-			
17. Tobacco products		-	-		-		-		-	-		
18. Tobacco raw		-	-		-							
19. Other agric. products		1.5	-		-			18.4	-	.3		-
20. Hides & skins, raw							-		-	-		-
21. Leather manufactures				-					-			
22. Straw	-				-				-	1.8		-
23. Raw jute		-	-						-			-
24. Other raw fibre		-	-		-					-		-
25. Cement	-			.4		2.1	.1			-		-
26. Firebricks	.9	18.2		23.5								.8
27. Lime & limestone	-	.2	-	.5	-				.2	-		-

Commodity												
28. Other mineral ores	-	-	-	2.5	2.5	.1	-	-	1.8	.1		.2
29. Non-metallic minerals	-	4.2	-	1.1	-			66.9		-	72.8	.5
30. Coal & coke	56.0	10.9	60.0	27.3	35.5	16.6		14.8	37.2	.3		45.2
31. Iron, steel, cast iron	.5			10.9	.1				2.0	.3		10.0
32. Scrap iron									4.1			1.0
33. Non-ferrous metals						7.8						.5
34. Machinery				.2		4.3		1.4	.1			-
35. Elec. & tel. goods						6.0		.1	.3	.2		-
36. Chemicals, explosives	.8			1.5		3.0	.1	-	1.1			.3
37. Medicine, cosmetics							.1					-
38. Paper & paper products		3.5										-
39. Glass		.6										-
40. Kerosene								2.7				-
41. Other petroleum fuels								.4				-
42. Rubber manufactures						.9		.1				-
43. Wood manufactures	-	.1		.4		.7		.1				-
44. Wood & timber, raw						.2		2.3		1.1		-
45. Gunnies, jute products		.7				.5		3.1		.1		-
46. Other textiles						2.5		.3				-
47. Non-wood bldg. material	.3	30.6			6.1	1.1	.1	1.4	.9	4.4		.5
48. Miscellaneous	-	4.2		.1	8.8	.1		4.8		2.7		.2
Percentage of total	58.9	76.9	60.1	46.2	78.2	47.3	67.2	50.8	49.2	69.2	72.8	63.3
Metric tons (100's)	1044	83	4337	907	745	26	5162	14	1560	168	3733	17831
State percentage totals												
Assam	.4	.1	5.4	1.8	1.3	0.0	4.3	0.0	.4	0.0	-	2.6
Bihar	4.5	6.3	7.0	6.6	26.3	7.3	24.2	14.0	15.5	1.7	39.8	19.3
Orissa	2.4	1.3	.3	2.3	2.8	.6	5.3	.7	9.1	.4	20.2	6.5
Uttar Pradesh	8.6	9.6	26.7	7.3	3.3	4.8	18.2	.8	4.7	.7	3.0	14.3
West Bengal	43.0	59.6	20.7	28.2	44.5	34.6	15.2	35.3	19.5	66.4	9.8	20.6

1. Excludes the city of Calcutta.

Source: Data compiled from individual station records for April, July, and October, 1962.

* Dash indicates less than .1 per cent.

TABLE 18

FLOWS BY COMMODITY TO STUDY-AREA STATIONS FROM OUTSIDE CALCUTTA AND THE CALCUTTA
REGION AS A PERCENTAGE OF TOTAL FLOWS FROM ALL OF INDIA TO STUDY-AREA STATIONS

Commodities	Durga-pur	Rani-ganj	Asan-sol	Burn-pur	Bara-kar	Chitta-ranjan	Dhan-bad	Ranchi	Jamshed-pur	Khar-agpur	Adra	Study-Area Total
1. Other foods	1.1	1.3		-*	.1	.1	1.0	.2	.2	4.4		.3
2. Wheat		.5	.1	-	-		3.4	.5	.7	1.6	-	.2
3. Wheat flour									.1	-		-
4. Rice in husk					-		.3	-				-
5. Rice not in husk							.2	.4	.2	.5		.1
6. Other grains		-			-							-
7. Gram, pulses		2.0	.9		.6		1.2		.5	3.1		.2
8. Sugar		.7					.3	.5		.4		-
9. Tea		-										-
10. Coffee					-		-					-
11. Groundnut seed					-		-					-
12. Rape & mustard seed	7.1			.2	.1		1.1	.3	.1	4.2		.4
13. Other seeds								-				-
14. Salt		.5					.3	2.3	.1	.5		.1
15. Groundnut oil								.3	.3	.6		.1
16. Other vegetable oil		.2	-		-		.3	-				-
17. Tobacco products		.1	-		-		.1	-				-
18. Tobacco raw		.1					.2	-				-
19. Other agric. products		.1			-		.1	.1	.1		-	-
20. Hides & skins, raw											-	-
21. Leather manufactures	.1										-	.1
22. Straw				-			.1		.1			-
23. Raw jute	-											-
24. Other raw fibre												-
25. Cement				-		-						-
26. Firebricks				.1	.1	.3			.1			-
27. Lime & limestone	17.7	7.4	.7	45.1	.1		.4		1.0	.9		15.1

Table (rotated). Column headers do not appear on this page; the eleven data columns are anchored by the "Percentage of total" and "Metric tons (100's)" rows.

Commodity											
28. Other mineral ores	.5	.3	–	.5	3.9	1.3	.2	–	1.6	–	.7
29. Non-metallic minerals		–	–	6.8	.7	–	–		1.1	–	1.3
30. Coal & coke	.5	.2	.4	4.2	–	3.0	.8	3.4	.7	.2	1.0
31. Iron, steel, cast iron	.5	.3	–				.1				–
32. Scrap iron	–		–	.1	.3	.3					.1
33. Non-ferrous metals	.2			.9		.4					.1
34. Machinery	–	–	–			.1	.4	.3	.4	.2	.1
35. Elec. & tel. goods	–	1.6	.5	2.3		.5		.2	.1		.1
36. Chemicals, explosives	.6				.1	–	3.3	.6	1.2	.2	.9
37. Medicine, cosmetics		–	–				.1	.1	–	.1	–
38. Paper & paper products	.1	.1		.1				.1			.1
39. Glass								1.5			
40. Kerosene							–				
41. Other petroleum fuels	.1	.1					.1	.1		.1	.1
42. Rubber manufactures			–	–	–		.1	–	.2		
43. Wood manufactures	–	1.1	–	–		.6	.1	.7	.1	.1	
44. Wood & timber, raw	–	1.7	.6	.1		1.5		.5	.1	.1	
45. Gunnies, jute products		–						.5		.5	
46. Other textiles		–	–		–		.7				
47. Non-wood bldg. material	–	.1		.1	–		.4	.2		.2	
48. Miscellaneous	–	.1	.1		–		.2	.5		.7	
Percentage of total	19.9	28.6	4.7	60.7	6.3	8.1	16.0	14.5	9.9	18.8	22.6
Metric tons (100's)	1291	155	19	1281	65	12	53	88	819	20	3872
State percentage totals											
Andhra Pradesh	.4	2.1	–	.1	–	0.0	2.2	.5	.8	2.1	.5
Bombay	–	4.4	1.1	.8	.2	1.4	4.6	2.7	2.6	1.7	1.0
Delhi	–	1.0	.4	.1	.1	.5	1.6	1.0	.1	.4	.2
Kerala	0.0	0.0	0.0	–	–	0.0	–	.1	.2	.2	–
Madras	.1	1.2	0.0	.9	–	–	.1	3.7	.4	1.7	.5
Mysore	–	.2	0.0	–	.1	0.0	.1	.1	.6	.1	.1
Punjab	–	8.6	1.7	6.8	.9	2.2	3.5	.4	1.1	6.1	1.9
Rajasthan	–	2.9	.5	.2	.2	.1	.3	.6	.2	1.8	.3
Madhya Pradesh	19.4	8.2	1.0	51.8	5.1	3.9	3.7	5.4	3.9	4.7	18.1

Source: Data compiled from individual station records for April, July, and October, 1962.

*Dash indicates less than .1 per cent.

TABLE 19

FLOWS BY COMMODITY FROM STUDY-AREA STATIONS TO POINTS OUTSIDE CALCUTTA AND THE CALCUTTA REGION AS A PERCENTAGE OF TOTAL FLOWS TO ALL OF INDIA FROM STUDY-AREA STATIONS

Commodities	Durga-pur	Rani-ganj	Asan-sol	Burn-pur	Bara-kar	Chitta-ranjan	Dhan-bad	Ranchi	Jamshed-pur	Khar-agpur	Adra	Study-Area Total
1. Other foods				-*	-			.1				-
2. Wheat									-			-
3. Wheat flour												-
4. Rice in husk				-								-
5. Rice not in husk										1.2		-
6. Other grains												
7. Gram, pulses				-					-			-
8. Sugar												
9. Tea				-								-
10. Coffee												
11. Groundnut seed												
12. Rape & mustard seed				-								-
13. Other seeds												
14. Salt		.4										-
15. Groundnut oil												
16. Other vegetable oil							-					-
17. Tobacco products							-					-
18. Tobacco raw												
19. Other agric. products									-			-
20. Hides & skins, raw								1.5		.1		-
21. Leather manufactures												
22. Straw						-						
23. Raw jute									-			-
24. Other raw fibre												
25. Cement	-											
26. Firebricks		.4			5.9		.1					.2
27. Lime & limestone				1.4	-							.1

28. Other mineral ores	–			–	–	1.7						–
29. Non-metallic minerals	–		–	–				–				–
30. Coal & coke	20.3		23.2			28.9	11.8	28.9			22.8	17.7
31. Iron, steel, cast iron			37.2	37.2	10.3	–	11.8	–	37.1	1.3		8.3
32. Scrap iron				.2	.2				.1			
33. Non-ferrous metals	.1		–	–	–	–	.1	–	.3			
34. Machinery	–		–	1.0	–	3.0		.1	–			
35. Elec. & tel. goods					.1	7.3	.1	1.2	1.3			.1
36. Chemicals, explosives	1.1	1.1	–	.1	.1	.5		.1	1.3	.1		.1
37. Medicine, cosmetics	–		–	–	–	–	–					
38. Paper & paper products	6.3	6.3										
39. Glass	–	–										
40. Kerosene												
41. Other petroleum fuels			–				.1			.1		
42. Rubber manufactures	–		–				–			–		
43. Wood manufactures	1.1	1.1		–	–	.4	1.9	1.9		.1		
44. Wood & timber, raw					.4	.7	1.2	1.2				
45. Gunnies, jute products	–		–		.7		–		–			
46. Other textiles							–	–				–
47. Non-wood bldg. material	–		–	.2				–	–			
48. Miscellaneous	–		–			.1	.1	.8	.1			
Percentage of total	20.7	9.6	23.2	40.4	16.5	13.7	18.6	29.1	39.7	3.0	22.8	26.9
Metric tons (1001s)	368	10	1682	788	155	7	5	2219	1250	7	1172	7667
State percentage totals												
Andhra Pradesh	1.3	0.0	3.2	2.0	.6	0.0	.6	.1	1.8	0.0	1.5	1.5
Bombay	5.1	5.5	0.0	16.1	4.3	1.1	8.0	0.0	15.3	1.1	–	3.3
Delhi	1.9	.2	2.4	2.4	0.0	3.7	1.0	10.0	1.3	.1	.1	3.8
Kerala	.7	0.0	0.0	.2	.1	–	–	0.0	.9	–	.2	.2
Madras	1.7	1.7	0.0	5.0	.8	0.0	1.5	0.0	5.8	.2	–	1.1
Mysore	.1	.1	.6	1.4	.1	–	–	.4	1.4	–	1.1	.7
Punjab	3.6	1.5	4.7	4.7	2.8	3.8	.9	11.2	6.0	.1	.2	5.8
Rajasthan	.4	0.0	9.7	2.9	1.1	1.7	–	4.1	4.3	–	.2	4.4
Madhya Pradesh	2.9	.6	2.6	5.7	6.7	3.4	6.6	3.3	2.9	1.5	19.5	6.1

Source: Data compiled from individual station records for April, July, and October, 1962.

*Dash indicates less than .1 per cent.

CHAPTER V

THE BENGAL-BIHAR INDUSTRIAL AREA IN THE

INDIAN NATIONAL ECONOMY

Chapters III and IV dealt with various roles played by the Bengal-Bihar Industrial Area's specialized activities, exchange patterns associated with these roles, and the study area's linkages with other complementary areas throughout India. For the surrounding Calcutta region, this analysis indicated the general organization of exchange as it related to study-area specialization. However, the study-area specialization and exchange patterns may also be affected by its location and relative accessibility to other areas of specialized production and consumption in India. Measures of the study area's relative accessibility to the Indian economy will be based on the potential model. Since this technique has been developed and evaluated primarily for the United States economy, it will be well to consider some of the differences in spatial organization between the United States and Indian economies.

The Indian and United States Economies: Comparison of Spatial Organization

Using the potential model, Harris measured the relative accessibility of various points in the United States to the national retail market. [1] He found that the United States markets for manufacturing, agricultural, and mining activities tended to be centralized in the northeastern manufacturing belt. Except in their immediate vicinity, other regional market concentrations (Atlanta, Dallas, Los Angeles, etc.) tended to be eclipsed in their influence on industrial location patterns by the effect of the great market concentration of the northeast. Ullman's mapping and analysis also indicated the major influence

---

[1] Harris, op. cit.

96

of this market and manufacturing concentration in the northeast upon the organization of interstate commodity flows in the United States and the lesser influence which regional markets have upon the total organization of these flows.[1] Duncan et al. in their analysis of the exchange of funds in the United States again indicated the major influence of the northeastern market in organizing the nationwide system of financial flows.[2]

The great concentration of market in the northeastern United States, noted by Harris and others, reflects the general historical development of the United States as a single integrated and rapidly expanding economy. In the expansion westward, newly developing activities of the economy were dependent for support and market upon the prior, established economic activities of the northeast.

The history of Indian economic development was quite different. The subcontinent has been extensively peopled for over 3000 years. India's early economy can be described as a collection of subsistence agricultural economies organized at a village level. From the surplus agricultural and handicraft production of these villages various areas of specialized production arose, as did regional exchange. However, extensive interregional trade did not develop and these agricultural regions were never organized into an integrated national economy.[3]

Under British rule, commercial agriculture and industrial development spread from India's major ports (Calcutta, Bombay, and Madras). Each port encouraged the development of specialized activities in the surrounding hinterland. Commodity flows associated with these activities by and large passed through the local port.[4] During the later 1800's, the Calcutta hinterland specialized in the production of jute, coal, tea, other agricultural products, and machinery repair. The Bombay hinterland specialized in the production of cotton textiles and food grains, whereas the Madras hinterland remained heavily agricultural, producing cotton and spices.[5] This new system of commercially oriented agriculture and industry had little impact on the pre-existing system of village subsistence agriculture, and dual systems of economic activity developed through-

---

[1] Ullman, op. cit.

[2] Duncan, op. cit.

[3] D. R. Gadgil, The Industrial Evolution of India in Recent Times (London: Oxford University Press, 1924); K. A. Nilakanta Sastri, The Culture and History of the Tamils (Calcutta: F. K. L. Mukhopadhyay, 1964), pp. 87-105; and William H. Moveland, India at the Death of Akbar (London: Macmillan, 1920).

[4] Gadgil, op. cit., VI, 83-98.

[5] Spate, op. cit., X-XII, 257-326.

out India.

Each hinterland specialized in the export of goods which were not generally complementary with activities in other Indian regions. Without a nationwide system of rapid
land communication, each of the major port hinterlands functioned as a relatively closed
economic region.

With the development of India's rail network and completion of the transcontinental main lines early in the 1900's came the possibility of rapid rail communication
throughout India and the integration of regional economies into a national economy. [1] Although a rapid nationwide expansion of textile trade was experienced along with the development of the railway system, trade in other commodities expanded slowly. This may
have been due in part to the limited consumer and industrial market available in India and
in part to the structure of freight rates on the Indian railways. The rate structure greatly favored the shipment of raw materials from hinterland areas to ports and discouraged
the establishment of industrial activities outside port areas. [2] During the period of industrial revolution, India experienced a slow rather than a rapid industrial expansion into
previously established but little developed port hinterlands. This expansion took place
from not one but four older industrial port areas.

During the early 20th century, each of India's port-oriented economic regions
continued to specialize along prior, established lines. As described in Chapter II, Calcutta and its mineral-rich hinterland developed iron and steel works and a large machinery and metal working industry geared to supplying the jute textile industry of Calcutta and rolling stock and rails to the Indian railways. In the Bombay region, chemical
and light machinery manufactures were developed to support the expanding textile industry. Much of this light machinery industry developed in the Punjab and Rajasthan areas
focused partially on Delhi as the regional metropolis. In the Madras region, cotton textiles, leather, machinery, and an aluminum industry based on westcoast electric power
were developed. However, limited complementarity continued to exist between the spe-
cializations of each region. [3]

Since independence, Indian government policies have aimed at balanced regional
development and integration of the Indian economy through planned dispersal of comple-

[1] J. N. Sahni, Indian Railways: One Hundred Years (New Delhi: Ministry of Railways (Railway Board), 1953).

[2] Gadgil, op. cit., IX, 145-157, and R. D. Tiwari and C. N. Vakil, Railway
Rates in Relation to Trade and Industry in India (Calcutta: Longman's Green & Co.,
1937).

[3] Spate, op. cit., X-XII, 257-326.

mentary economic activities in each of its economic regions.[1] Although the systems of village subsistence agriculture and of commercial agriculture and industry are now considerably more integrated, elements of both persist and India is not free of aspects of a dual economy. Economic development and integration is a slow process; and exchange within the Indian economy still exhibits strong intraregional orientation. The study area's industrial specialization and flow patterns are expected to reflect the influence of India's strong regional economies.

Relative Location, Specialization and Exchange

By assuming that each individual producer or consumer in an economy can exchange freely with all others, the potential model may be used to measure the accessibility of any point to all other points in the economy. The general form of the potential model, $P_i = a \sum_{j=i}^{n} \frac{P_j}{d_{ij}}$, indicates that the potential or relative accessibility of an activity at point i (P_i) to all similar activities at points j throughout the system is equal to a constant a times the sum of the concentration of these activities at points j (P_j) divided by a measure of the friction of overcoming the distance separating points i and j, (d_{ij}).

Harris argued that relative accessibility to a total market will greatly affect an industry's location pattern.[2] Using the potential model, he measured the relative accessibility of any point in the United States to the retail market at all other points in the economy. By comparing the relative accessibility of the location of various industries to national markets, Harris demonstrated in the United States context the affinity of these industries for locations near the highest point of accessibility to markets.

Using Harris's market potential as the measure of relative accessibility for various points in the United States to the total national retail market, Pred identified areas of high, medium, and low relative accessibility to this market.[3] He classified industries into three types: raw material-and-fuel, market, and labor-and-agglomeration-oriented industries on the basis of Weberian industrial location factors. Combining this classification with the classification of relative accessibility to market, Pred proposed a

---

[1] India (Republic), Planning Commission, The Third Five Year Plan (New Delhi: Government of India Press, Manager of Publications, 1961).

[2] Harris, op. cit.

[3] Pred, op. cit.

nine-fold classification of expected volume and length of commodity flows from each type of industry at each relative location.

Both Harris and Pred were concerned with measuring relative accessibility to a nationwide distribution of demand. Warntz's analysis of the geographical and temporal distribution of agricultural prices in the United States used the potential model to measure not only relative accessibility to a national distribution of demand but also to nationwide distribution of supplies.[1] Warntz found close correlation between local prices and local supply, demand, and time potentials. Thus not only demand space but also supply space and supply time potentials were relevant to the analysis of local commodity exchanges and would be expected to influence the type and scale of local specialization.

Although exchange within the Indian economy appears to be more regionally oriented than is true for the United States, the possibility certainly exists for exchange between the Bengal-Bihar Industrial Area and any part of India. Given India's cultural diversity and the existence of strong regional trading areas, one would expect differences in the propensity toward trade between various parts of the country. However, there are no clear criteria for evaluating the exact propensity for interdistrict, interstate, or interregional trade in various commodities. Although unrealistic to some degree, a national economy with equal possibilities of exchange between all supply and market areas of the system has been assumed and the study area's location relative to it computed using the potential model.

In the potential model the most sensitive variable is the measure of distance or friction to be overcome by a flow. In his study of commodity flow in Southern Ontario, Ray argues that simple exponential distance rather than transport costs is the most useful measure of friction in the exchange of commodities.[2] It was not within the scope of this study to test various distance-decay models in the context of India's nationwide pattern of exchange. Hence, simple straight line distance has been used as the distance measure in computing various potentials reported in this study.

Measures of production and consumption activity throughout India were drawn from a number of sources. Data on the concentration of population, urban population, and

[1] William Warntz, Toward a Geography of Price, A Study in Geo-Econometrics (Philadelphia: University of Pennsylvania Press, 1959).

[2] D. Michael Ray, Market Potential and Economic Shadow: A Quantative Analysis of Industrial Location in Southern Ontario (Chicago: Department of Geography, University of Chicago, Research Paper No. 101, 1965), p. 64.

manufacturing employment by district were drawn from the Indian Census of 1961.[1] The latest available data by district on employment in other activities were drawn from the 1958 Survey of Industries.[2] District data on agricultural production were last published in Area and Production of Crops in India, 1955-56,[3] and income figures by district were published in Inter-District and Inter-State Income Differentials, 1955-56.[4]

Having established the study area's relative access to market and supply areas throughout India, inferences can be drawn concerning the impact of this accessibility upon its specialization and flow patterns. Following Harris' argument, one would expect that accessibility to a market would lead an area to specialize in supplying that market.[5] Bengal-Bihar Industrial Area specialization should reflect nearby markets and supplies. Following Stouffer and Ullman's argument concerning intervening opportunity, one would expect inputs for specialized activities to come from the nearest available source and outputs to flow to the nearest markets.[6] However, given the possibility of scale economies, nearby points might not provide adequate supplies or market thresholds, and apparent intervening opportunities would be passed over for the nearest large concentration of supply or market. Thus study-area flows might well reflect exchanges with centers of high supply and market concentrations rather than nearest available source.

One would expect principles such as these to underly industrial location both in the United States and India. Given the study area's specialization and relative accessibility to Indian markets, the length and volume of its commodity exchanges should be in agreement with Pred's analysis of United States manufacturing exchange and his typology of manufacturing flows.[7]

---

[1] India (Republic), Office of the Registrar General, Census of India, 1961, Vol. I, Part IIA (i), "General Population Tables" (Delhi: Government of India Press, 1964).

[2] India (Republic), Ministry of Labor and Employment, Labor Bureau, op. cit.

[3] India (Republic), Ministry of Food and Agriculture, Directorate of Economics and Statistics, Estimates of Area and Production of Principle Crops in India, 1955-56 (Delhi: Government of India Press, 1960).

[4] National Council of Applied Economic Research, Inter-District and Inter-State Income Differentials, 1955-56, Occasional Paper No. 6 (Delhi: National Council of Applied Economic Research, 1963).

[5] Harris, op. cit.

[6] Samuel A. Stouffer, "Intervening Opportunities and Competing Migrants," Journal of Regional Science, II, No. 1 (Spring, 1960), 1-26 and Ullman, op. cit.

[7] Pred, op. cit.

The Bengal-Bihar Industrial Area and the Spatial
Structure of the Indian Economy

The distribution of various Indian demand and supply space potentials are presented in Figures 43-78. Two patterns are clearly indicated. For certain goods such as gram, wheat, or coal whose production is localized due to climatic or geologic conditions, single production concentrations serve the nation, Figures 51, 72, 73 . However, for many other goods a pattern of four nearly equal regional supply and demand spaces are evident. Each region has developed a large concentration of market for urban and industrial goods and to some extent has specialized in the production of such goods within the region. For example, Figures 47 and 48 indicating the pattern of urban and manufacturing market spaces may be compared with Figures 43, 46, and 74 indicating the pattern of machinery, limestone, and cement supply spaces. Against these maps of Indian supply and demand spaces have been plotted Bengal-Bihar Industrial Area exchange patterns for various commodities.

The study area is located at or near the point of highest accessibility to India's supply areas for heavy metallurgical raw materials and to markets for industrial goods. This accessibility appears to have greatly encouraged its specialization in the production and consumption of metals and machinery. The study area's high accessibility to the urban and industrial market of the Calcutta region is reflected in the large volume of short outflows of coal and industrial goods which tie the area strongly to the Calcutta region. Nearby sources of supply appear to have been developed to meet study-area needs and are reflected in the short inflows of raw materials to the area.

Study-area flows do not appear to violate the expectation of trade with nearest opportunity. Flows passing over apparent intervening opportunities may be explained by economies of scale provided by larger and more specialized markets beyond and by governmental regulation. With considerable distances separating the study area from India's other regional supply and market concentrations and with these regions traditionally relatively self-sufficient in production and consumption, it is not surprising to find a limited degree of complementarity between the study area and the Indian national market outside the Calcutta region. Of the commodities studied, the highest degree of interregional complementarity was found in the exchange of machinery and metals. For these commodities the pattern of trade is between similarly specialized areas. Interregional trade based on dissimilar specialization was limited mainly to food grains and coal. Both of these commodities exhibit single national concentrations of supply and the study area appears to trade with the nearest suitable supply or market opportunities, Figures 72, 73 and 51 . Exchanges of raw materials and agricultural products appear to persist in the

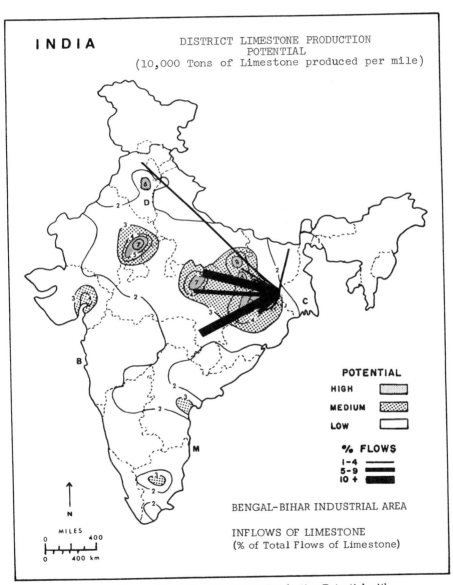

Figure 43. Indian Limestone Production Potential with
Study-Area Inflows of Limestone

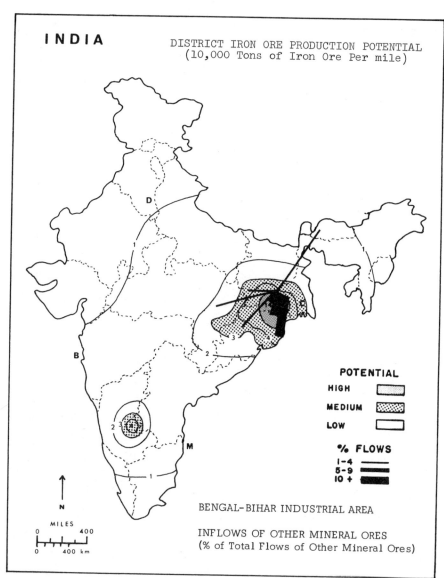

Figure 44. Indian Iron Ore Production Potential with
Study-Area Inflows of Other Mineral Ores

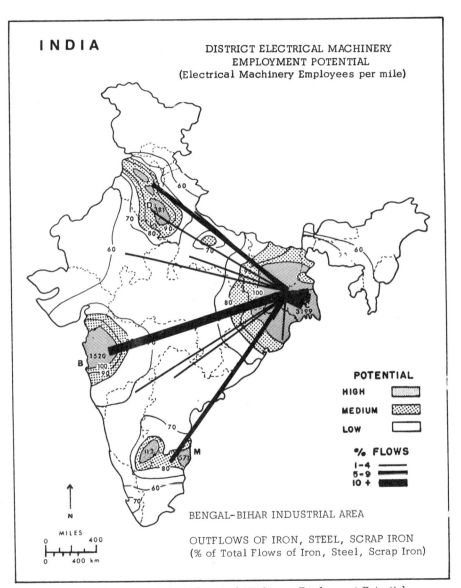

Figure 45. Indian Electrical Machinery Employment Potential
with Study-Area, Outflows of Iron, Steel, Scrap Iron

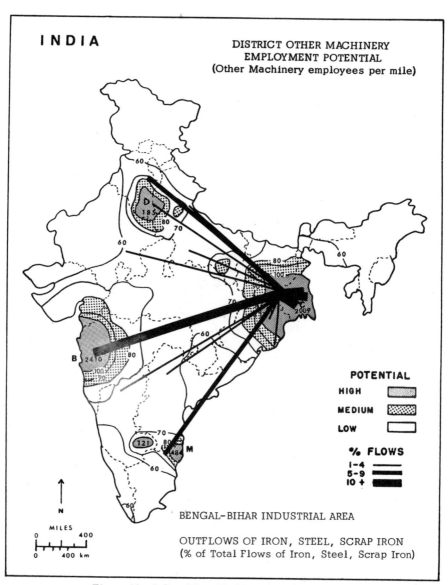

Figure 46. Indian Other Machinery Employment Potential
with Study-Area Outflows of Iron, Steel,
Scrap Iron

107

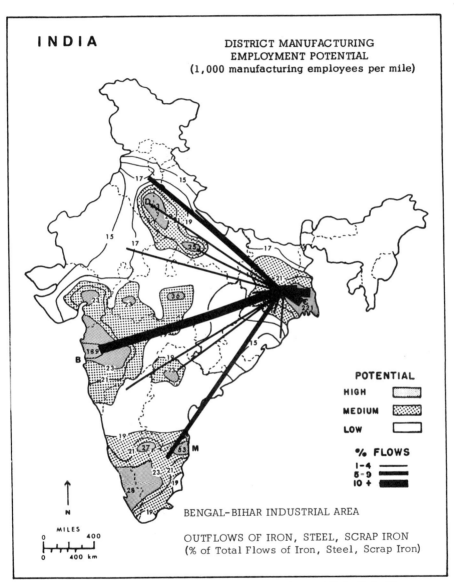

Figure 47. Indian Manufacturing Employment Potential with
Study-Area Outflows of Iron, Steel, Scrap Iron

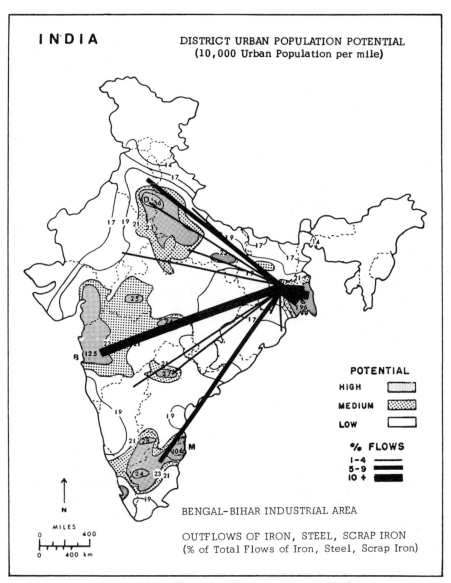

Figure 48. Indian Urban Population Potential with Study–
Area Outflows of Iron, Steel, Scrap Iron

109

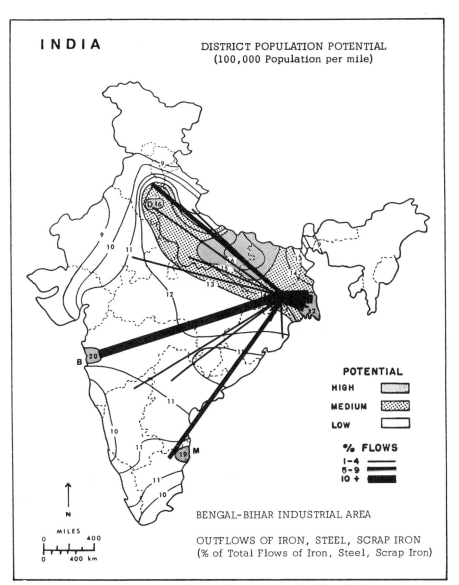

Figure 49. Indian Population Potential with Study-Area
Outflows of Iron, Steel, Scrap Iron

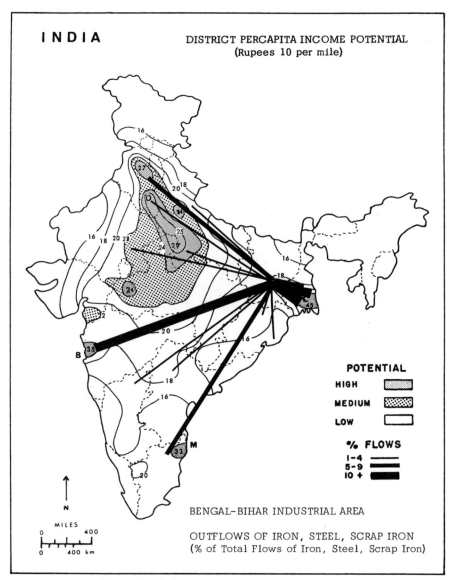

Figure 50. Indian Per Capita Income Potential with Study-
Area Outflows of Iron, Steel, Scrap Iron

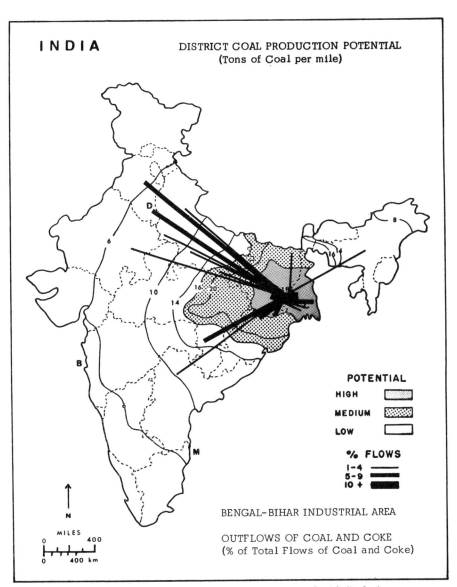

INDIA DISTRICT COAL PRODUCTION POTENTIAL
(Tons of Coal per mile)

POTENTIAL

HIGH

MEDIUM

LOW

% FLOWS

1-4

5-9

10 +

BENGAL–BIHAR INDUSTRIAL AREA

OUTFLOWS OF COAL AND COKE
(% of Total Flows of Coal and Coke)

N

MILES
0   400

0   400 km

Figure 51.   Indian Coal Production Potential with Study-Area
Outflows of Coal and Coke

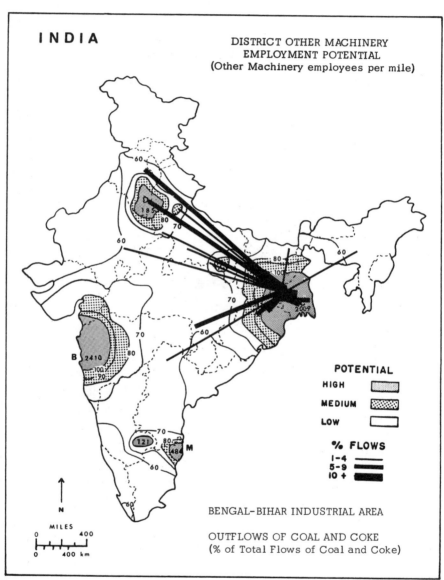

Figure 52. Indian Other Machinery Employment Potential with
Study-Area Outflows of Coal and Coke

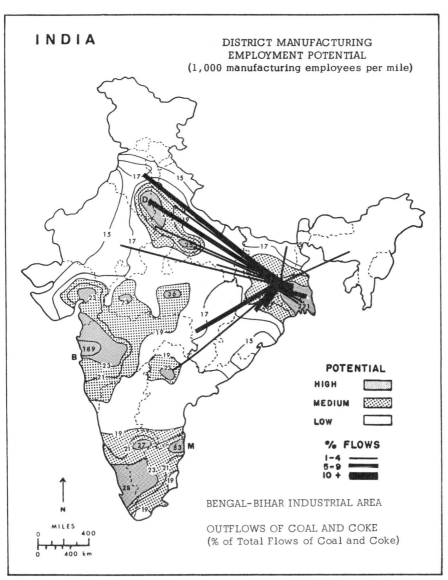

Figure 53.   Indian Manufacturing Employment Potential with
Study-Area Outflows of Coal and Coke

114

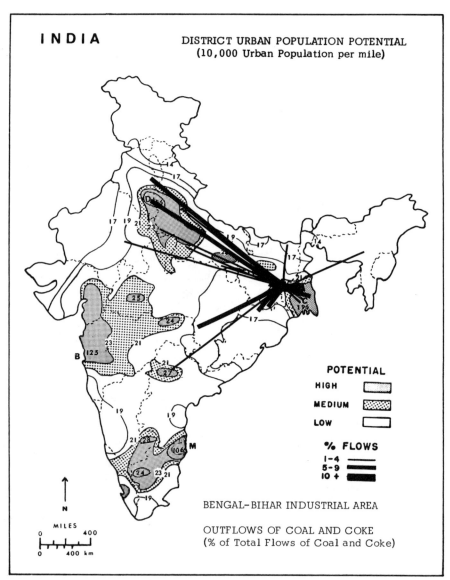

Figure 54. Indian Urban Population Potential with Study-
Area Outflows of Coal and Coke

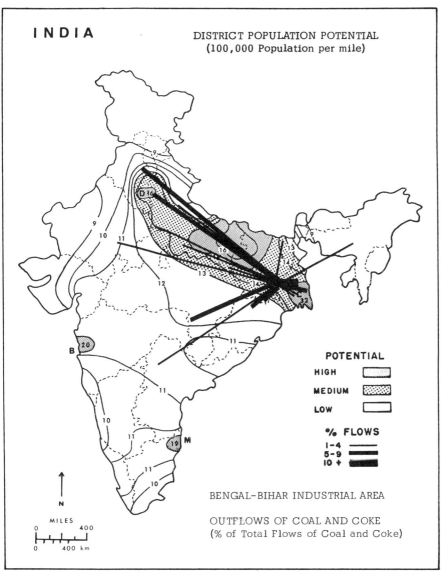

INDIA

DISTRICT POPULATION POTENTIAL
(100,000 Population per mile)

POTENTIAL

HIGH

MEDIUM

LOW

% FLOWS

1-4
5-9
10 +

BENGAL-BIHAR INDUSTRIAL AREA

OUTFLOWS OF COAL AND COKE
(% of Total Flows of Coal and Coke)

N

MILES
0   400

0   400 km

Figure 55.   Indian Population Potential with Study-Area
Outflows of Coal and Coke

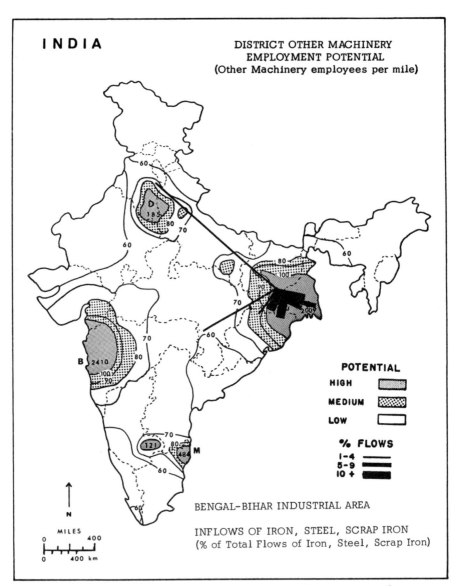

Figure 56. Indian Other Machinery Employment Potential
with Study-Area Inflows of Iron, Steel, Scrap Iron

117

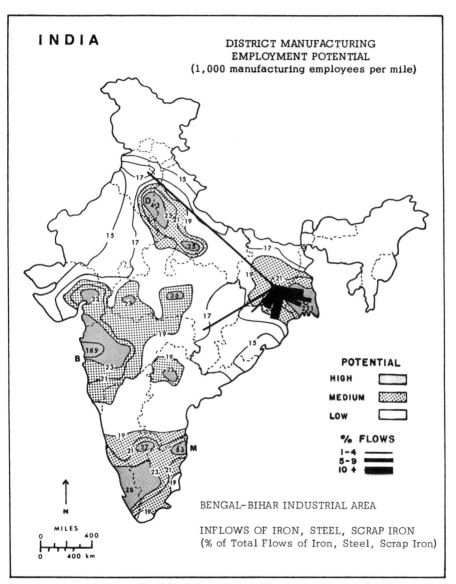

Figure 57. Indian Manufacturing Employment Potential with
Study-Area Inflows of Iron, Steel, Scrap Iron

118

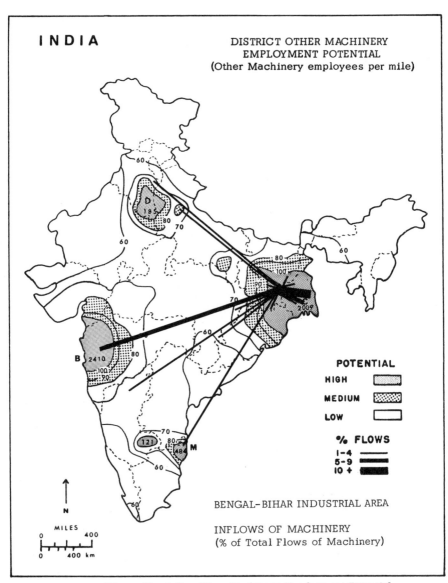

Figure 58. Indian Other Machinery Employment Potential
with Study-Area Inflows of Machinery

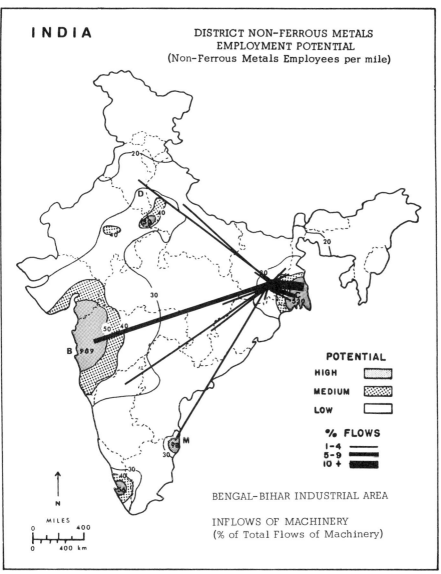

INDIA

DISTRICT NON-FERROUS METALS
EMPLOYMENT POTENTIAL
(Non-Ferrous Metals Employees per mile)

POTENTIAL

HIGH

MEDIUM

LOW

% FLOWS
1-4
5-9
10 +

BENGAL-BIHAR INDUSTRIAL AREA

INFLOWS OF MACHINERY
(% of Total Flows of Machinery)

N

MILES
0   400

0   400 km

Figure 59.   Indian Non-Ferrous Metals Employment Potential
with Study-Area Inflows of Machinery

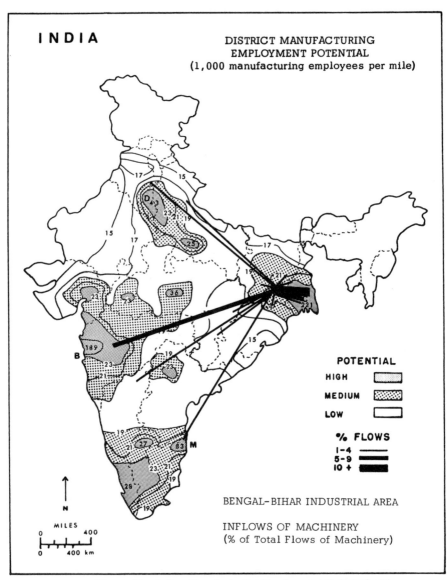

Figure 60.   Indian Manufacturing Employment Potential with
Study-Area Inflows of Machinery

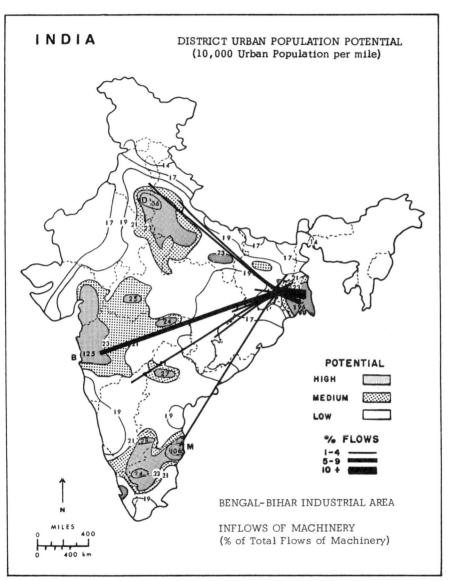

Figure 61. Indian Urban Population Potential with
Study-Area Inflows of Machinery

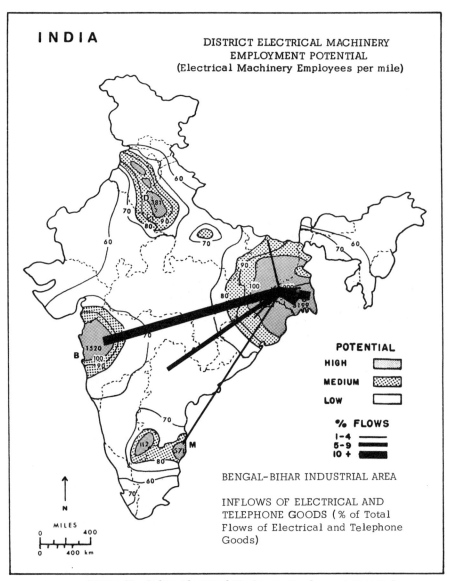

Figure 62. Indian Electrical Machinery Employment Potential
with Study-Area Inflows of Electrical and Telephone Goods

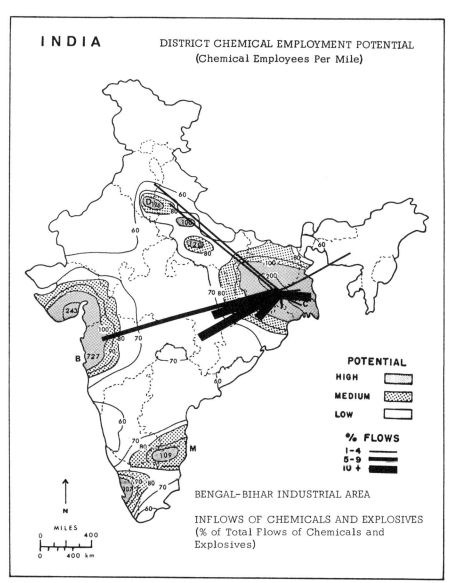

Figure 63.   Indian Chemical Employment Potential with Study-
Area Inflows of Chemicals and
Explosives

124

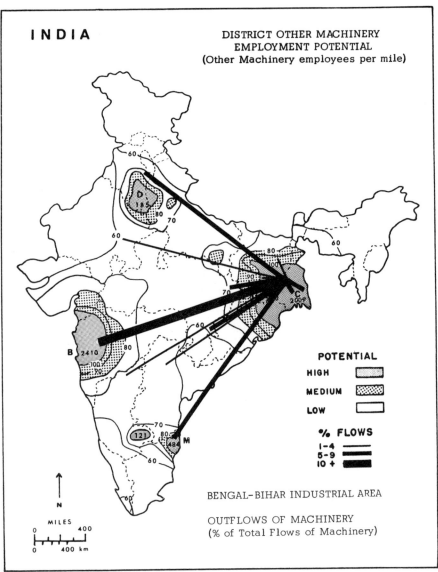

Figure 64. Indian Other Machinery Employment Potential
with Study-Area Outflows of Machinery

125

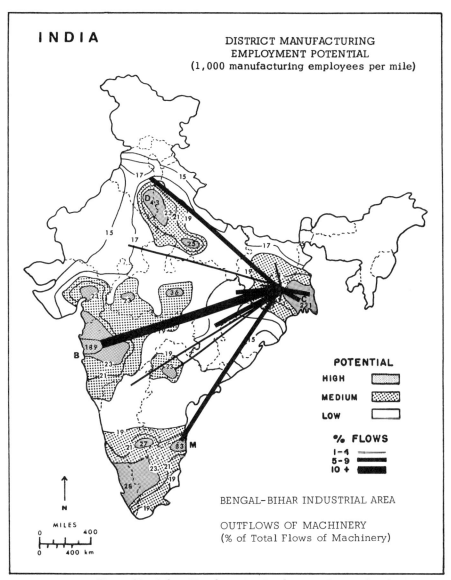

Figure 65. Indian Manufacturing Employment Potential with
Study-Area Outflows of Machinery

126

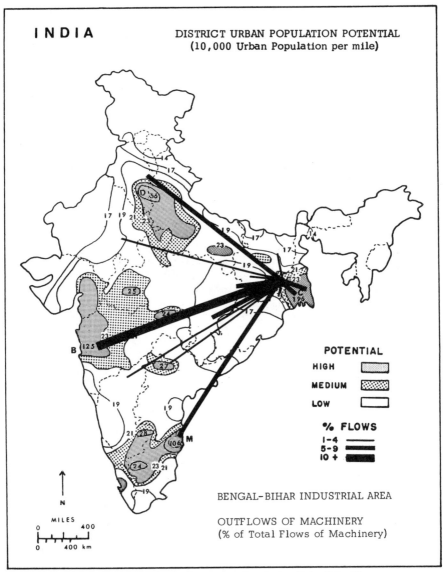

Figure 66. Indian Urban Population Potential with
Study-Area Outflows of Machinery

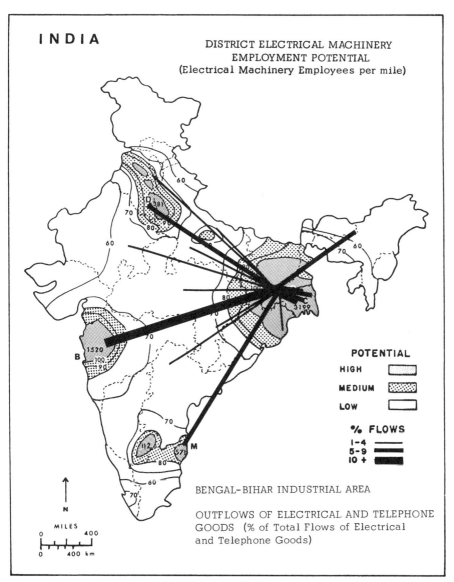

Figure 67.   Indian Electrical Machinery Employment Potential
with Study-Area Outflows of Electrical
and Telephone Goods

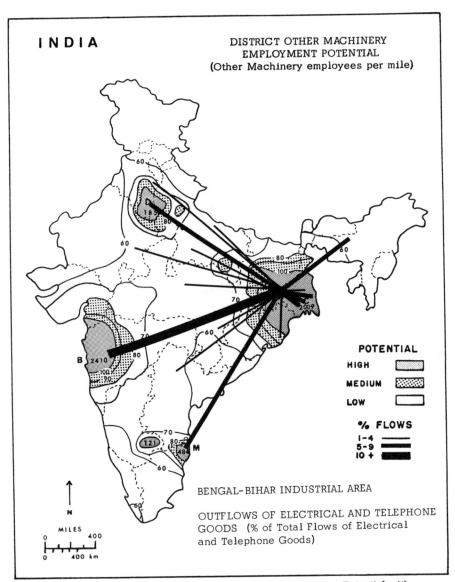

INDIA

DISTRICT OTHER MACHINERY
EMPLOYMENT POTENTIAL
(Other Machinery employees per mile)

POTENTIAL

HIGH

MEDIUM

LOW

% FLOWS
1-4
5-9
10 +

BENGAL-BIHAR INDUSTRIAL AREA

OUTFLOWS OF ELECTRICAL AND TELEPHONE
GOODS (% of Total Flows of Electrical
and Telephone Goods)

MILES
0   400

0   400 km

N

Figure 68.   Indian Other Machinery Employment Potential with
Study-Area Outflows of Electrical
and Telephone Goods

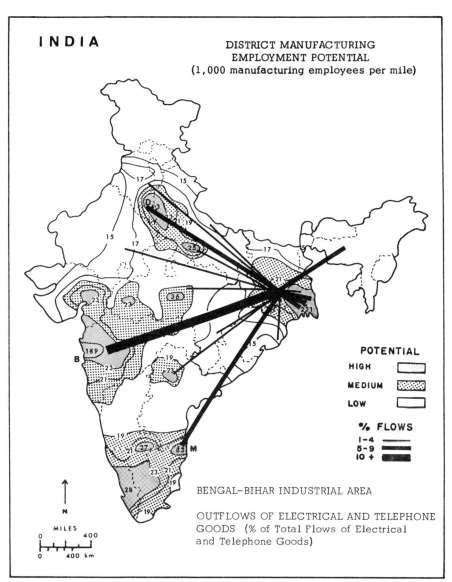

Figure 69. Indian Manufacturing Employment Potential with
Study-Area Outflows of Electrical
and Telephone Goods

130

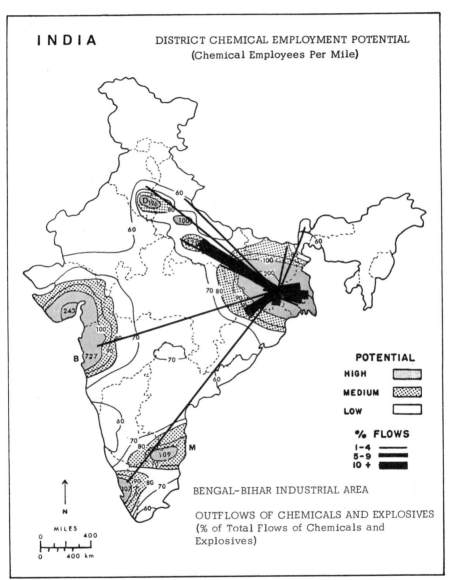

Figure 70.   Indian Chemical Employment Potential
with Study-Area Outflows of Electrical
and Telephone Goods

131

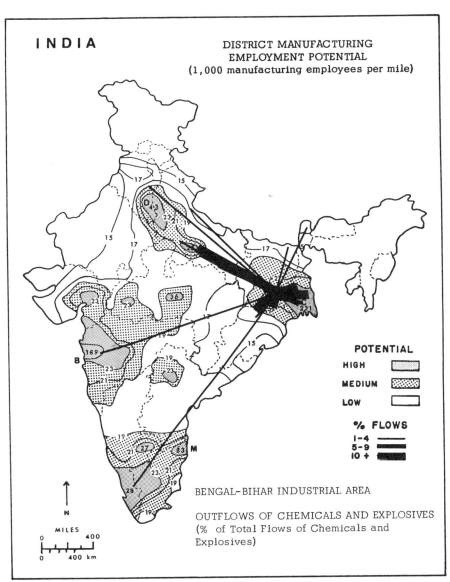

Figure 71. Indian Manufacturing Employment Potential with
Study-Area Outflows of Chemicals
and Explosives

132

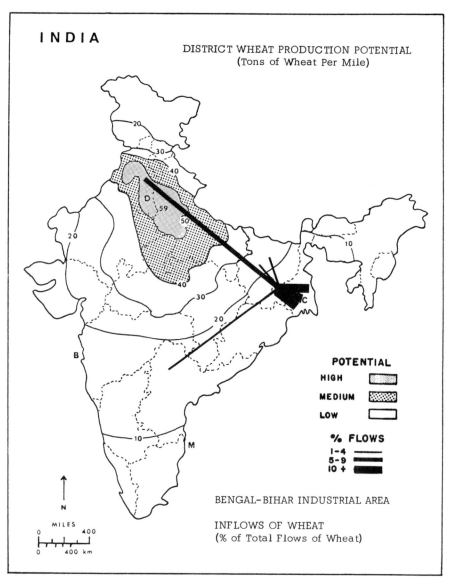

Figure 72.   Indian Wheat Production Potential with Study-
Area Inflows of Wheat

133

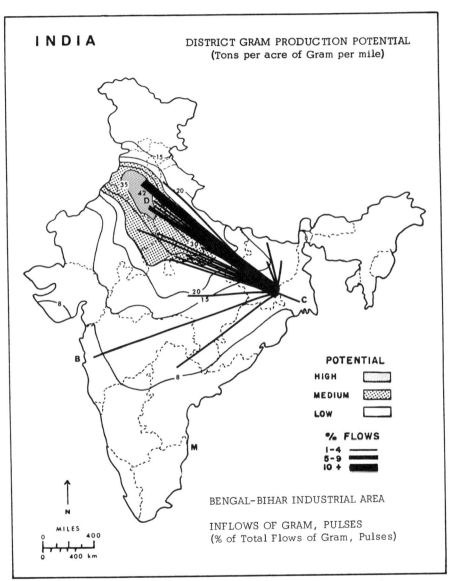

Figure 73. Indian Gram Production Potential with Study-
Area Inflows of Gram, Pulses

134

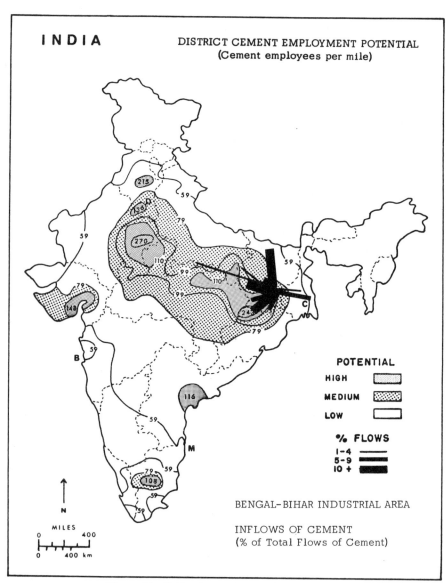

Figure 74.   Indian Cement Employment Potential with
Study-Area Inflows of Cement

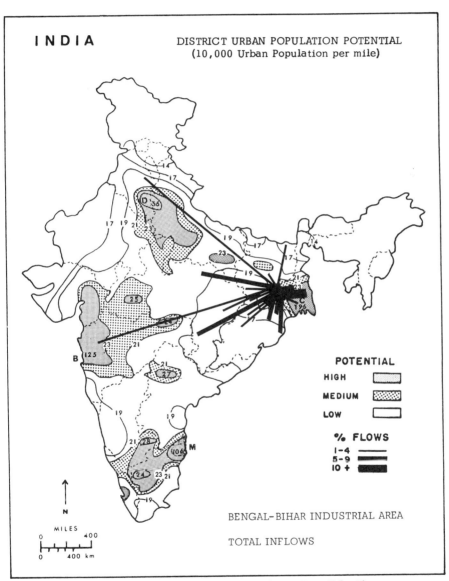

INDIA

DISTRICT URBAN POPULATION POTENTIAL
(10,000 Urban Population per mile)

POTENTIAL

HIGH

MEDIUM

LOW

% FLOWS

1-4
5-9
10 +

BENGAL-BIHAR INDUSTRIAL AREA

TOTAL INFLOWS

MILES

0   400

0   400 km

N

Figure 75. Indian Urban Population Potential with
Study-Area Total Inflows

136

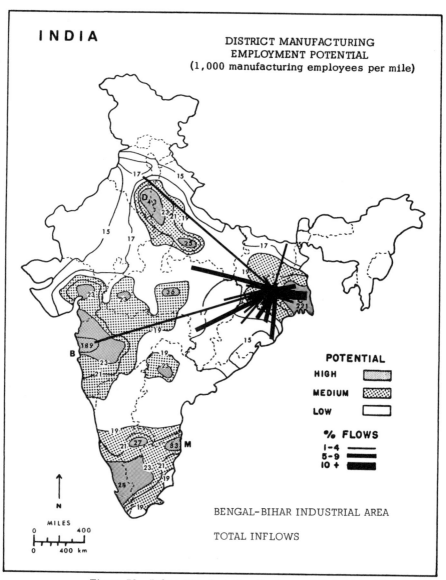

Figure 76.   Indian Manufacturing Employment Potential with
Study-Area Total Inflows

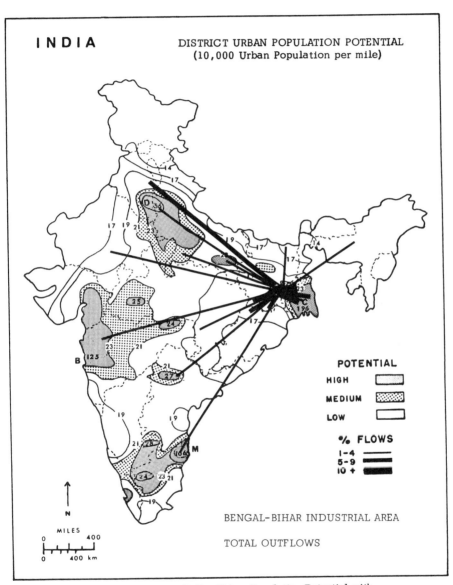

Figure 77. Indian Urban Population Potential with
Study-Area Total Outflows

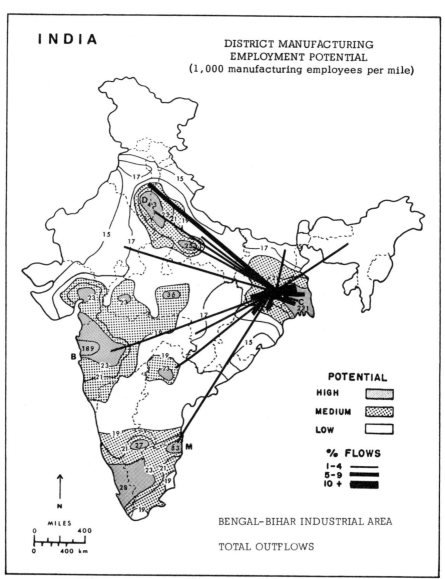

Figure 78. Indian Manufacturing Employment Potential
with Study-Area Total Outflows

traditional highly intraregional exchange patterns. Within the Calcutta region, study-area exchanges of these goods were with dissimilarly specialized areas, while exchanges of manufactured goods were with similarly specialized urban areas, primarily the Calcutta metropolitan area.

Given its specialization and its location relative to national markets, the length and volume of study-area commodity exchanges closely follow Pred's typology of manufacturing flows. However, the strong regional markets in India appear to have modified the flow pattern expected for "raw-material-and-power-oriented industries in areas of high market accessibility."[1]

As Pred notes, "a raw-material-processing industry in the manufacturing heart of a region or nation generally will not have sufficient cost advantage over competitors in areas of intermediate and low accessibility to enter much of its production into competition in these more distant areas." In a footnote he adds, "This would not be true however if concentration of the raw material happened to be particularly great in the high accessibility areas."[2] Such concentration could arise either from economies of scale in production, from a series of relatively strong regional market concentrations rather than one large national market, or from a combination of the two. Thus with a relatively large concentration of supply, strong regional markets would reduce the relative demand of a national or immediately adjacent regional market concentration and increase the importance of competing in other areas of high accessibility. Apparently in an economic system with large-scale economies in raw-material-and-power-oriented industries and strong regional rather than a single national market concentration as in the United States, location of a large-scale plant at a point of high accessibility to a regional market leads to a higher percentage of long distance flows to other regional markets than would be anticipated by Pred's typology. The flow patterns associated with each of the study-area specialized activities present interesting and varied pictures from which the influence of location within India's demand and supply spaces upon the study-area specialization and exchange patterns may be discerned.

Iron and Steel Production

In the manufacture of iron and steel, the study area is potentially complementary with raw material sources throughout India. Figures 43 and 44 indicate the relative accessibility of various points in India to limestone and iron ore production. Within these

---

[1] Pred, op. cit., p. 76.

[2] Ibid.

supply spaces have been plotted the proportion of the study area's inflows of limestone and other mineral ores including iron ore. Figure 43 indicates sources of limestone have been developed in each of the four regions of India to serve local needs. However, the greatest concentration of production has been developed in close proximity to the steel mills of the study area and Calcutta region. The large limestone flow from outside this area of highest concentration represents flow from a mine opened after 1958, the year for which the limestone supply potentials were computed. Figure 44 indicates sources of iron ore have been developed both in the Calcutta and Madras regions. Again the greatest concentration of iron ore production has been developed in close proximity to steel mills of the study area and the Calcutta region. Study-area receipt patterns for both of these goods are based on complementarity between dissimilarly specialized areas.

In its shipments of steel, the study area could be complementary with various metal-using industries located mainly in similarly specialized urban areas. Figures 45-50 present various approximations of the national demand space for steel. They indicate the relative accessibility of points throughout India to concentrations of electrical and other machinery employment, total manufacturing employment, urban population, total population, and per capita income. Within these demand spaces, the study area's pattern of steel outflow has been plotted. These figures indicate the four regional concentrations of electrical and other machinery production, manufacturing in general, and urban population focused on each of the major metropolitan areas. The figure of population potential indicates the nearly uniform distribution of total population, over 70 per cent rural, throughout India with a slightly higher concentration of population and wealth in its most fertile area, the Ganges Valley.

With respect to each of these possible markets for steel, the study area is located at or near the point of greatest accessibility to its regional as well as to the Indian national market. The early specialization of the Calcutta metropolitan area and its region in heavy machinery manufacture provided a large market for an area specialized in steel production and has clearly influenced study-area flow patterns to this market. Due to development of metal-using industries elsewhere in India, increase in the capacity of study-area plants and reduction of steel imports through the ports of Bombay and Madras, the study area now ships considerable quantities of steel to manufacturing and other urban activities throughout India. With its total population heavily rural and with the majority of its gross national product and per capita income agriculturally derived, the correlation between steel flows and India's total population and per capita income is not particularly strong.

Comparing the figures of limestone and iron ore supply space, Figures 43 and 44, with figures of various manufacturing and urban market potentials, Figures 45-50, the short distance shipments of raw materials to the study area accords nicely with Pred's expected pattern for raw-material-and-power-oriented industries at points of high market accessibility. However, even though the study area is located in or near the area of highest market accessibility, the number of long distance steel shipments from the study area does not fit this pattern.

With considerable economies of scale built into its steel plants, the study area produces more steel than the Calcutta regional market can or is allowed to absorb under governmental regulation. The limited production in India's other regional markets coupled with governmental regulation of steel prices and shipments resulted in a rather high proportion of long distance interregional steel outflows from the study area.

The study area's steel outflows within the context of India's strong regional markets suggest that given many discontinuous (regional) points of high market accessibility and excess capacity in a raw-material-and-power-oriented industry located at any such point of high regional accessibility, one would expect both a large proportion of short intraregional flows and a high proportion of long distance interregional flows.

Coal Production

Study-area outflows of coal, India's main industrial fuel, might again be expected to be complementary with urban and manufacturing concentration. Figure 51 indicates the relative accessibility of Indian points to coal production (coal supply space) and the distribution pattern of coal from the study area. As discussed in Chapter III, coal is produced in some quantity to the west and south of the study area, and under government control the distribution of study-area coal was heavily oriented to local and Ganges Valley points with reduced competition from other coal fields. Figures 52-55 indicate the outflow of study-area coal in relation to accessibility to other machinery and total manufacturing employment, urban population, and total population. Location at the point of highest accessibility to regional markets clearly influences the outflows of study-area coal with flows going to non-mining, or dissimilarly specialized areas.

As in the case of steel, there is less correlation between coal outflows and total population concentration than with concentrations of urban activity. These flows of coal, over 70 per cent of the study area's outflows, show only limited complementarity with points outside the Ganges Valley, and the study area does not participate fully in the national market for coal. The short length high volume flows of study-area coal conform nicely to Pred's expectation for a raw-material-oriented industry at a point of high accessibility to its market.

Machinery and Other Manufactures Exchange
==

In its role as producer of machinery and other manufactures, the study area would most likely engage in complementary exchange with concentrations of machinery, chemicals, other manufacturing, and with urban areas in general. Figures 56-63 indicate inflows of steel, electrical and other machinery, and chemicals from points of different relative accessibility to total manufacturing, machinery, electrical machinery, chemicals, and non-ferrous metals employment and urban and total population throughout India. Inflows of steel relate to the concentration of steel production in the study area and Calcutta region. Although produced in south India and in re-rolling mills in the Bombay and Punjab areas, there appears to be little cross hauling of steel for use in the study area. Its location in the Calcutta region at the point of highest concentration of urban and industrial activities appears to have influenced the many short inflows of non-electrical machinery to the study area, Figures 58-61. However, to support local production, the study area exhibits considerable complementarity in the exchange of machinery with all four similarly specialized major urban industrial concentrations of India. This pattern is in close agreement with the pattern anticipated by Pred's category of labor-and-agglomeration-economy-oriented industries at sites of high accessibility.[1] Study-area receipts of electrical machinery, Figure 62, came mainly from local and Bombay area sources, the two areas of highest potential for this good. Chemical receipts, Figure 63, were even more oriented to production within the Calcutta region and in nearby Madhya Pradesh. Chemical specialization in the other regions of India is apparently not complementary with study area activities.

Although the study area is located at the point of highest accessibility to urban industrial markets in India and the Calcutta region, outflows of electrical and other machinery as discussed in Chapter III, went extensively outside the Calcutta region, Figures 64-69. These exchanges may reflect road hauls in the Calcutta area and indicate a rather high degree of complementarity between similarly specialized industrial activities throughout India. Apparently considerable cross hauling occurs at different stages in the production of machinery. The Bombay region received the largest share of interregional shipments of machinery from the study area, and nearly equal flows were sent to the Delhi and Madras regions. Figures 70 and 71 indicate the limited complementarity of study-area chemical production with chemical and other manufacturing production in areas outside the Calcutta region.

Surrounded by India's greatest concentration of supplies and manufacturing

[1] Ibid.

markets and with the historic specialization of the Calcutta region in machinery manufacture, it is not surprising to find the study area specialized in this line of activity. Given the relative absence of complementary activities outside the major industrial urban places of India, as expected these exchanges were mainly with areas of highest urban and industrial accessibility. In this role, the small volume lengthy exchanges in which the study area engages conform with those hypothesized by Pred for labor-and-agglomeration-oriented industries in areas of high market accessibility.

Consumer Goods Receipts

Gram and wheat were the study area's main receipts of consumer goods by rail. Figures 72 and 73 indicate that the national supply spaces for wheat and gram are dominated by large single production concentrations rather than multiple regional concentrations. Both gram and non-imported wheat were received from points of highest supply potential. Comparing the maps of gram and wheat supply potential, Figures 72 and 73, with the maps of urban population or demand space potential, Figure 75, it is apparent that this agricultural industry is located at a point of high accessibility to a regional market. However, this regional market is not large enough to absorb all local production, and long distance flows to other points of high market accessibility throughout India take place. Production of gram and wheat is oriented to a much more diffuse national market than is found in the United States.

Although cement was produced in each of India's major economic regions, study-area cement receipts generally came from the nearest point of high cement supply space potential, Figure 74 . Comparing cement supply space and urban population or market potentials, Figures 74 and 75, Pred's expectation of short flows for raw-material-and-power-oriented industries in areas of high market accessibility adequately describe the pattern of study-area cement receipts.

Total Flows

Figures 75 and 76 indicate the aggregate pattern of study-area inflows against the pattern of accessibility to urban population and total manufacturing employment potentials in India. Reflecting the mix of individual commodity receipts, the area's total receipts come in large part from industrial and urban markets in the Calcutta region with limited receipts from other regional concentrations of industrial production. Figures 77 and 78 indicate the aggregate pattern of study-area outflows again in relation to urban population and manufacturing employment potentials. Reflecting its specialization in coal, steel and machinery production, the aggregate outflow pattern shows the study area closely tied to regional and Gangetic Valley manufacturing. In its outflows, the area is much more closely tied to India's other regional markets than was true of its inflows. As expected, the study area's flows are oriented to points of highest accessibility to industrial raw materials and markets.

CHAPTER VI

BENGAL-BIHAR INDUSTRIAL AREA EXCHANGES,

SUPPLY, DEMAND AND DISTANCE EFFECTS

The figures and tables in earlier chapters strongly suggest that exchanges of the
Bengal-Bihar Industrial Area vary in a regular fashion subject to conditions of supply,
demand, distance, and governmental regulation found throughout India. The relationship
between variation in these conditions and variation in the volume of study-area exchange
can be specified much more exactly.

Outflows

As noted in Chapter I, it has often been postulated that the volume of goods
shipped from any given area to other areas of an economic system should be directly related to the demand for such goods in these other areas and inversely related to the diffi-
culty of overcoming intervening distance in reaching them. [1] The potential model ex-
pressing this hypothesis would be expected to predict adequately observed exchanges of
goods between a particular place, such as the Bengal-Bihar Industrial Area, and places
in the surrounding economic system. However, in the few studies of commodity flows
which have been undertaken, the demand and distance variables in the potential model
have not proved equally powerful in accounting for observed variation in flow patterns.

In their studies of flows of commodities by rail from major parts of Australia and
Ghana, Smith and Gould found that intervening distance had almost no effect upon

---

[1] Isard, Methods, pp. 394-568.

observed variation in the volume of goods shipped to towns in the surrounding hinterlands.[1]
Smith noted that for towns in southern New South Wales variation in distance was weakly
correlated with variation in the tonnage of commodities received from Sydney and Melbourne. He found that variation in the population of these towns was sufficient to account
for approximately 68 per cent of the variation in tonnage received from either Sydney or
Melbourne and for approximately 77 per cent of the variation in tonnages which they received from Sydney and Melbourne combined.[2] In the case of commodity flows to hinterland towns from Ghana's port of Takoradi, Gould observed that the distances involved
were too short to have any effect upon the volume of flow. He found that variation in the
population of receiving towns alone accounted for approximately 49 per cent of the variation in the volume of goods which they received from Takoradi.[3]

Although Smith and Gould observed no significant distance effect upon variation
in the commodity flows they were studying, their experience does not rule out the possible importance of distance as a variable inversely influencing the flow of goods. The
absence of a distance effect suggests that particular spatial arrangements of activities
and costs of operating specific modes of transport may minimize the difficulties of overcoming distance for certain commodity flows. One would expect intervening distance to
have little or no effect upon the volume of flows to a set of destinations if there is but
one major originating source (as in the case of a port with a relatively closed hinterland); if all the destinations are located relatively close to that source so that operating
costs for the mode of transport used are mainly starting, stopping and terminal costs;
or if all of the destinations are at relatively equal distances from the source due either
to large intervening distance or to the operation of some form of transport subsidy. Alternatively, for a set of destinations enjoying many competing sources of supply and located at substantially varying distances from each source, one would expect that variation in distance would have considerable effect upon the volume of goods which a set of
destinations will receive from any one source. For example, within the large Canadian
economy, Ray found that 58 per cent of the variation in the volume of commodity flows
by rail from Southern Ontario to points throughout the rest of Canada could be accounted

---

[1] Robert H. T. Smith, Commodity Movements in Southern New South Wales
(Sydney: Department of Geography, Australian National University, 1962); Peter R.
Gould, The Development of the Transportation Pattern in Ghana (Evanston: Northwest-
ern University Studies in Geography No. 5, 1960).

[2] Smith, op. cit., pp. 104-122.

[3] Gould, op. cit., p. 98.

for simply by variation in the distance to receiving points.[1] Given the diverse results of the Smith, Gould, and Ray studies, it appears that before proceeding to an evaluation of the ability of the potential model to account for variation in study-area outflows, an examination should be undertaken of the separate effect on these flows of the demand and distance variables used in the model.

Demand Effects

Examining first the effects of demand, Table 20 indicates that the regression of log of urban population[2] in receiving districts (k) throughout India (the same model used by Smith and Gould) accounted for approximately 49 per cent (r^2) of the total variation in log of study-area outflows, significant at the .01 level. Thus variation in demand measured simply by urban population was able to account for nearly half of the variation in the Bengal-Bihar Industrial Area's total mix of outflows.

TABLE 20

RELATION OF TOTAL OUTFLOWS TO URBAN
POPULATION AND DISTANCE

Independent Variable with Respect to k	Correlation Coefficient	Coefficient of Determination	Regression Coefficient	Standard Error of	Variance Ratio Test
	r	r^2	b	b	F
Urban Population	.70	.49	1.54	.12	151.61*
Distance	.21	.04	-1.01	.37	7.46*
Potential Model:					
Urban population	.73	.53	1.53	.12	163.11*
Distance			-.97	.25	14.04*
(Step 2 of stepwise regression)					

* = significant at the .01 level for 156 and 155 degrees of freedom.

Note: Variables all log transformed.

[1] Ray, op. cit., p. 65.

[2] Throughout this analysis variables have been transformed to logarithms to the base 10 to approximate normal distributions.

Because the study-area commodity mix consisted largely of industrial goods, coal, steel and machinery, it was hypothesized that measures of demand other than urban population might provide a higher level of explanation for variation in the volume of study-area outflows. Other available measures of the demand for industrial goods included total population, total manufacturing employment, employment in specific manufacturing industries, total income, and per capita income for each district and state. However, each of these measures was closely correlated with urban population. When variation in these measures was separately correlated with variation in study-area outflows, none provided a higher level of explanation than did urban population, and it was concluded that urban population was the most satisfactory predictor of study-area outflows using this simple demand model.

Applying this demand model to individual rather than total study-area commodity flows, one might expect considerable difference in the relative contribution of different demand measures. Tables 21 and 22 indicate the various measures of demand and correlations which accounted for the greatest amount of variation in major study-area outflows.[1] The demand effect alone ranged from explaining 38 per cent of the variation in coal outflows to explaining approximately 51 per cent of the variation of electrical machinery. These results reflect India's limited number of specialized urban industrial markets and the large proportion of study-area machinery flows to these few markets noted in Figures 66 and 69. The lower correlation between the area's coal and steel outflows and concentrations of urban demand reflect the larger proportion of steel flows to rural demands, Figure 48, and coal flows to urban and rural demands mainly in northern India, Figure 54. As noted earlier, this diffusion in the demand pattern for coal and steel was to some degree regulated by government controls.

Distance Effects

Given a range of values and degrees of specialization in the study-area commodity mix and the existence of numerous points of consumption as well as competing sources for many of its goods in other economic regions of India, one might expect considerable distance effects upon study-area outflows. However, the regression of log of total tonnage received from the study area upon the log of distance to receiving district alone accounted for slightly over 4 per cent of the variation in study-area outflows, significant at the .01 level, Table 20. Again, considering flow patterns of individual rather than

---

[1]Commodities selected for analysis in this chapter represented either a large portion of the volume or were typical of the "traditional" or "modern" components of study area outflows or inflows.

TABLE 21

RELATION OF SELECTED OUTFLOWS TO URBAN POPULATION
AND OTHER SELECTED DEMAND VARIABLES

Commodity	Demand Variable with Respect to k	Correlation Coefficient	Coefficient of Deter- mination	Regression Coefficient	Standard Error of	Variance Ratio Test
		r	r^2	b	b	F
Coal	Urban population	.59	.35	1.50	.16	81.7*
	Manufacturing employment	.62	.38	1.52	.15	102.5*
Iron and Steel	Urban population	.67	.45	1.37	.12	130.2*
Electrical Machinery	Urban population	.66	.44	.87	.07	124.0*
	Electrical machinery employment	.73	.53	.66	.05	173.8*
Other Ma- chinery	Urban population	.64	.41	.69	.06	110.6*
	Manufacturing employment	.69	.48	.69	.05	139.7*

* = significant at the .01 level for 156 degrees of freedom.
Note: Variables all log transformed.

TABLE 22

SIMPLE CORRELATION OF OUTFLOWS AND SELECTED
DEMAND AND DISTANCE VARIABLES[a]

Commodities and Independent Variables	Urban Population	Distance	Total Manufacturing Employment	Electrical Machinery Employment
Total Commodities	.7020	-.2137	.7188	
Coal	.5063	-.1958	.6297	
Iron and Steel	.6746	-.2322	.6739	
Electrical Machinery	.6654	-.1011	.6913	.7260
Other Machinery	.6440	-.1773	.6874	
Urban Population		-.0120		
Distance	-.0120		-.0745	-.0489
Total Manufacturing Employ- ment		-.0745		
Electrical Machinery Employ- ment		-.0489		

a = for Tables 20 through 24.
Note: Variables all log transformed.

total commodities, one might expect that in accounting for these flow patterns the relative contribution of distance would be quite variable. However, Table 23 indicates that in the case of those commodities for which distance does make a significant contribution to explaining variation in flows, the range of explanation is quite small, from 2 to 7 per cent.

TABLE 23

RELATION OF SELECTED OUTFLOWS TO DISTANCE

Commodity	Correlation Coefficient r	Coefficient of Determination r^2	Regression Coefficient b	Standard Error of b	Variance Ratio Test F
Coal	.20	.04	-1.08	.43	6.22*
Iron and Steel	.23	.05	-1.02	.34	8.82*
Electrical Machinery	.10	.01	-.28	.22	1.61[ns]
Other Machinery	.18	.03	-.41	.18	5.06**

* = significant at the .01 level for 156 degrees of freedom.
** = significant at the .05 level for 156 degrees of freedom.
ns = Not statistically significant.
Note: Variables all log transformed.

The major study-area outflows consisted of some of India's highest value products least subject to variation in the cost of transport. As noted in earlier chapters, the study-area location at or near the center of urban industrial demand in the Calcutta economic region led to a large volume of short distance, high value shipments to this market. Shipments to centers of demand in India's other economic regions occurred over considerable distances with relatively few intervening demands. In addition, governmental controls over the allocation and pricing of the area's two largest flows, coal and steel, reduced the influence of distance upon variation in these flows. On the basis of this analysis, it is clear that those commodities least affected by variation in distance were the high value commodities (machinery), commodities for which the study area supplied a high proportion of regional or nationwide production (steel), and commodities for which shipment patterns were regulated (coal) or transportation subsidized (steel).

Distance Decay Rates

The fact that distance does make a small though significant contribution in accounting for variation in the volume of most study-area outflows lends interest to the value of the distance coefficient in the regression model. With respect to outflows of total commodities and steel, the coefficients are not significantly different from 1.0 at the .01 level of confidence, and the coefficient for coal is only slightly greater than 1.0, Tables 20 and 23. Thus shipments of the study area's two major commodities appeared to decline very nearly proportionate to increasing distance. The distance coefficient for electrical machinery was not statistically significant, while that for other machinery, .41, was considerably less than 1.0. If data were available, it would be extremely interesting to examine the rates of distance decay for these same commodities originating in India's other regions and changes in such rates resulting from changes in government regulations.

The Potential Model

The preceding analysis indicates that both demand and distance variables are significantly correlated with variation in total study-area outflows. When the full potential model

$$\log f_{1k} = \log a + b \log P_k - c \log d_{1k}$$

$$\text{where } f_{1k} = \text{tonnage of commodity flow}$$

$$a = \text{constant term}$$

$$P_k = \text{population or demand at a given destination k}$$

$$d_{1k} = \text{distance point 1 (the study area) to k}$$

(all variables log transformed to insure normality)

was applied to study-area outflows, correlation of log of total tonnage received from the study area with the log of urban population in districts throughout India and log of distance from the study area was 0.7314 significant at the .01 level, Table 20. The potential model was able to account for approximately 53 per cent of the variation in total study-area outflows, representing an increase in (r) of 0.03 over the model without distance. The ability of the potential model to account for only one-third to one-half of the total variation in individual outflows reflects the minimal effect of distance on these flows, Table 24. Table 25 indicates the actual values of the potential model's parameters for individual commodity outflows.

Regional Differences in Outflow Patterns

Chapters III, IV and V described the high percentage of Bengal-Bihar Industrial Area commodities exchanged within the Calcutta economic region. Although these intra- and interregional exchange patterns generally conformed to the models of regional and

TABLE 24

RELATION OF SELECTED OUTFLOWS TO COMBINED
DEMAND AND DISTANCE EFFECTS
(second step of stepwise regression)

Commodity	Independent Variable with Respect to k	Correlation Coefficient r	Coefficient of Determination r^2	Regression Coefficient b	Standard Error of b	Variance Ratio Test F
Coal	Urban population	.62	.38	1.50	.16	85.2*
	Distance			-1.04	.35	8.9*
Iron and Steel	Urban population	.71	.50	1.36	.11	141.4*
	Distance			-.98	.24	15.7*
Electrical Machinery	Urban population	.67	.45	.86	.07	124.7*
	Distance			-.26	.16	2.4 ns
Other Machinery	Urban population	.67	.45	.69	.06	114.8*
	Distance			-.39	.14	8.0*

* = significant at the .01 level for 155 degrees of freedom.
ns = Not statistically significant.
Note: Variables all log transformed.

TABLE 25

THE POTENTIAL MODEL FOR SELECTED OUTFLOWS

Commodity Flow Study Area to k F_{1k}	Demand at k P_k	Distance Study Area to k d_{ik}
Total Commodities	F_{1k} = a (Urban Pop.)$^{1.53}$ (distance)$^{-.97}$	
Coal	F_{1k} = a (Urban Pop.)$^{1.50}$ (distance)$^{-1.04}$	
Iron and Steel	F_{1k} = a (Urban Pop.)$^{1.36}$ (distance)$^{-.98}$	
Electrical Machinery	F_{1k} = a (Urban Pop.)$^{.86}$	
Other Machinery	F_{1k} = a (Urban Pop.)$^{.69}$ (distance)$^{-.39}$	

commodity exchange presented in Chapters I and III, no attempt was made to evaluate actual intra- and interregional differences in study-area flow patterns.

To test the actual significance of observed differences in intra- and interregional outflow patterns, one-way analysis of variance was applied to the various outflows (log transformed) sent to two groups of districts and states corresponding to the Calcutta economic region and to the rest of India, Figure 1. Table 26 indicates that flow patterns within and between region were significantly different for total outflows and for individual

TABLE 26

VARIATION IN THE VOLUME OF SELECTED COMMODITY
OUTFLOWS TO THE CALCUTTA ECONOMIC
REGION AND TO THE REST OF INDIA
(one way analysis of variance, 2 regions)

Commodity	Sum of Squares	Degrees of Freedom	Mean Square	T Test
Total Commodities				
Between Regions	24.96	1	24.96	
Within Regions	294.51	156	1.88	3.63*
Total	319.47	157		
Coal				
Between Regions	52.28	1	52.28	
Within Regions	387.56	156	2.48	4.58*
Total	439.84	157		
Iron and Steel				
Between Regions	1.89	1	1.89	
Within Regions	273.19	156	1.75	1.04^{ns}
Total	275.08	157		
Electrical Machinery				
Between Regions	.26	1	.26	
Within Regions	113.43	156	.72	$.60^{ns}$
Total	113.69	157		
Other Machinery				
Between Regions	1.84	1	1.84	
Within Regions	76.16	156	.48	1.94^{**}
Total	78.00	157		

* = significant at the .01 level.
** = significant at the .05 level.
ns = not statistically significant.
Note: Variables all log transformed.

flows of coal and other machinery. Reflecting the figures in Tables 17 and 19, no significant difference was observed in flows of steel and electrical machinery to the region and to the rest of India.

If, as suggested in Chapters I and V, activities in the four major economic regions of India have historically been organized to maximize intraregional exchange and regional self-sufficiency, significant intra- and interregional differences would be expected in both distance and demand effects upon study-area exchanges. To test for regional differences in these effects, the logs of various flows were regressed upon the logs of urban population and distance (the potential model) for the Calcutta region and for the rest of India separately. Regression coefficients of demand and distance from these two regressions were compared for significant differences using a Z test.[1]

Table 27 indicates that for total outflows and for outflows of coal there was no significant difference in the effects of demand between regions even though significant regional differences in volume were noted in Table 26. Conversely, although regional differences in volume were not significant, regional differences in demand effects for steel and electrical machinery were significant at the .05 or .01 level. Regional demand and volume difference were both significant for outflows of electrical machinery. Although these commodities were widely demanded and encouraged to flow through India, the results indicate that regional specialization has led to regional differentiation of demand for the area's more specialized goods. On the other hand, even though demand for study-area coal appeared uniform throughout India, regulation encouraged a more regional pattern in its distribution.

Regional differences in the effects of distance upon study-area outflows present quite another picture. With respect to outflows of electrical machinery, distance effects were not significant within the region but were significant outside the region. As noted earlier, the limited effect of distance upon study-area outflows of electrical and other machinery to the Calcutta region reflects the high value of these goods and the generally short distances to regional centers of demand. The distance effect upon other machinery was significant for both regions and significantly different between them. With respect to steel outflows, distance was significant within the region but not significant for flows

---

[1] With a null hypothesis of no significant difference between the values of b_1 and b_2

$$z = \frac{b_1 - b_2}{\sqrt{Se_{b_1}^2 + Se_{b_2}^2}}$$

TABLE 27

RELATION OF SELECTED OUTFLOWS TO COMBINED DEMAND
AND DISTANCE EFFECTS FOR THE CALCUTTA
ECONOMIC REGION AND THE REST OF INDIA
(second step of stepwise regression)

Commodity and Region	Independent Variable with Respect to k	Correlation Coefficient r	Coefficient of Determination r^2	Regression Coefficient b	Standard Error of b	Variance Ratio Test F
Total Commodities						
Calcutta Region	Urban population	.78	.61	1.49	.12	144.9*
	Distance			-.32	.22	2.1ns
Rest of India	Urban population	.76	.58	1.96	.25	60.4*
	Distance			-2.61	1.31	3.9ns

Regional difference in demand effect $Z = 1.74^{ns}$
Regional difference in distance effect $Z = .-^{ns}$

Coal						
Calcutta Region	Urban population	.71	.50	1.76	.17	100.3*
	Distance			.01	.31	.0ns
Rest of India	Urban population	.61	.37	1.60	.32	24.3*
	Distance			-1.85	1.65	1.2ns

Regional difference in demand effect $Z = .44^{ns}$
Regional difference in distance effect $Z = .-^{ns}$

Iron and Steel						
Calcutta Region	Urban population	.69	.48	1.16	.14	63.9*
	Distance			-.95	.26	13.2*
Rest of India	Urban population	.75	.56	1.76	.23	54.3*
	Distance			-2.12	1.23	2.9ns

Regional difference in demand effect $Z = 2.22^{**}$
Regional difference in distance effect $Z - ncz$

---

* = significant at the .01 level for 104 and 48 degrees of freedom.
** = significant at the .05 level for 104 and 48 degrees of freedom.
ns = not statistically significant.
ncz = not comparable using Z test.
Note: Variables all log transformed.

TABLE 27 -- <u>Continued</u>

Commodity and Region	Independent Variable with Respect to k	Correlation Coefficient r	Coefficient of Determination r^2	Regression Coefficient b	Standard Error of b	Variance Ratio Test F
Electrical Machinery						
Calcutta Region	Urban population	.55	.30	.70	.11	38.2[*]
	Distance			-.25	.20	1.5[ns]
Rest of India	Urban population	.88	.77	1.32	.10	169.3[*]
	Distance			-2.68	.52	26.0[*]

Regional difference in demand effect Z = 4.13[*]
Regional difference in distance effect Z = ncz

Commodity and Region	Independent Variable with Respect to k	Correlation Coefficient r	Coefficient of Determination r^2	Regression Coefficient b	Standard Error of b	Variance Ratio Test F
Other Machinery						
Calcutta Region	Urban population	.60	.36	.43	.08	27.6[*]
	Distance			-.62	.14	17.6[*]
Rest of India	Urban population	.86	.74	1.15	.10	132.0[*]
	Distance			-2.43	.52	21.7[*]

Regional difference in demand effect Z = 6.00[*]
Regional difference in distance effect Z = 3.35[*]

to the rest of India. Based upon either of the above conditions (statistically significant distance effects in one region only or significant statistical differences between the regression coefficients for the two regions), one can argue that the distance effect upon study-area outflows of total commodities and outflows of iron and steel, electrical, and other machinery was significantly different between regions of India. The strong influence of governmental regulation upon the distribution of both coal and steel was reflected in the lack of regional differences in the distance effect for coal and the lack of distance effect for steel shipments outside the Calcutta region to the rest of India.

Given the existence of significant regional differences in distance and demand effects upon variation in iron and steel, electrical, and other machinery outflows, one might expect that for the separate regions the potential model would predict outflows of these commodities more adequately than for the whole of India. However, comparing Table 24 with Table 27 for each of these commodities, the potential model performed less well within the region and considerably better for flows to the rest of India. This poorer performance of the model within the Calcutta region reflects the high value of steel and machinery, the large concentration of demand for these goods found within the region, considerable movement of these goods by truck within the region, and the long hauls to relatively equal concentrations of demand outside the Calcutta region noted in earlier chapters. For outflows of total commodities and coal, the potential model performed better for flows to the Calcutta region rather than areas outside it, apparently reflecting the minimal effect of distance upon coal outflows and the importance of government regulation oriented to supplying regional demand.

The actual difference between regions in the regression coefficients of distance and demand are striking, Table 27. Within the Calcutta region, goods tended to move more than in proportion to distance and demand. However, when shipped outside the region, flows tended to diminish more than proportionate to the square of distance and more than proportionate to demand.

Inflows

Just as the potential model might be expected to adequately account for variation in the outflow of goods from one area to other areas of an economic system, the variables of this model might also be expected to adequately account for the variation in inflows of goods from other areas of the system to a specific place such as the study area. Within the framework of the potential model, the volume of supplies received from a set of sources should be proportionate to the volume of supply available at each source and inversely proportionate to the cost of overcoming the intervening distance from the source.

One would expect the amount of variation in inflows accounted for by the supply variable to decrease with increases in the degree of specialization of local input needs and in the degree to which ownership, licensing, and other management procedures link local firms with specific suppliers elsewhere. This argument relating specialization and linkages inversely to flow appears more relevant to supply than to demand situations. Local purchasers may be expected to seek out the minimum number of suppliers which can satisfy local demands at the lowest price. Even though supplies may exist at numerous other points, this practice links the local firm with one or at most a few suppliers. It is likely that the area with the greatest supply will provide the best source of supply.

However, it is less likely that supplies will come from a range of sources. With respect to demand, a supplier would be expected to seek out and supply the largest concentration of demand. However, where capacity exists to produce beyond the demands of any one place, as in the case of study-area coal and steel, other demands for the available supplies would be sought. Thus one would expect that the concentrations of demand with which a firm acting as supplier would establish links would be much more variable than the concentrations of supply with which it would establish links acting as a consumer. As in the case of outflows, one would expect that the ability of distance to account for variation in inflows would be inversely related to the value of the commodity, the number of suppliers available, and the degree to which transport subsidies are operating. Before proceeding to an evaluation of the ability of the potential model to explain variation in study-area inflows, the separate effects of the model's demand and distance variables upon these inflows will be examined.

Demand Effects

Regression of the log of tonnage upon the log of urban population in supplying areas accounted for approximately 33 per cent of the variation in total commodity inflows to the study area, significant at the .01 level, Table 28. Thus urban population (as the

TABLE 28

RELATION OF TOTAL INFLOWS TO URBAN
POPULATION AND DISTANCE

Independent Variable with Respect to k	Correlation Coefficient r	Coefficient of Determination r^2	Regression Coefficient b	Standard Error of b	Variance Ratio Test F
Urban Population	.58	.34	1.23	.13	78.9*
Distance	.41	.17	-1.86	.33	30.8*
Potential model: Urban population	.70	.49	1.22	.12	101.4*
Distance			-1.83	.26	48.8*
(Step 2 of stepwise regression)					

* = significant at the .01 level for 156 and 155 degrees of freedom.

Note: Variables all log transformed.

measure of an area's ability to produce the mix of goods received by the study area) accounted for only one-third of the variation in total inflows. Because this mix of inflows contains large quantities of heavy raw materials, steel, and other manufactured goods, other measures of supply were tested. However, supplies of steel, metallic and non-metallic minerals, machinery manufacturing, and total manufacturing employment produced no higher level of explanation of variation in total study-area inflows than simply urban population.

For analyzing inflows of individual commodities, better measures of supply than urban population were available. Tables 29 and 30 indicate correlations and the regression of the logs of major study-area inflows on the logs of different supply variables.

TABLE 29

SIMPLE CORRELATION OF INFLOWS, SUPPLY
AND DISTANCE VARIABLES[a]

Commodity Inflows	with	Distance	Supply Variables	with	Distance
Total Commodities		-.4059	Urban Population		-.0120
Iron and Steel		-.3894	Steel Production		-.0426
Electrical Machinery		-.2489	Electrical Machinery Employment		-.0489
Other Machinery		-.2389	Other Machinery Employment		-.0745
Chemicals		-.2751	Chemical Employment		-.0630
Cement		-.3147	Cement Employment		-.0604
Limestone		-.2794	Limestone Production		-.0449
Metallic Ores		-.2440	Metallic Ore Production		-.1076
Non-Metallic Minerals		-.3812	Non-Metallic Mineral Production		-.1825
Gram		.1107	Gram Production		.2974

Commodity Inflows with Supply Variables

Total Commodities with Urban Population	.5796
Iron and Steel with Steel Production	.5891
Electrical Machinery with Electrical Machinery Employment	.6864
Other Machinery with Other Machinery Employment	.6464
Chemicals with Chemical Employment	.5368
Cement with Cement Employment	.3851
Limestone with Limestone Production	.5339
Metallic Ores with Metallic Ore Production	.6037
Non-Metallic Minerals with Non-Metallic Mineral Production	.5120
Gram with Gram Production	.4285

a = For Tables 27 through 33.

Note: Variables all log transformed.

TABLE 30

RELATION OF SELECTED INFLOWS TO SELECTED
SUPPLY VARIABLES

Commodity	Demand Variable with Respect to k	Correlation Coefficient r	Coefficient of Determination r^2	Regression Coefficient b	Standard Error of b	Variance Ratio Test F
Iron and Steel	Steel production	.59	.35	1.03	.11	82.9*
Electrical Machinery	Electrical machinery employment	.68	.46	.46	.03	139.0*
Other Machinery	Other machinery employment	.65	.42	.45	.04	112.0*
Chemicals	Chemical employment	.54	.29	.55	.06	63.1*
Cement	Cement employment	.63	.40	.84	.10	70.5*
Limestone	Limestone production	.53	.28	1.19	.15	62.2*
Metallic Ores	Metallic ore production	.60	.36	.78	.08	89.5*
Non-Metallic Minerals	Non-metallic mineral production	.51	.26	1.39	.18	55.4*
Gram	Gram production	.42	.18	.63	.10	35.0*

* = Significant at the .01 level for 156 degrees of freedom.

Note: Variables all log transformed.

Variation in supply alone accounted for 14 to 46 per cent of the variation in these inflows. As expected, lower correlations of flows with supplies were observed where more numerous sources of supply existed. The higher correlation of electrical machinery with supply reflected the pattern noted earlier of large receipts from India's two largest concentrations of supply, the Calcutta and Bombay areas, Figure 62. Reflecting the pattern

of Figure 61, inflows of other machinery, a rather diverse category, were closely correlated with the numerous machinery-producing areas throughout India. The limited correlation between supplies of steel and inflows to the study area may be explained by the
fact that, although concentrations of imported steel were found in the Bombay and Madras
regions, the study area received nearly all its imported steel from the port of Calcutta
rather than from these other areas. The low correlation between inflows of limestone,
metallic and non-metallic minerals and concentrations of these raw materials appeared
to reflect specific linkages to large-scale plants in the study area and with specific mines
rather than with the full set of mines available throughout India. The specialized chemical needs of the study area appeared to be satisfied by a limited number of India's available chemical plants. Again, a similar argument may hold with respect to gram inflows
where it appeared that study-area traders had established links with a limited number of
markets in Ganges Valley producing areas.

     Compared to the effect of demand on variation in the volume of study area out-
flows the availability of supplies had considerably less influence on variation in inflows,
Tables 21 and 30. Although inflows did generally vary in a regular fashion with availability of supplies, it is clear that other effects including links with specific suppliers
were also very important in accounting for variation in the volume of these inflows.

Distance Effects

     As noted in earlier chapters, the study area is immediately surrounded by India's
largest concentration of industrial raw materials and industrial production. Considerable distance effects upon study-area inflows would therefore not be expected. The regression of log of total inflows upon the log of distance from suppliers throughout India
accounted for 15 per cent of the variation in total study-area inflows, significant at the
.01 level, Table 28. Although this effect is not large, distance did account for considerably more of the variation in inflows than in outflows, Table 23. This higher correlation
of distance with variation in inflows appeared to be the result of a mix of inflows consisting of a greater proportion of low value commodities with movement more subject to
varying transport costs and to a smaller proportion of commodities with movements subject to governmental controls. However, the amount of total variation explained by distance is still quite small.

     Considerable differences were observed in the effect of distance upon individual
commodities, inflows to the study area, Table 31. Based on high value, a limited distance effect was observed for inflows of electrical machinery, other machinery, and
chemicals. In addition, because of the small number of available sources and the location of these sources in areas either immediately surrounding or at great distance from

TABLE 31

RELATION OF SELECTED INFLOWS TO DISTANCE

Commodity	Correlation Coefficient r	Coefficient of Determination r^2	Regression Coefficient b	Standard Error of b	Variance Ratio Test F
Iron and Steel	.38	.14	-1.49	.28	27.8[*]
Electrical Machinery	.25	.06	-.51	.16	10.2[*]
Other Machinery	.24	.05	-.69	.22	9.4[*]
Chemicals	.28	.08	-.90	.25	12.7[*]
Cement	.31	.09	-.79	.19	17.1[*]
Limestone	.28	.08	-1.08	.29	13.2[*]
Metallic Ore	.24	.05	-.96	.30	9.8[*]
Non-Metallic Minerals	.38	.14	-1.08	.26	26.5[*]
Gram	.11	.01	-.48	.22	4.8[**]

* = significant at the .01 level for 156 degrees of freedom.
** = significant at the .05 level for 156 degrees of freedom.
Note: Variables all log transformed.

the study area, the distance effect on chemicals and electrical machinery receipts appeared to have been reduced even further. The larger distance effect upon steel inflows appeared to be the result of the study area's location with respect to India's few steel mills and the necessity of drawing steel from each of them to supply the total range of study-area needs. The small effect of distance upon inflows of limestone and other mineral ores appeared to follow from the argument of links with specific mines, while the larger distance effect upon cement inflows appeared to be the result of a larger number of sources for similar grades of cement and controls over cement allocation. The larger distance effect for inflows of non-metallic minerals appeared to reflect receipts from numerous sources of the diverse mixture of commodities subsumed under this category. Distance was weakly correlated with inflows of gram, apparently because of specific linkages with a few markets and the long distance to India's one major producing area. Because of the large receipts from nearby Calcutta, distance was again not correlated with wheat inflows, Figure 72. Distance explained more of the variation in total inflows than for individual commodity inflows, clearly reflecting the larger number of links with more diverse sources which were associated with this total mix of inflows. Comparing Table 31 and Table 23, the better performance of distance in accounting for variation in inflows than for outflows appears to be a reflection of the greater influence of distance on inflows of steel, cement, metallic and non-metallic minerals.

Distance Decay Rates

Because distance was significantly correlated with a number of study-area inflows, the coefficients of distance in the regression model for these inflows are of considerable interest. For total commodity inflows and for individual inflows of lime-stone, non-metallic minerals, and steel, the decrease in tonnage with increasing distance was more than proportionate to distance but significantly less than the square of distance, Table 31. This result does not seem out of line for total inflows and inflows of the two heavy raw materials. However, in the face of controlled pricing for steel, the coefficient does seem somewhat surprising and may reflect specific linkages or local demands for a specific range of products. Receipts of machinery, cement, chemicals, and metallic ores were all more than proportionate to distance, reflecting the specialized linkages or high value noted earlier.

The Potential Model

Analysis of individual supply and distance effects indicates that both are corre-lated with variation in study-area inflows. The correlation of the log of total tonnage received from various origins with the log of urban population and log of distance was .7036, significant at the .01 level, Table 28. The potential model thus accounts for just 50 per cent of variation in total study-area inflows, representing an increase in (r) of .12 over the model without distance. With respect to inflows of individual commod-ities, Table 32 indicates the potential model was able to account for between 14 and 52 per cent of variation in these inflows. Although the percentage of variation explained is not large, study-area inflows clearly do vary in a regular fashion with distance and supply conditions throughout India. For individual commodities, comparison of Table 32 with Table 24 indicates that except for machinery the potential model performed less well with respect to inflows than it did for outflows. This result reflects the smaller effect of supply variables upon inflows than was observed for demand variables upon outflows. Table 33 indicates the actual parameters of the potential model for these major study-area inflows.

TABLE 32

RELATION OF SELECTED INFLOWS TO COMBINED
SUPPLY AND DISTANCE EFFECTS
(second step of stepwise regression)

Commodity	Independent Variable with respect to k	Correlation Coefficient r	Coefficient of Determination r^2	Regression Coefficient b	Standard Error of b	Variance Ratio Test F
Iron and Steel	Steel production	.63	.40	.88	.11	63.3*
	Distance			-1.47	.24	37.8*
Electrical Machinery	Electrical machinery employment	.72	.52	.45	.03	146.4*
	Distance			-.44	.11	14.8*
Other Machinery	Other machinery employment	.69	.48	.45	.04	124.0*
	Distance			-.70	.17	17.2*
Chemicals	Chemical employment	.58	.34	.53	.06	64.2*
	Distance			-.79	.21	13.8*
Cement	Cement employment	.51	.26	.33	.05	34.4*
	Distance			-.85	.17	24.1*
Limestone	Limestone production	.61	.37	1.22	.14	74.5*
	Distance			-1.17	.24	22.9*
Metallic Ores	Metallic ore production	.64	.41	.78	.08	95.2*
	Distance			-.90	.24	14.1*
Non-Metallic Minerals	Non-metallic mineral production	.58	.34	1.24	.17	48.1*
	Distance			-1.08	.23	20.3*
Gram	Gram production	.46	.21	.71	.11	41.0*
	Distance			-.56	.24	5.1**

* = significant at the .01 level for 155 degrees of freedom.
** = significant at the .05 level for 155 degrees of freedom.
Note: Variables all log transformed.

TABLE 33

THE POTENTIAL MODEL FOR SELECTED INFLOWS

Commodity Flow k to Study Area F_{kl}	Supply at k S_k	Distance k to Study Area d_{kl}
Total Commodities	F_{kl} = a (Urban Pop.)$^{1.22}$ (distance)$^{-1.83}$	
Iron and Steel	F_{kl} = a (Steel Prod.)$^{.88}$ (distance)$^{-1.47}$	
Electrical Machinery	F_{kl} = a (Elect. Mach. Empl.)$^{.45}$ (distance)$^{-.44}$	
Other Machinery	F_{kl} = a (Other Mach. Empl.)$^{.45}$ (distance)$^{-.70}$	
Chemicals	F_{kl} = a (Chemical Empl.)$^{.53}$ (distance)$^{-.79}$	
Cement	F_{kl} = a (Cement Empl.)$^{.33}$ (distance)$^{-.85}$	
Limestone	F_{kl} = a (Limestone Prod.)$^{1.22}$ (distance)$^{-1.17}$	
Metallic Ores	F_{kl} = a (Met. Ore Prod.)$^{.78}$ (distance)$^{-.90}$	
Non-Metallic Minerals	F_{kl} = a (Non-Met. Min. Prod.)$^{1.24}$ (distance)$^{-1.08}$	
Gram	F_{kl} = a (Gram Prod.)$^{.71}$ (distance)$^{-.56}$	

Regional Differences in Inflow Patterns

As with outflows, regional differences might be expected in the patterns of study-area inflows. Possible regional differences in the volume of inflows were tested by applying one-way analysis of variance to the log of various inflows from the Calcutta economic region and from the rest of India. Table 34 indicated significant regional differences in the volume of inflows for total commodities and limestone only. The remaining inflows to the study area appeared to come in similar volume from regional and extra-regional sources.

To test for regional differences in the effects of supply and distance upon inflows to the study area, the logs of various inflows were regressed upon the logs of supply and distance variables (the potential model) for the Calcutta region and the rest of India separately. Using the Z test, the regression coefficients of supply and distance from these separate regressions were compared for significant differences.

TABLE 34

VARIATION IN THE VOLUME OF SELECTED INFLOWS FROM THE
CALCUTTA ECONOMIC REGION AND THE REST OF INDIA
(one-way analysis of variance, 2 regions)

Commodity	Sum of Squares	Degrees of Freedom	Mean Square	T Test
Total Commodities				
Between Regions	12.59	1	12.59	
Within Regions	287.98	156	1.84	2.61^{*}
Total	300.57	157		
Iron and Steel				
Between Regions	.01	1	.01	
Within Regions	211.51	156	1.35	$.09^{ns}$
Total	211.52	157		
Electrical Machinery				
Between Regions	.01	1	.01	
Within Regions	62.22	156	.39	$.10^{ns}$
Total	62.23	157		
Other Machinery				
Between Regions	1.01	1	1.01	
Within Regions	121.39	156	.77	1.13^{ns}
Total	122.40	157		
Chemicals				
Between Regions	.01	1	.01	
Within Regions	154.96	156	.99	$.07^{ns}$
Total	154.97	157		
Cement				
Between Regions	1.86	1	1.86	
Within Regions	89.62	156	.57	1.80^{ns}
Total	91.48	157		
Limestone				
Between Regions	.95	1	.95	
Within Regions	213.04	156	1.36	$.83^{ns}$
Total	213.99	157		
Metallic Ores				
Between Regions	.55	1	.55	
Within Regions	221.75	156	1.42	$.62^{ns}$
Total	222.30	157		
Non-Metallic Minerals				
Between Regions	.13	1	.13	
Within Regions	188.22	156	1.20	$.32^{ns}$
Total	188.35	157		
Gram				
Between Regions	.40	1	.40	
Within Regions	158.67	156	1.01	$.62^{ns}$
Total	159.07	157		

* = significant at the .01 level.
ns = not statistically significant
Note: Variables all log transformed.

Earlier chapters noted the tremendous concentrations of steel, machinery, cement, and gram production within the Calcutta region. Study-area receipts of these goods from the surrounding Calcutta region clearly differentiated this region from other regions of India, Table 35. With respect to study-area receipts of electrical machinery

TABLE 35

RELATION OF SELECTED INFLOWS TO COMBINED SUPPLY AND DISTANCE
EFFECTS FOR THE CALCUTTA ECONOMIC REGION
AND THE REST OF INDIA
(second step of stepwise regression)

Commodity and Region	Independent Variable with respect to k	Correlation Coefficient r	Coefficient of Determination r^2	Regression Coefficient b	Standard Error of b	Variance Ratio Test F
Total Commodities						
Calcutta Region	Urban population	.68	.46	1.06	.16	43.7*
	Distance			-1.53	.29	27.9
Rest of India	Urban population	.77	.59	1.81	.21	71.2*
	Distance			-4.81	1.11	18.5
	Regional difference in supply effect			Z = 2.88*		
	Regional difference in distance effect			Z = 2.87*		
Iron and Steel						
Calcutta Region	Steel production	.67	.45	.81	.14	31.2*
	Distance			-1.61	.27	34.2
Rest of India	Steel production	.79	.62	1.27	.14	79.6*
	Distance			-2.17	.71	9.1
	Regional difference in supply effect			Z = 2.42**		
	Regional difference in distance effect			Z = .74 ns		

* = significant at the .01 level for 104 and 48 degrees of freedom.
** = significant at the .05 level for 104 and 48 degrees of freedom.
ns = not statistically significant.
ncz = not comparable using Z test.
Note: Variables all log transformed.

TABLE 35 -- Continued

Commodity and Region	Independent Variable with respect to k	Correlation Coefficient r	Coefficient of Determination r^2	Regression Coefficient b	Standard Error of b	Variance Ratio Test F
Electrical Machinery						
Calcutta Region	Electrical machinery employment	.70	.49	.43	.05	62.1[*]
	Distance			-.49	.13	12.3[*]
Rest of India	Electrical machinery employment	.75	.56	.48	.06	53.3[*]
	Distance			-.61	.50	1.4[ns]
	Regional difference in supply effect			$Z = .07^{ns}$		
	Regional difference in distance effect			$Z = ncz$		
Other Machinery						
Calcutta Region	Other machinery employment	.67	.45	.37	.05	50.9[*]
	Distance			-.90	.19	21.7[*]
Rest of India	Other machinery employment	.78	.61	.61	.07	70.6[*]
	Distance			-2.13	.69	9.3[*]
	Regional difference in supply effect			$Z = 3.00^{*}$		
	Regional difference in distance effect			$Z = 1.73^{ns}$		
Chemicals						
Calcutta Region	Chemical employment	.58	.34	.41	.09	19.9[*]
	Distance			-.99	.24	16.0
Rest of India	Chemical employment	.63	.40	.64	.12	28.2[*]
	Distance			-.74	.92	.6[ns]
	Regional difference in supply effect			$Z = 1.53^{ns}$		
	Regional difference in distance effect			$Z = ncz$		
Cement						
Calcutta Region	Cement employment	.65	.42	.79	.10	61.5[*]
	Distance			-.49	.21	5.3[**]
Rest of India	Cement employment	.30	.09	.07	.03	4.6[**]
	Distance			-.20	.28	.5[ns]
	Regional difference in supply effect			$Z = 7.20^{*}$		
	Regional difference in distance effect			$Z = ncz$		

TABLE 35 -- Continued

Commodity and Region	Independent Variable with respect to k	Correlation Coefficient r	Coefficient of Determination r^2	Regression Coefficient b	Standard Error of b	Variance Ratio Test F
Limestone						
Calcutta Region	Limestone production	.63	.40	1.29	.21	37.1*
	Distance			-1.14	.25	19.8*
Rest of India	Limestone production	.61	.37	1.22	.22	28.5**
	Distance			-2.67	1.07	6.1
	Regional difference in supply effect			$Z = .23^{ns}$		
	Regional difference in distance effect			$Z = 1.40^{ns}$		
Metallic Ores						
Calcutta Region	Metallic ore production	.66	.44	.92	.12	53.0*
	Distance			-.91	.28	10.0*
Rest of India	Metallic ore production	.64	.41	.62	.11	31.5*
	Distance			-.07	.85	.0^{ns}
	Regional difference in supply effect			$Z = 1.87^{ns}$		
	Regional difference in distance effect			$Z = ncz$		
Non-Metallic Minerals						
Calcutta Region	Non-metallic mineral production	.64	.41	1.48	.27	29.3*
	Distance			-1.19	.29	16.6*
Rest of India	Non-metallic mineral production	.46	.21	.87	.24	12.3*
	Distance			.21	.83	.1^{ns}
	Regional difference in supply effect			$Z = 1.69^{ns}$		
	Regional difference in distance effect			$Z = ncz$		
Gram						
Calcutta Region	Gram production	.49	.24	.74	.12	33.4*
	Distance			-.48	.27	3.1^{ns}
Rest of India	Gram production	.42	.18	.70	.22	9.8*
	Distance			.20	.88	.0^{ns}
	Regional difference in supply effect			$Z = .16^{ns}$		
	Regional difference in distance effect			$Z = ncz$		

and chemicals, the absence of regional differentiation in the supply effect appears to reflect close links with each of the few producing centers throughout India noted earlier. For inflows of heavy minerals, the lack of regional differences in the supply effect reflected large volume receipts of these goods from supplies located in nearby Madhya Pradesh just outside the Calcutta region.

Regional differences in the distance effect upon study-area inflows were inferred either from the lack of a significant distance effect in one region or from statistically significant differences between the regression coefficients of distance for both regions. Significant regional differences were observed in the inflows of all commodities except steel, other machinery, limestone, and gram. With respect to limestone, large inflows from the limited number of sources inside the Calcutta region and from Madhya Pradesh outside the region resulted in the lack of a significant regional distance effect. Regarding inflows of steel and other machinery, the distance effects were significant within each region but not significant between the regions. The lack of a distance effect upon gram in either region reflects the influence of the one large concentration of production and the linkage noted earlier. Electrical machinery and chemicals showed no significant distance effect outside the Calcutta region, reflecting the high value of these commodities. The lack of a distance effect for inflows of cement, metallic, and non-metallic minerals from outside the Calcutta region appears to reflect demands for specific supplies of these goods located outside the Calcutta region.

Given these observed regional differences in the effects of distance and supply upon variation in study-area inflows, it was hypothesized that the potential model would predict these inflows more adequately for the separate regions than for the whole of India. However, comparing Tables 32 and 35, it was found that the potential model predicted inflows of total commodities and individual inflows of electrical machinery, other machinery, chemicals, and gram from the Calcutta region less well or at the same level as had been predicted for the whole of India. This result appears to reflect the limited supply and distance effects upon these goods noted earlier. For receipts from outside the region, the level of prediction was somewhat higher than for the whole of India, reflecting large concentrations of supplies outside the region. For cement, limestone, metallic ores, and non-metallic minerals, the model performed the same or less well for flows from outside the region and better for flows from within the region. For steel receipts, the potential model performed better for both regions than for the nation as a whole, reflecting the importance of the effects of concentrated steel supplies within the study area and of distance outside the region.

With respect to inflows of total commodities, steel, and limestone, the study area appeared to have relatively weak links with each of its suppliers. As indicated in Table 35, the regional regression coefficients of both supply and distance for receipts of each of these goods were less than proportionate to supplies and distance. Receipts of electrical, other machinery, chemicals, cement, and metallic ores were more than proportionate to supply and in most cases to distance, indicating much closer study-area linkages with suppliers of these goods.

Explaining Additional Variation in Study-Area Exchange

Theoretically, the supply or demand and distance variables of the potential model should account for all of the variability in study-area exchanges. However, this model was able to explain little more than half of the observed variation in total study-area trade and approximately one-third to two-thirds of the variation in its individual commodity flows. It is clear that sources of variation exist other than those summarized by the simple supply, demand, and distance measures available to this study. Attempts to achieve a higher level of explained variation would appear to call either for improving the measures, for changing the model, or for a combination of both approaches.

Modifications in Measurement of Variables

Possible improvements in the supply, demand, and distance measures were considered first. As noted earlier, important additional sources of variation include governmental regulation of commodity pricing and distribution, transportation subsidies, competition from road movement and the licensing practices, branch plant ownership and other specific inter-firm linkages of study-area activities. Unfortunately, it was not within this study's scope to assess the exact impact of each of these conditions on study-area exchanges. No reasonable way could be found to incorporate such effects directly into available supply and demand measures derived from census and other official reports. However, it appeared that other sources of variation could be taken into account through modification of the supply, demand, and distance measures.

Stouffer, Ray, and Ullman[1] suggest that the effects of intervening and otherwise competing supplies and demands may be possible sources of variation not effectively summarized by the distance measure used in this study. Stouffer argues that measures of relative location based upon the potential model with its distance variable

---

[1] Stouffer, op. cit.; Ray, op. cit.; and Ullman, op. cit.

recognize neither the uneven distributions of demand nor the directionality of movement found within an economic system. With respect to migration flows between points i and j, Stouffer demonstrates that the demand exerted at point j upon possible flows from point i is directly related to the total supply of migrants at i and demand for migrants at j. Further, these flows will be inversely related to the number of possible destinations or opportunities for migrants from i, intervening between it and j, and inversely related to the combined effects of all migrants located within a circle of radius i to j, competing for demand at j. [1]

Without incorporating a distance effect directly, Stouffer's model attempts to take into account the location of various concentrations of competition relative to both points i and j. As in the Stouffer study, intervening opportunities (supplies and demands intervening between the study area and various origins or destinations k) were measured by counting the total supply or demand occurring within a circle with a diameter equal to the distance: study area to k. However, as Stouffer's results suggest[2] and as one would expect given the distribution over the entire nation of the origins and destinations for study-area supplies and demands, the measures of various intervening opportunities were closely correlated with the simple linear distance measure already employed in the potential model, Table 36.

Given the absence of a distance effect on flows of several study-area commodities, government controls over the distribution of others, and the considerable distances separating the demand centers of its major economic regions, the Indian economy is obviously far from a perfect market. Thus a measure such as a supply potential taking into account competition throughout the entire Indian economy appeared a more suitable gauge of the study area's competitive position at k than did a measure limiting competitive possibilities to a circle with a radius: study area to k.

The combined effects of both measures, intervening opportunity between the study area and k, and competition given by the supply or demand potential at k were substituted for distance in the potential model. Comparison of Tables 37 and 38 with Tables 20, 24, 28, and 32 indicates as expected that the measures of intervening opportunity performed approximately as well as distance with respect to both outflows and inflows. This measure of intervening opportunity might be used interchangeably with distance; however, the use of distance is much simpler.

---

[1] Stouffer's model is: log flows i to j = a + b log (total migrants from i times total migrants to j) - c log (all migrants within a circle between i and j of diamter i to j) - d log (all migrants within a circle of radius ij centered at j).

[2] Stouffer, op. cit., p. 12.

TABLE 36

SIMPLE CORRELATION OF DISTANCE WITH INTERVENING
OPPORTUNITY MEASURES

Measures of Supply or Demand Intervening Between the Study Area and Point k	Correlation with Distance
Intervening Urban Population	.7925
Intervening Manufacturing Employment	.6097
Intervening Electrical Machinery Employment	.5847
Intervening Chemical Production Employment	.6976
Intervening Steel Production	.7559
Intervening Metallic Ore Production	.2679
Intervening Non-Metallic Mineral Production	.6601
Intervening Cement Employment	.6703
Intervening Limestone Production	.6475
Intervening Gram Production	.7952

Note: Variables all log transformed.

In most cases, the measure of competition was correlated at the .3 to .4 level with the measures of demand or supply and at a .05 to .2 level with the measures of intervening opportunity, Table 39. The competition measure, Tables 37 and 38, made no significant contribution to the potential model except in the case of outflows of electrical machinery and inflows of other machinery and limestone where it was closely correlated with the demand or supply measure. Thus relative accessibility at k to nationwide demand and supply distributions did not appear to be a useful measure of the study area's competitive position at point k; and, although not tested, Stouffer's measure based on competition within a circle of radius study area to k, centered on k, might prove a better measure even in the context of the Indian economy. These attempts at improving the measure of distance did not lead to any significant improvement in the potential model's explanatory power with respect to study-area exchanges.

Stouffer's methodology also suggests that account should be taken of the total supply of migrants available at i and the total demand for migrants at j. With respect to this study, this measure would require information on the total number and origin or destination of the exchanges of points k. Unfortunately, such data were not available, and no further modifications in the measurement of variables appeared feasible.

TABLE 37

RELATION OF SELECTED OUTFLOWS TO COMBINED DEMAND AND
INTERVENING OPPORTUNITY EFFECTS
(third step of stepwise regression)

Commodity	Independent Variable with respect to k	Correlation Coefficient by step r	Coefficient of Determi- by step r^2	Regression Coefficient 3rd step b	Standard Error of b	Variance Ratio Test F
Total Commodities	Urban pop.	.68	.46	1.56	.13	134.2*
	IV+ urban pop.	.70	.49	-.38	.12	5.1**
	Urban pop. potential	.70	.49	-1.73	2.39	.5ns
Coal	Urban pop.	.58	.34	1.49	.16	78.4*
	IV+ urban pop.	.60	.36	-.07	.17	.1ns
	Mfg. empl. potential	.60	.36	-13.97	15.96	.7ns
Iron and Steel	Urban pop.	.67	.45	1.38	.12	124.9*
	IV+ mfg. empl.	.70	.49	-.32	.12	6.9*
	Mfg. empl. potential	.70	.49	9.29	11.50	.6ns
Electrical Machinery	Urban pop.	.66	.44	.80	.08	95.7*
	IV+ mfg. empl.	.66	.44	-.09	.09	.9ns
	Mfg. empl. potential	.68	.46	16.88	7.38	5.2**
Other Machinery	Urban pop.	.64	.41	.69	.06	102.2*
	IV+ urban pop.	.67	.45	-.23	.07	8.6*
	Mfg. empl. potential	.67	.45	4.65	6.16	.5ns

* = significant at .01 level for 155 degrees of freedom.
** = significant at .05 level for 155 degrees of freedom.
ns = not statistically significant.
+ = IV stands for Intervening.
Note: Variables all log transformed.

Modification of the Potential Model

Attempts to modify the measurement of variables resulted in no significant improvement in the potential model's ability to explain variation in study-area exchanges. It thus appeared that changes in the model itself might be the way to achieve higher levels of explanation. A modification which considered the effects to competition in addition to, rather than as a part of, the potential model seemed the most reasonable change.

TABLE 38

RELATION OF SELECTED INFLOWS TO COMBINED SUPPLY AND
INTERVENING OPPORTUNITY EFFECTS
(third step of stepwise regression)

Commodity	Independent Variable with respect to k	Correlation Coefficient by step r	Coefficient of Determination by step r^2	Regression Coefficient 3rd step b	Standard Error of b	Variance Ratio Test F
Total Commodities	Urban pop.	.57	.33	1.30	.12	107.8^{*}
	IV^{+} urban pop.	.72	.51	-.91	.15	35.6^{*}
	Mfg. empl. potential	.72	.51	-7.23	11.30	$.4^{ns}$
Iron and Steel	Steel prod.	.58	.34	.99	.11	72.2^{*}
	IV^{+} steel prod.	.66	.44	-.35	.09	12.3^{*}
	Mfg. empl. potential	.66	.44	8.98	11.58	$.6^{ns}$
Electrical Machinery	Elec. machinery employment	.68	.46	.44	.04	101.4^{*}
	IV^{+} elec. mach. employment	.70	.49	-.05	.03	3.5^{ns}
	Mfg. empl. potential	.70	.49	9.64	5.60	2.9^{ns}
Other Machinery	Mfg. empl.	.68	.46	.79	.07	112.0^{*}
	IV^{+} urban pop.	.71	.50	-.27	.09	7.9^{*}
	Mfg. empl. potential	.73	.53	3.45	1.22	8.8
Chemicals	Chem. empl.	.53	.28	.52	.07	48.4^{*}
	IV^{+} chem. empl.	.56	.31	-.06	.07	$.9^{ns}$
	Chem. empl. potential	.56	.31	3.51	3.62	$.9^{ns}$
Cement	Cement empl.	.38	.14	.33	.05	32.6^{*}
	IV^{+} cem. empl.	.50	.25	-.34	.09	13.7^{*}
	Mfg. empl. potential	.50	.25	5.82	7.49	$.6^{ns}$

$*$ = significant at the .01 level for 155 degrees of freedom.
ns = not statistically significant
+ = IV stands for Intervening.
Note: Variables all log transformed.

176

TABLE 38 -- Continued

Commodity	Independent Variable with respect to k	Correlation Coefficient by step r	Coefficient of Determi- by step r²	Regression Coefficient 3rd step b	Standard Error of b	Variance Ratio Test F
Limestone	Lime. prod.	.53	.28	.99	.15	41.3^{*}
	IV^{+} lime. prod.	.59	.35	-.39	.09	17.0^{*}
	Lime. prod. potential	.62	.38	3.02	1.95	7.4^{*}
Metallic Ore	Met. ore prod.	.60	.36	.75	.08	82.1^{*}
	IV^{+} met. ore production	.60	.36	.05	.07	$.6^{ns}$
	Met. working employment potential	.60	.36	32.20	108.22	$.1^{ns}$
Non-Metallic Minerals	Non-met. min. production	.51	.26	1.34	.18	51.4^{*}
	IV^{+} non-met. min. prod.	.55	.30	-.37	.12	8.6^{*}
	Mfg. empl. potential	.55	.30	116.08	115.39	1.0^{ns}
Gram	Gram prod.	.42	.18	.82	.14	30.6^{*}
	IV^{+}gram prod.	.43	.19	-.14	.10	1.7^{ns}
	Gram prod. potential	.43	.19	-27.10	39.83	$.4^{ns}$

Another approach to evaluating the effects of competition and intervening opportunity on commodity flows is suggested by Linneman's study of international trade.[1] In computing the value of a demand potential for any point i within a system $\sum_{j} \frac{P_i}{d_{ij}}$, the contribution of demand at a given point k to the total demand potential at i,

[1] Hans Linnemann, An Econometric Study of International Trade Flows (Amsterdam: North-Holland Publishing Co., 1966).

TABLE 39

CORRELATION OF SELECTED STUDY-AREA FLOWS AND DEMAND,
SUPPLY, INTERVENING OPPORTUNITY, AND COMPETITION
VARIABLES WITH RESPECT TO K

	IV[+] Urban pop.	Urban pop. Potential	Total Commodity Outflows
Urban Population	.0458	.3522	.6834
IV Urban Population		-.0219	-.1510
Urban Population Potential			.2084

	IV Urban pop.	Mfg. Empl. Potential	Coal Outflows
Urban Population	.0458	.3271	.5863
IV Urban Population		-.0972	-.1145
Mfg. Empl. Potential			.2179

	IV Mfg. Empl.	Mfg. Empl. Potential	Steel Outflows
Urban Population	.0309	.3271	.6746
IV Mfg. Employment		-.0566	-.1663
Mfg. Empl. Potential			.2553

	IV Mfg. Empl.	Mfg. Empl. Potential	Electrical Machinery Outflows
Urban Population	.0309	.3271	.6654
IV Mfg. Employment		-.0566	-.0297
Mfg. Empl. Potential			.3509

	IV Urban pop.	Mfg. Empl. Potential	Other Machinery Outflows
Urban Population	.0458	.3271	.6440
IV Urban Population		-.0972	-.1793
Mfg. Empl. Potential			.2761

+ = IV stands for Intervening.
Note: Variables all log transformed.

178

Table 39 -- <u>Continued</u>

	IV Urban pop.	Mfg. Empl. Potential	Total Commodity Inflows
Urban Population	.0458	.3271	.5796
IV Urban Population		-.0972	-.4109
Mfg. Empl. Potential			.2054

	IV Steel prod.	Mfg. Empl. Potential	Iron and Steel Inflows
Steel Production	.0305	.3783	.5891
IV Steel Production		-.1212	-.2951
Mfg. Empl. Potential			.3218

	IV Elec. mach. Empl.	Mfg. Empl. Potential	Electrical Machinery Inflows
Elec. Machinery Empl.	.1113	.4498	.6864
IV Elec. Machinery Empl.		-.0438	-.0632
Mfg. Empl. Potential			.4107

	IV Urban pop.	Mfg. Empl. Potential	Other Machinery Inflows
Mfg. Employment	.0145	.3582	.6838
IV Urban Population		-.0972	-.1974
Mfg. Empl. Potential			.4178

	IV Chem. Empl.	Chem. Empl. Potential	Chemical Inflows
Chemical Employment	.0328	.3212	.5368
IV Chemical Employment		-.3177	-.1581
Chemical Empl. Potential			.3529

TABLE 39 -- Continued

	IV Cement Empl.	Mfg. Empl. Potential	Cement Inflows
Cement Employment	.0403	-.0047	.3851
IV Cement Employment		-.1985	-.3116
Mfg. Empl. Potential			.1162

	IV Limestone Production	Limestone Production Potential	Limestone Inflows
Limestone Production	-.0142	.3888	.5339
IV Limestone Production		.0239	-.2730
Limestone Prod. Potential			.3486

	IV Metallic Ore Production	Metal Working Empl. Potential	Metallic Ore Inflows
Metallic Ore Production	.2160	.0328	.6037
IV Metallic Ore Production		-.1317	.1379
Metal Working Empl. Potential			.2281

	IV Non- Met. Min Production	Mfg. Empl. Potential	Non-Metallic Mineral Inflows
Non-Metallic Mineral Prod.	-.1246	.1174	.5120
IV Non-Met. Mineral Prod.		-.3850	-.2815
Mfg. Empl. Potential			.1672

	IV Gram Production	Gram Prod. Potential	Gram Inflows
Gram Production	.4972	.6998	.4285
IV Gram Production		.6479	.0761
Gram Production Potential			.2145

$$\frac{\dfrac{P_k}{d_{ik}}}{\displaystyle\sum_j \dfrac{P_j}{d_{ij}}}, \text{ may be viewed as the competitive position of k vis à vis all other points}$$

j for supplies available at i. In this expression, the combined effects of distance and demand at k upon the supply at i are weighted by the total of all demands and distances upon i. Because of the distance effect, if these demands are large and concentrated closer to i than k, they will reduce the effect of demand at k more than if they are small or are located further away from i than k.

Alternatively, one may compute a supply potential at any point j. The contribution of supplies at a given point k to this total supply potential at j is

$$\frac{\dfrac{S_k}{d_{jk}}}{\displaystyle\sum_i \dfrac{S_i}{d_{ji}}}.$$

With respect to demand exerted by k, this expression may be viewed as a measure of the competitive position of supplies at k vis à vis all other supply points i. In this expression, the combined effects of supply at k and distance upon demand at j are weighted by the sum of all supplies and distance upon j. Again because of the distance effect, if these supplies are large and closer to j than k, they will reduce the effect of supply at k more than if they are small or located further away from k than j. These two measures should be more sensitive to the competitive position of any given k at points i and j with respect to supplies and demands elsewhere throughout the system than either the simple demand or supply potential at k.

Outflows

Berry has proposed a commodity exchange model which incorporates these competition measures suggested by Linneman within Stouffer's framework of intervening opportunity and competition.[1] For an entire economic system, it is hypothesized that commodity flows from point i to point k should be directly related to some constant (a), to the supply (S_i) at i available to demand at k, and to the demand (P_k) at k attracting the supply at i. These flows should be inversely related to the distance (d_{ik}) separating i and k. Distance was shown earlier to be closely correlated with, and a reasonable alternative for, measures of intervening opportunity. Further, these flows should be

---

[1] Berry, Essays, pp. 157-58; Linnemann, op. cit., and Stouffer, op. cit.

directly related to the contribution of demand at k to the demand potential (AP_k) at i and to the contribution of i to the supply potential (AS_i) at k, both measures of competition within the system affecting i and k. The model would thus be:

$$F_{ik} = a \cdot S_i^{b_1} \cdot P_k^{b_2} \cdot d_{ik}^{-b_3} \cdot AS_i^{b_4} \cdot AP_k^{b_5} \tag{1}$$

Where n equals all points in the system, operationally the model would become:

$$F_{ik} = a \cdot \frac{S_i^{b_1} \cdot P_k^{b_2}}{d_{ik}^{b_3}} \cdot \left(\frac{\dfrac{S_i}{d_{ik}}}{\displaystyle\sum_n \dfrac{S_n}{d_{kn}}} \right)^{b_4} \cdot \left(\frac{\dfrac{P_k}{d_{ik}}}{\displaystyle\sum_n \dfrac{P_n}{d_{in}}} \right)^{b_5} \tag{2}$$

Except for Linneman's studies of the flow of funds associated with international trade,[1] this model has not been tested either within an international or national economic system.

A further extension of this model can be suggested. Along with the demand effect created by conditions within k itself, one might expect that an additional demand effect would be created by k's ability to redistribute commodities received from elsewhere. Thus a better account of demand at k should result from the inclusion of both a measure of demand generated at k and a measure of k's access to outside markets (redistribution effect) such as a market potential at k. Similarly, besides the supply produced locally at i, one might expect an additional supply effect based on i's ability to concentrate within itself supplies produced elsewhere. A better accounting of supply at i would then include a measure of the supply produced at i and a measure of i's access to other supplies (concentration effect) such as a supply potential.

Both the concentration and redistribution effects should be directly related to variation in outflow. Thus expanding model (1), within an entire economic system flows from i to k should also be directly related to the concentration effect (or supply potential) C at point i and the redistribution effect (or market potential) R at point k.[2] The full model would thus be:

$$F_{ik} = a \cdot S_i^{b_1} \cdot P_k^{b_2} \cdot d_{ik}^{-b_3} \cdot AS_i^{b_4} \cdot AP_k^{b_5} \cdot C_i^{b_6} \cdot R_k^{h_7} \tag{3}$$

---

[1] Linnemann, op. cit.

[2] Ray has also developed a model combining two measures of potential. To explain the location of industrial activity in southern Ontario, Canada, Ray argues that both relative accessibility to markets and to investment capital must be taken into account. He develops a dual potential model which takes account separately of the accessibility of points in Southern Ontario to markets within Canada and to the concentrations of industrial plants located in specific sectors of the United States as Ray defines them. Ray's model is manufacturing at i = a + b log (sum of all markets j in Canada

Operationally, the model would become:

$$F_{ik} = a \cdot \frac{S_i^{b_1} \cdot P_k^{b_2}}{d_{ik}^{b_3}} \cdot \left(\frac{\dfrac{S_i}{d_{ik}}}{\sum_n \dfrac{S_n}{d_{kn}}}\right)^{b_4} \cdot \left(\frac{\dfrac{P_k}{d_{ik}}}{\sum_n \dfrac{P_n}{d_{in}}}\right)^{b_5} \cdot \left(\sum_n \frac{S_n}{d_{in}}\right)^{b_6} \cdot \left(\sum_n \frac{P_n}{d_{kn}}\right)^{b_7} \quad (4)$$

Again this model has yet to be tested using flows of an entire economic system.

In applying this model to the outflows of a single point within the system, all of the terms involving only i will become constants and drop out. For flows from the study area (point 1) to all k, the model become:

$$F_{1k} = a \cdot \frac{P_k^{b_2}}{d_{1k}^{b_3}} \cdot \left(\frac{\dfrac{S_1}{d_{1k}}}{\sum_n \dfrac{S_n}{d_{kn}}}\right)^{b_4} \cdot \left(\sum_n \frac{P_n}{d_{kn}}\right)^{b_7} \quad (5)$$

Thus, outflows from the study area to the rest of India should be directly related to demand at i, the contribution of the study area to supply at k (competitive effect), and to the market potential at k (redistribution effect) and inversely related to the distance study area to k.

Inflows

As with outflows for an entire economic system, one might also hypothesize that inflows to point j from point k would be directly related to some constant (a), to the supply (S_k) at k, and to the demand (P_j) at j attracting supplies from k. Implying the effects of intervening opportunity, these flows should be inversely related to the distance (d_{kj}) k to j. Further, such inflows should be directly related to the contribution of supply at k to the supply potential (AS_k) at j and to the contribution of demand at j to the demand potential (AP_j) at k. Again assuming that the greater the market potential at j, the greater will be the possibilities for j to redistribute goods received from k (redistribution effect). Also, the greater the supply potential at k, the more likely is

divided by distance ij) + c log (sum of all industrial plants in the United States at k times a binary measure of sectoral affinity between U.S. city k and i divided by distance ik), Ray, op. cit., p. 138.

k to be able to supply j (concentration effect). Thus, inflows from j to k should be directly related to the concentration effect (C_k) at k and the redistribution effect (R_j) at j. The full model would thus be:

$$F_{kj} = a \cdot S_k^{b_1} \cdot P_j^{b_2} \cdot d_{kj}^{-b_3} \cdot AS_k^{b_4} \cdot AP_j^{b_5} \cdot C_k^{b_6} \cdot R_j^{b_7} \qquad (6)$$

Operationally, the model would be:

$$F_{kj} = a \cdot \frac{S_k^{b_1} \cdot P_j^{b_2}}{d_{kj}^{b_3}} \cdot \left(\frac{\dfrac{S_k}{d_{jk}}}{\sum_n \dfrac{S_n}{d_{jn}}} \right)^{b_4} \cdot \left(\frac{\dfrac{P_j}{d_{kj}}}{\sum_n \dfrac{P_n}{d_{kn}}} \right)^{b_5} \cdot \left(\sum_n \frac{S_n}{d_{kn}} \right)^{b_6} \cdot \left(\sum_n \frac{P_n}{d_{jn}} \right)^{b_7} \qquad (7)$$

This model has not been tested for an entire economic system where n equals all points in the system.

Applying this model to inflows to a single point j within an economic system, all of the terms involving only j will again become constants and drop out. For inflows to the study area (point 1) from all points k, the model becomes

$$F_{k1} = a \cdot \frac{S_k^{b_1}}{d_{k1}^{b_3}} \cdot \left(\frac{\dfrac{P_1}{d_{k1}}}{\sum_n \dfrac{P_n}{d_{kn}}} \right)^{b_5} \cdot \left(\sum_n \frac{S_n}{d_{kn}} \right)^{b_6} \qquad (8)$$

Thus, inflows to the study area should be directly related to supplies at k, to the contribution of the study area to demand at k (competition effect), and to the supply potential at k (concentration effect). Further, the inflows should be inversely related to the distance study area to k.

In the formulation of equations (5) and (8), the distances 1 to k and k to n occur in more than one variable and the values of S_1 and P_1 are constants. Although inter-correlation exists among the variables, given the data available these formulations seemed the most reasonable modification of the potential model; and tests of these models using study-area inflows and outflows seemed worthwhile. In these tests, the least correlated sets of variables were used wherever possible.

Tests of the Expanded Potential Model

The study area's contribution to supply and demand potentials at k (compe-tition effects) and k's total supply and demand potentials (redistribution and concen-tration effects) were computed using a number of supply and demand measures. The correlation of these measures with each other and with simple supply, demand, and distance measures are presented in Table 40.

Data available to test the expanded model were organized by district within the Calcutta economic region, adjacent Madhya Pradesh and Delhi, and by state elsewhere throughout India. Grouped in this manner, the calculated values of most supply and demand potentials at k assume a maximum in the vicinity of the study area and Calcutta, decrease rapidly in all directions over the first 100 miles outward from this area, and then assume a very gradual decline outward over the remainder of the Calcutta region and rest of India. Thus, the various potential measures used in tests of the expanded model were distributed as though India possessed one large concentration of supply or demand centered on the study area and declining outward over the rest of India.

As noted earlier, the competition measures were formulated as a constant divided by the 1k distance again divided by the total supply or demand potential at k. Given the distribution pattern just noted with minor variation in the values of various potentials at k over much of India, these potentials in effect become near constants and the value of the competition measure reduces to approximately d_{ij}^{-b}. The high negative correlation of distance with various competition measures (SAC coal production potential at k, etc.) reflects this approximation, Table 40.

To test the expanded model, major study-area exchanges were regressed on a number of different sets of demand, supply, distance, redistribution, concentration, and competition variables for outflows[1]

$$\log F_{1k} = \log a + b_2 \log P_k - b_3 \log d_{1k} + b_7 \log R_k + b_4 SACS_k \tag{9}$$

and for inflows

$$\log F_{k1} = \log a + b_1 \log S_k - b_3 \log d_{k1} + b_6 \log C_k + b_5 SACP_k \tag{10}$$

where $SACS_k$ equals the study-area contribution to the supply potential at k, or AS_k, and $SACP_k$ equals the study-area contribution to the demand potential at k, or AP_k.

Tables 41 and 42 indicate that for a number of outflows and inflows, the additional variables of the expanded potential model did account significantly for additional variation over that explained by the potential model. However, the amount explained was small, 1 to 4 per cent, and generally weak statistically (at the .05 level of confidence). Tables 43 and 44 indicate the actual values of parameters in the expanded

---

[1]The competition measures $SACP_k$ and $SACS_k$ were expressed as a percentage and in the models used were not log transformed. Thus as they approach zero, the model reduces to the pure potential model plus the concentration or redistribution effect.

TABLE 40

CORRELATION OF SELECTED STUDY AREA FLOWS AND
SUPPLY, DEMAND, DISTANCE, COMPETITION,
REDISTRIBUTION AND CONCENTRATION
VARIABLES WITH RESPECT TO k

	Urban Pop.	Dis- tance	Mfg. [a] Empl. Potential	SAC[b] Coal Prod. Potential	SAC Steel Prod. Potential	SAC Elec. Mach. Empl. Potential
Distance	-.0120					
Mfg. Empl. Potential	.4395	-.3412				
SAC Coal Production Potential	.0950	-.7137	.2791			
SAC Steel Production Potential	-.1782	-.6702	-.2602	–		
SAC Elec. Machinery Empl. Potential	-.1129	-.8225	.0125	–	–	
Coal Outflows	.5863	-.1958	.3143	.3104	–	–
Steel Outflows	.6746	-.2322	.3293	–	.0053	–
Elec. Mach. Outflows	.5741	-.2485	.0125	–	–	-.0099

	Distance	Urban Pop. Potential	SAC Mfg. Empl. Potential	Total Commodities Outflows	Total Commodities Inflows
Urban Population	-.0120	.4117	.0503	.7020	.5796
Distance		-.1395	-.8310	-.2137	-.4059
Urban Population Potential			-.0379	.2603	.1573
SAC Mfg. Employment Potential				.0883	.2589

	Distance	Mfg. Empl. Potential	SAC Other Mach. Empl. Potential	Other Machinery Outflows
Urban Population	-.0120	.4395	-.0860	.6440
Distance		-.3412	-.8329	.1773
Mfg. Empl. Potential			.0343	.3535
SAC Other Mach. Empl. Potential				.0733

a = Total potential at k--redistribution or concentration measure.

b = SAC stands for study-area contribution to potential at k--competition measure.

Note: All variables except SAC variables log transformed.

186

TABLE 40--Continued

	Distance	Metal Working Potential	SAC Steel Prod. Potential	Iron and Steel Inflows
Steel Production	-.0426	.3338	-.2868	.5891
Distance		-.4841	-.6702	-.3894
Metal Working Potential			-.1422	.4065
SAC Steel Prod. Potential				.0158

	Distance	Elec. Mach. Potential	Mfg. Empl. Potential	Electrical Machinery Inflows
Elec. Mach. Empl.	-.0489	.4349	-.0644	.6864
Distance		-.6985	-.8310	-.2485
Elec. Mach. Empl. Potential			.4252	.5027
SAC Mfg. Empl. Potential				.0611

	Distance	Mfg. Empl. Potential	SAC Urban pop. Potential	Other Machinery Inflows
Other Machinery Empl.	-.0327	.4648	-.0562	.6464
Distance		-.3412	-.8068	-.2389
Mfg. Empl. Potential			.1904	.4737
SAC Urban Population Potential				.1534

	Distance	Chemical Potential	SAC Mfg. Empl. Potential	Chemical Inflows
Chemical Employment	-.0630	.3875	.2705	.5368
Distance		-.6981	-.1895	-.2751
Chemical Potential			.5610	.3583
SAC Mfg. Empl. Potential				.2010

	Distance	Limestone Production Potential	SAC Const. Empl. Potential	Cement Inflows
Cement Employment	.0604	.2696	.0017	.3851
Distance		-.3460	-.8488	-.3147
Limestone Prod. Potential			.2707	.2856
SAC Construction Empl. Potential				.1866

TABLE 40--Continued

	Distance	Limestone Production Potential	SAC Limestone Production Potential	Limestone Inflows
Limestone Production	.0449	.3108	.0063	.5339
Distance		-.3460	-.8310	-.2794
Limestone Prod. Potential			.2919	.2981
SAC Mfg. Empl. Potential				-.1988

	Distance	Metal Working Empl. Potential	SAC Steel Prod. Potential	Metallic Ore Inflows
Metallic Ore Prod.	-.1076	.1988	.1243	.6037
Distance		-.9546	-.6702	-.2440
Metallic Ore Product Potential			.6135	.3195
SAC Steel Prod. Potential				.0584

	Distance	Metal Working Empl. Potential	SAC Steel Prod. Potential	Non-Metallic Mineral Inflows
Non-Metallic Mineral Prod.	-.1825	.2167	.1286	.5120
Distance		-.9546	-.6702	-.3812
Non-Metallic Ore Prod. Potential			.6487	.4025
SAC Steel Prod. Potential				.1330

	Distance	Gram Potential	SAC Urban Pop. Potential	Gram Inflows
Gram Production	.2974	.7128	-.2695	.3765
Distance		.3980	-.8068	.1107
Gram Prod. Potential			-.3488	.1551
SAC Urban Pop. Potential				-.0715

	Urban Pop. Potential
SAC Steel Prod. Potential	-.4199

TABLE 41

RELATION OF SELECTED OUTFLOWS TO COMBINED DEMAND,
DISTANCE, COMPETITION AND REDISTRIBUTION EFFECTS
(Fourth step of stepwise regression)

Commodity	Independent Variable with Respect to k	Correlation Coefficient by step r	Coefficient of Determination by step r^2	Regression Coefficient 4th step b	Standard Error of b	Variance Ratio Test F
Total Commodities	Urban pop.	.70	.49	1.59	.13	149.6*
	Distance	.73	.53	-1.80	.48	13.8*
	Urban pop.[a] potential	.73	.53	-1.06	.65	2.6ns
	SAC[b] mfg. empl. potential	.74	.55	-3.21	1.69	3.8**
Coal	Urban pop.	.58	.34	1.45	.18	64.4*
	Distance	.62	.38	-.08	.51	.0ns
	Mfg. empl. potential	.62	.38	-.10	.86	.0ns
	SAC coal prod. potential	.63	.41	4.17	1.50	7.7*
Iron and Steel	Urban pop.	.67	.46	1.44	.12	133.9*
	Distance	.71	.51	-1.72	.42	16.4*
	Urban pop. potential	.71	.51	-1.88	.82	5.2**
	SAC steel prod. potential	.72	.52	-2.24	1.11	4.0**
Electrical Machinery	Urban pop.	.66	.44	.83	.08	93.7*
	Distance	.67	.45	-1.01	.35	7.9*
	Mfg. empl. potential	.67	.45	-.16	.46	.1ns
	SAC elec. mach. empl. potential	.69	.48	-4.12	1.57	6.8*

Other Machinery--Competition and Redistribution effects not significant.

* = significant at the .01 level for 153 degrees of freedom.

** = significant at the .05 level for 153 degrees of freedom.

ns = not statistically significant

a = total potential at k--redistribution or concentration measure.

b = SAC stands for study-area contribution to potential at k--competition measure.

Note: All variables except competition effect log transformed.

TABLE 42

RELATION OF SELECTED INFLOWS TO COMBINED SUPPLY,
DISTANCE, COMPETITION AND CONCENTRATION EFFECTS
(Fourth step of stepwise regression)

Commodity	Independent Variable with Respect to k	Correlation Coefficient by step r	Coefficient of Determination by step r^2	Regression Coefficient 4th step b	Standard Error of b	Variance Ratio Test F
Total Commodities	Urban pop.	.57	.32	1.37	.12	112.4*
	Distance	.70	.49	-2.83	.47	34.8*
	Urban pop. potential [a]	.71	.50	-2.07	.65	10.1*
	SAC [b] mfg. empl. potential	.73	.53	-5.89	2.66	4.8**
Electrical Machinery	Elec. machinery employment	.68	.46	.41	.04	85.5*
	Distance	.72	.52	-.68	.29	5.3**
	Elec. machinery potential	.72	.52	.27	.27	.9 ns
	SAC mfg. empl. potential	.73	.53	-2.48	1.25	3.9**
Other Machinery	Other machinery empl.	.64	.41	.40	.04	79.6*
	Distance	.69	.48	-.46	.30	2.4 ns
	Mfg. empl. potential	.70	.49	1.01	.43	5.4**
	SAC urban pop. potential	.70	.49	.82	2.44	.1 ns
Cement	Cement empl.	.38	.14	.33	.05	32.0*
	Distance	.51	.26	-1.52	.33	21.1*
	Limestone prod. potential	.51	.26	.38	.49	.5 ns
	SAC construction empl. potential	.54	.29	4.51	1.69	7.0*

* = significant at the .01 level for 153 degrees of freedom.

** = significant at the .05 level for 153 degrees of freedom.

ns = not statistically significant.

a = total potential at k--redistribution or concentration measure.

b = SAC stands for study-area contribution to potential at k--competition measure.

Note: All variables except competition effect log transformed.

TABLE 42--Continued

Commodity	Independent Variable with Respect to	Correlation Coefficient by step	Coefficient of Determination by step	Regression Coefficient 4th step	Standard Error of	Variance Ratio Test
	k	r	r^2	b	b	F
Metallic Ores	Metallic ore prod.	.60	.36	.72	.08	82.7*
	Distance	.64	.41	1.06	.85	1.5[ns]
	Metallic ore potential	.66	.44	3.34	1.18	7.9*
	SAC steel prod. potential	.67	.45	-.77	.77	1.0[ns]
Non-Metal. Minerals	Non-metallic mineral prod.	.52	.27	1.50	.26	32.3*
	Distance	.64	.41	-2.40	1.09	4.8**
	Non-metallic ore potential	.64	.41	-.89	1.46	.37[ns]
	SAC steel prod. potential	.67	.45	-2.56	.88	8.3*

Iron and Steel, Electrical Machinery, Chemicals, Limestone--competition and redistribution effects not significant.

potential model for these flows. However, for outflows of other machinery and inflows of steel, electrical machinery, chemicals, and limestone, the expanded model accounted for no additional statistically significant variation over that accounted for by the simpler potential model.

Redistribution or concentration effects except for outflows of steel and inflows of total commodities, other machinery, and metallic ores were not statistically significant. However, the effects of competition except for other machinery and metallic ore inflows were significant. For many flows, the signs of the regression coefficients for the redistribution, concentration, and competition variables were negative, just opposite to that hypothesized by the model. These sign changes appear to result from the formulation of these variables, the particular distribution of Indian supply and demand with respect to the study area, and the existence of trucking competition with rail flows in the vicinity of the study area.

In the expanded potential model it is hypothesized that supply and demand potentials

TABLE 43

THE EXPANDED POTENTIAL MODEL FOR SELECTED OUTFLOWS

Commodity Flow from Study Area to k	Demand at k	Distance Study Area to k	Redistribution Measure[a]	Competition Measure[b]
F_{1k}	P_k	d_{1k}	R_k	$SACS_k$

Total Commodities

$$F_{1k} = a \cdot (\text{Urban Pop.})^{1.59} \cdot (\text{distance})^{-1.80} \cdot 10^{-3.21 (\text{SAC Mfg. Empl. Potential})}$$

Coal

$$F_{1k} = a \cdot (\text{Urban Pop.})^{1.45} \cdot 10^{4.17 (\text{SAC Coal Prod. Potential})}$$

Iron and Steel

$$F_{1k} = a \cdot (\text{Urban Pop.})^{1.44} \cdot (\text{distance})^{-1.72} \cdot \left(\frac{\text{Urban Pop.}}{\text{Potential}}\right)^{-1.88} \cdot 10^{-2.24 \left(\begin{smallmatrix}\text{SAC Steel}\\\text{Prod.}\\\text{Pot.}\end{smallmatrix}\right)}$$

Electrical Machinery

$$F_{1k} = a \cdot (\text{Urban Pop.})^{.83} \cdot (\text{distance})^{-1.01} \cdot 10^{-4.12 (\text{SAC Elec. Mach. Empl. Pot.})}$$

a = Total demand potential at k.

b = $SACS_k$ stands for study-area contribution to supply potential at k.

at k represent k's relative access to supplies or markets throughout India and its relative opportunities for concentration or redistribution of goods. However, many of the meas-ures available to this study could represent concentrations of either supply or demand and thus could represent competition reducing exchanges of k with the study area rather than redistribution of concentration hypothesized to increase its flows. Given the nega-tive sign of the regression coefficient for urban population potential at k for both steel outflows and total commodity inflows, it appears that this supposed redistribution meas-ure is really a measure of proximity to competing sources of steel in other urban areas and competing markets for a diverse mix of commodities.

Contrary both to the hypothesis of the expanded model and to earlier findings with respect to distance effects on study-area flows, in those cases where the regression co-efficient of the competition measure was negatively signed, it appears that study-area

TABLE 44

THE EXPANDED POTENTIAL MODEL FOR SELECTED INFLOWS

Commodity Flows to the Study Area from k	Supply at k	Distance k to the Study Area	Concentration Measure[a]	Competition Measure[b]
F_{k1}	$= \quad S_k$	d_{k1}	C_k	$SACP_k$

Total Commodities

$$F_{k1} = a \cdot (\text{Urban Pop.})^{1.37} \cdot (\text{distance})^{-2.83} \cdot \left(\frac{\text{Urban Pop.}}{\text{Potential}}\right)^{-2.07} \cdot 10^{-5.89} \left(\frac{\text{SAC Mfg.}}{\text{Empl. Pot}}\right)$$

Electrical Machinery

$$F_{k1} = a \cdot \left(\frac{\text{Elec. Mach.}}{\text{Empl.}}\right)^{.41} \cdot (\text{distance})^{-.68} \cdot 10^{-2.48} (\text{SAC Mfg. Empl. Potential})$$

Other Machinery

$$F_{k1} = a \cdot \left(\frac{\text{Other Mach.}}{\text{Empl.}}\right)^{.40} \cdot \left(\frac{\text{Mfg. Empl.}}{\text{Potential}}\right)^{1.01}$$

Cement

$$F_{k1} = a \cdot (\text{Cement Empl.})^{.33} \cdot (\text{distance})^{-1.52} \cdot 10^{4.51} (\text{SAC Const. Empl. Pot.})$$

Metallic Ores

$$F_{k1} = a \cdot \left(\frac{\text{Met. Ore}}{\text{Prod.}}\right)^{.72} \cdot \left(\frac{\text{Met. Ores}}{\text{Prod. Pot.}}\right)^{3.34}$$

Non-Metallic Minerals

$$F_{k1} = a \cdot \left(\frac{\text{Non-met.}}{\text{Min. Prod.}}\right)^{1.50} \cdot (\text{distance})^{-2.40} \cdot 10^{-2.56} (\text{SAC Steel Prod. Potential})$$

a = Total supply potential at k.

b = $SACP_k$ stands for study area contribution to demand potential at k.

exchanges increase with increasing distance. However, given that this competition measure approximates d_{1k}^{-b} and is correlated with supply, demand, redistribution and concentration measures and given India's particular pattern of demand and trucking competition in the study area for certain goods, this supposed competition factor may actually be an approximation of simple demand or supply.

Although its exact magnitude is not known, throughout the vicinity of the study area, trucking competed with rail movements. Thus in the area of highest values for the competition factor, the flow by rail was reduced by trucking competition. Outside the study area where values of the competition factor were considerably smaller, goods were exchanged with the study area almost exclusively by rail. In addition, with respect to the study area, India's distribution of the demand and supply measures used in this study tended to be at a minimum in the area immediately beyond the core of the Calcutta region and increase gradually outward toward the core of India's other regions. Thus outside the immediate vicinity of the study area, the demand or supply components of the competition measure increase with increasing distance.

With respect to outflows of steel and electrical machinery and inflows of electrical machinery and non-metallic minerals, it can be argued that because of the rail bottlenecks which existed within the vicinity of the study area and because of their high value these goods were the most subject to trucking movement. Within the study area, although the value of the competition figure would be high, the flows of these goods by rail were reduced by trucking competition. As Table 26 indicates, shipments of steel outside the region were not subject to distance effects. Thus as demand outside the Calcutta region increases, so would flows of steel. Although distance did affect flows of electrical machinery to the rest of India, the effect of large-scale demand appears to have overwhelmed the distance effect. Inflows of electrical machinery and non-metallic minerals from outside the region were found to have no distance effects, Table 33. Again these goods would tend to come in considerable quantity from the few available sources located at great distance from the study area and thus be inversely related to d_{1k}^{-b}. Apparently the negative regression coefficient of the competition measure for total outflows and inflows reflects the influence in these mixed commodity groups of various commodities affected minimally by distance.

The regression coefficient of the competition measure for coal outflows and cement inflows were positive as expected. Because of government regulation of coal and cement movements and the location of coal producing areas outside the study area and cement plants nearby, relatively few large-volume long distance flows took place to supply the area with cement or to distribute its coal. Thus as distance increased and the contribution of the study area to demand and supply potentials at k decreased, flows of these goods also decreased.

For a number of study-area commodity flows the expanded potential model did explain additional statistically significant variation beyond that explained by the simple potential model. However, the amount of additional explanation was small and at best more than 40 per cent of the variation in study-area trade remained to be explained. The limited success in testing this expanded model appears to stem from both the formulation of the model which resulted in inter-correlated variables and from the lack of satisfactory data. Results of tests of the model were difficult to interpret because of the summarization in the single value of the competition, redistribution, or concentration measure of the complex interaction of distance, demand and supply; because of the particular distribution of Indian supplies and markets with respect to the study area; and because of an unknown amount of trucking competition. Given the problems of data availability, of inter-correlation among the variables, and of interpretation of these complex variables, for analyzing study-area exchanges the expanded potential model has little to recommend it over the simple potential model. Until better data becomes available or a modification of the potential model free of inter-correlated variables can be developed, analysis of regularity in flows associated with individual places in India might better rely upon the potential model.

Summary

Commodity exchanges of the Bengal-Bihar Industrial Area were found to vary inversely with the distance shipped and directly with demand or supply conditions throughout India. The potential model summarizing this relationship was found appropriate for analyzing both inflows and outflows of the area and was able to account for over 50 per cent of the variation in the volume of individual and total commodity flows. Reflecting the influence of India's strong economic regionalization, clear differences were found in the volume and in the effects of distance, demand or supply on goods exchanged with the Calcutta region and with the rest of India. Regional differences in these effects were most pronounced for agricultural and heavy, low-value industrial commodities and were absent or minimal for modern industrial goods such as machinery or for government controlled goods such as steel.

Attempts were made to account for additional variation in study-area flows both by improving measurement of the variables used in the potential model and by changing the model itself. Substituting measures of intervening opportunity and competition for distance, as Stouffer suggests,[1] provided no increased explanation. The measure of intervening opportunity was closely correlated with distance,while competition, as measured by a supply or demand potential at points outside the study area, was found to have minimal correlation with the flows. Within the framework of this study other modifications in measurement were not feasible.

---

[1] Stouffer, op. cit.

An attempt was made to improve the potential model through the addition of two new variables measuring the study area's competitive position vis à vis other points in India and the relative ability of these points to redistribute or concentrate goods exchanged with the study area. The addition of these competition, concentration, or redistribution effects to the potential model did explain small but statistically significant additional variation in study-area exchanges over that provided by the simpler potential model. However, partly because of the formulation of the expanded model and partly because of the lack of adequate data, the added variables were closely correlated with the distance, supply or demand variables of the potential model. For analyzing the flows of a single point in India this expanded model proved of limited value over the simpler potential model.

Need for Further Studies

With changes both in the measures used and in the potential model itself, over 40 per cent of the variations in study-area exchanges still remain to be explained outside the framework of this model. Within the context of the Indian economy the effects of various government regulations on the production and distribution of commodities and the effects of competition from other modes of transport, particularly trucking, must explain much of this remaining variation. Improved measurement of the distance, demand, and supply effects regulating commodity flows of the Bengal-Bihar Industrial Area or other areas throughout India should take into account the actual impact of different types of government policies upon the movement of goods, the different linkages between industrial and other establishments which would encourage trade between specific areas, and the effects of competition between various modes of transport.

The fact that the expanded potential model did explain some additional variation in study area flows strongly indicates that this model might prove useful in analyzing flows between all parts of an economic system. For an entire system the problem of inter-correlation among the model's variables would be greatly reduced. Such analysis could be undertaken immediately with data recorded in the Accounts[1] relating to the exchange of agricultural and heavy raw materials among India's major trade blocks. Extension of this line of analysis should concentrate on improvements in measurement as suggested earlier and on the collection of nationwide flow data for sub-state areas including the larger metropolitan areas. Such data should relate not only to the commodities

---

[1] India (Republic) Department of Commercial Intelligence and Statistics, Accounts, op. cit.

reported in the Accounts[1] but also to more modern industrial and consumer goods.

For these sub-state areas, analysis of individual and total commodity flows within the framework of the expanded potential model should provide a number of important insights into the regulation and movement of goods within the Indian economy. Analysis of the effects of government regulation on commodity flows in different regions and areas could provide background for assessing the value of these regulations. Studies could be undertaken of the effect on various commodity flows of regional differences in the availability and quality of transport. Of special interest would be the effect on flows resulting from changes in railway gauge or strong competition among modes of transport either within or between regions. Considerable differences have been noted in the major activities of India's economic region, yet flows of similar foods, cloth, machinery, etc. occur in each. Studies of the effect of differences in economic base upon such flows might also be undertaken. Although barely scratching the surface, this study of Bengal-Bihar Industrial Area commodity flows did establish that well-known economic principles underly the movement of goods in India. The next step should be a broader analysis of individual and total commodity movements among sub-state areas of the entire Indian economy.

---

[1] Ibid.

CHAPTER VII

BENGAL-BIHAR INDUSTRIAL AREA TRADE AND

AREAL INTERACTION IN INDIA

The early economic history of India is one of regional economies based on village-organized, near-subsistence agriculture. Within each region were produced and traded all of the foodstuffs, raw materials, and craft items necessary to support the villages of the region. Interregional trade consisted of a trickle of luxury items and high-value raw materials.

Under early British colonial administration large-scale commercial activities were developed, based on the production of specialized raw materials. This new commerce was oriented to the exchange of Indian raw materials for foreign manufactures. Major ports and administrative centers (Calcutta, Bombay, Madras and Delhi) grew up to organize this export trade. Subsistence agriculture persisted in pre-British patterns while the new commercial activities were oriented to the major port cities, leading to the spatial organization of India's commerce into four major urban-centered economic regions. Few of the new commercial activities complemented those in India's other regions so that neither the village agricultural sector nor the commercial sector constituted a base for extensive interregional trade.

During the 20th Century, and especially since Independence, substantial industrial and commercial development has taken place in India. It is this development which has generated regional and interregional exchange to the extent that Indian trading patterns may now be cited as a classic example of the different levels of exchange within a dual economy. Exchanges of foodstuffs and necessities for village agriculture persist in age-old regional patterns; areas producing specialized raw materials exchange these goods for the domestic and foreign manufactures obtainable from India's industrial and port cities; and these same cities exchange manufactured goods with each other for further fabrication and marketing.

The Bengal-Bihar Industrial Area lies within the larger Calcutta economic region, and as India's largest coal and steel producer, it trades at each of the country's three levels of exchange and with each of its specialized areas and major regions. The Area lies adjacent to the urban industrial market and port of Calcutta and is nearly equidistant from the urban cores of India's other three regions. Some of India's richest deposits of coal and the iron ore, limestone and other minerals basic to a heavy metals industry are found within the Area. Surrounding sections of Bihar and Orissa contain additional deposits of raw materials for the manufacture of both steel and aluminum.

During the late 1800's the developing jute and tea industries centered themselves in Calcutta, stimulating the growth of that metropolis. The Bengal-Bihar Industrial Area developed initially to supply coal for Calcutta industries and for export through the port of Calcutta. With the major expansion of industry in India during the 20th Century, new functions were added to the Bengal-Bihar Industrial Area. The development within the Area of large-scale coal mining, steel, light metals and machinery industries was a clear attempt by public and private industry to maximize both the Area's proximity to local raw materials and its accessibility to growing industrial markets in the Calcutta Metropolitan Area.

Coupled with this major expansion and the shift in India's economy from a colonial to a national orientation, major changes have taken place in the exchange patterns of the Bengal-Bihar Industrial Area. The Area now functions as a large-scale consumer of regional minerals, building materials, and foodstuffs, and as a major supplier of coal, metals and machinery, both to its region and to the rest of India. By volume, coal accounts for over 70 per cent and iron and steel over 22 per cent of its shipments. Machinery and building materials constitute much of the remainder. Over 60 per cent of the Area's receipts were raw materials for steel production. Steel itself accounted for an additional 13 per cent of receipts, and the remaining receipts were mainly food grains and building materials.

Both the pattern and scale of study-area inflows and outflows reflect those of "raw-material-and-power-oriented industries in areas of high market accessibility" suggested by Pred's typology of manufacturing flows. [1] Located near the center of the Calcutta region and specialized in the manufacture of heavy metals and machinery, the Area traded its largest volume of goods over short distances within the region. The major receipts of the Area were limestone, iron ore, coal, bauxite, building materials

---

[1] Pred, op. cit.

and steel from the Area itself and from immediately surrounding districts of West Bengal, Bihar and Orissa. Receipts of machinery and imported wheat and petroleum came from the port and industrial activities of the Calcutta metropolitan area. Receipts of rice, gram, and other foodstuffs linked the Area to northern Bihar, West Bengal and Uttar Pradesh. Small amounts of food and wood products were received from Assam and from coastal and southern Orissa.

Under government regulation, coals from West Bengal were distributed within the study area and sent to the Calcutta metropolitan area and to southern Bihar and Orissa. Coals produced in the Bihar portion of the study area were sent throughout the Ganges Valley. Steel from West Bengal mills was sent in large quantity to Calcutta and the Ganges Valley whereas the Bihar mill at Jamshedpur in the southern part of the Area sent many of its products to southern portions of the region and to the rest of India. Within the Calcutta region, Bengal-Bihar Industrial Area trade in agricultural goods continued to reflect long-standing regional exchange patterns as well as a newer pattern of import receipts. The Area's exchanges of manufactured goods for the raw materials of surrounding mining areas and for the manufactures of urban industrial centers of the region clearly reflect the developing pattern of "modern" industrial exchange within the region.

The Area's trade in manufactured goods, raw materials, and food with India's other regions reflects the large-scale demand and supply generated by its activities, the large concentrations of market and supply in the other regions, and the long distances separating them from the study area. The considerable volume of heavy coal and steel shipments outside the region reflects government policy. Much Area coal was sent the length of the Ganges Valley to Delhi, Punjab, and Rajasthan; smaller amounts were sent to western and southern India. Under government control, steel was delivered throughout India at a uniform price. Thus, Area steel was sent in considerable quantity to each of India's other regional markets. However, since India's largest concentration of industry is in western and northern India, most interregional steel shipments went to these areas.

Except for coal and steel, the Area's interregional shipments were mainly high-value machinery and other manufactures sent to areas of highest market concentration in India's other regions. The Area's interregional receipts, except for heavy limestone and steel from nearby Madhya Pradesh, consisted of high-value raw materials, machinery, chemicals, and specialized foods. As noted earlier, with little industrial development in south India the majority of Area receipts were from western and northern India. Study-area receipts from the south were mainly raw minerals and some electrical machinery from Mysore, Madras, and Andhra Pradesh. In its interregional patterns

Bengal-Bihar Industrial Area exchanges mirror the developing national integration of specialized mining areas with specialized manufacturing centers and the integration of these manufacturing centers with other urban industrial areas throughout India. At the interregional level, the older pattern of village agricultural trade did not appear.

Underlying each of these observed patterns is the fact that the Bengal-Bihar Industrial Area flows behave in a predictable fashion with respect to supply, demand, and distance conditions throughout India. Flows were found to vary directly with supply and demand conditions and inversely with distance. The potential model summarizing this relationship accounted for approximately 50 per cent of the variation in total inflows and outflows of the area and up to 70 per cent of the variation in flows of individual commodities. The effects of demand in controlling outflows were considerably greater than the effects of supply in controlling inflows. Distance effects were found to be least for high-value commodities such as machinery, commodities such as steel for which the study area supplied a large proportion of regional or national production, and commodities such as coal and steel for which shipment patterns were regulated or transportation subsidized.

Indicating the relative self-sufficiency of India's economic regions, considerable differences appeared in the volume of outflows and inflows which the Area traded with the Calcutta region and other major regions of India. Important differences were also noted between the effects of distance, demand and supply on exchanges with the region and rest of India. However, these regional differences were absent or minimal for high-value goods and for government-regulated flows of coal and steel.

Between 30 and 50 per cent of the variation in study-area trade remained to be explained outside the framework of the potential model, and attempts were made to account for this unexplained variation. The Indian economy is far from the idealized "perfect market." If a way could have been found to account directly for effects of government regulation, competition from other modes of transport, and specific linkages between Indian firms, much of this additional variation might have been explained. Attempts were made both to modify the measures used in the potential model and to change the model itself. Measures of intervening opportunity suggested by Stouffer were found to be closely correlated with simple linear distance. [1] Measures of competition based on the supply or demand potential at points outside the study area were found to have little or no statistically significant effect on flows. Thus, attempts to modify the measures used in the potential model resulted in no improved explanation.

Modification of the potential model by adding a measure of the Bengal-Bihar

---

[1] Stouffer, op. cit.

Industrial Area's contribution to the supply or demand potential in other areas of India and a measure of the ability of such areas to redistribute or concentrate goods exchanged with the study area led to small but statistically significant additional explanation. Many of the measures available to this study were inter-correlated, and their use rendered this expanded model of limited value over the simpler potential model. In this study of Indian commodity flows, as in most studies, better data were needed to achieve more satisfactory results whether simple or complex models were used. Better account of the effects of government regulation on commodity flows appears to be the most fruitful avenue for improvement.

Planning and Bengal-Bihar Industrial Area Exchanges

Within the Indian economy and especially within the Bengal-Bihar Industrial Area the government plays a major role in developing and regulating economic activities. Government regulation and planned economic development can effect striking changes in the commodity flows of an area in a rather short time. Although the study area is closely linked with the Calcutta metropolitan area and surrounding districts of the Calcutta region, certain changes are currently underway or planned which will considerably alter its trade patterns.

Short-term Changes

Within the near future many of the activities of the port of Calcutta are expected to transfer to the newly developing port of Haldia in West Bengal to the south of the study area or to ports in nearby Orissa. The Area's imported wheat, industrial raw materials, and petroleum receipts from Calcutta would thus diminish. The development of an oil refinery at Baurani in northern Bihar will further reduce the Area's dependence on Calcutta or Haldia. Completion of the Faraka Barrage across the Ganges river will provide the study area with improved access to northern West Bengal and Assam, expanding the directly accessible markets for its coal, steel, and machinery. The net effect of these changes should be to reduce the Area's overall dependence upon the Calcutta metropolitan area and to increase its dependence upon other intraregional areas to the north and south.

Since Independence, much of regional and national planning for eastern India has been concerned with the increasing concentration of industry, administration, and population in the over-crowded Calcutta metropolitan area.[1] Many current planning schemes and government policies aim at stemming increase in this concentration and possibly

---

[1] West Bengal, Calcutta Metropolitan Planning Organization, Basic Development Plan for the Calcutta Metropolitan District 1966-1986. (Calcutta: Calcutta Metropolitan Planning Organization, 1966).

reducing it through the provision of employment alternatives and urban development else-where in eastern India. [1]

With its established industrial base, the Bengal-Bihar Industrial Area is con-sidered the most likely location for development of large-scale alternative urban indus-trial employment. To make the Area a viable counter-magnet for the streams of funds and migrants now flowing to Calcutta, a major increase is needed in the opportunities for secondary and tertiary employment. Plans call for achieving much of this increase in secondary industrial employment through the development of ancillary industry to serve the Area's larger plants. [2] However, except for the few totally integrated plants, little ancillary industry exists within the Area, and as its exchanges of metals and machinery indicate, it is highly dependent upon Calcutta for ancillary manufacturing. MacDougall indicates that strong cultural and operational constraints currently prevent the rapid de-velopment of ancillary industry within the area. [3] Until these constraints are overcome and ancillary industry is widely established it is not expected that the Area's commodity flows will be reoriented to resemble those of a counter-magnet independent of Calcutta.

Among the alternative proposals concerned with developing the Bengal-Bihar Industrial Area as a counter-magnet is the argument that it need not function as a single unit. Viewed from outside, the Area functions as an integrated producer of coal, metals, and machinery and consumer of raw materials, metals, and foods. However, viewed by its activities at specific locations, many of the goods produced elsewhere within the area are not necessarily complementary, and in the case of coal, steel, and certain machin-ery may be directly competitive. Through control over allocation and financing of many of the area's industries the Indian Government has greatly influenced trade patterns of the Area. Both an east-west and north-south split were noted in the flow of many com-modities. Given the location of activities within the study area, the location and special-ization of places complementary to it, and the observed pattern of its exchanges, depend-ing upon the policy which the government might wish to pursue, the Area could reason-ably function either as a single integrated unit or as multiple units along a number of pos-sible divisions. Should development be encouraged along an east-west cultural linguistic division between West Bengal and Bihar, each component of the Area could be developed

---

[1] West Bengal, Asansol Planning Organization, Interim Development Plan: Asansol-Durgapur (Calcutta: Calcutta Metropolitan Planning Organization, 1966); West Bengal, Siliguri Planning Organization, Interim Development Plan: Siliguri (Calcutta: Calcutta Metropolitan Planning Organization, 1965).

[2] West Bengal, Asansol Planning Organization, op. cit.

[3] MacDougall, op. cit.

separately since each would have coal, steel, and machinery industries. West Bengal activities could continue their close integration with the Calcutta metropolitan area and West Bengal ports. Parallel to this north-south industrial corridor in West Bengal,[1] a Bihar-Orissa industrial corridor could be developed with industry in both states using Orissa ports. Alternatively, exchange patterns of the activities of the northern and southern parts of the Area suggest another possible division into well-integrated northern and southern industrial complexes which could use either West Bengal or Orissa ports.

Long-Term Changes

Because much of India's investment capital is licensed and controlled by the central and state governments, the greatest long-range impact on area flows is expected to result from governmental policies related to the location of industries and the development of transport systems. Despite anticipated changes in the Indian economy, major changes in specialization are not foreseen for the Bengal-Bihar Industrial Area. Considerable industrial growth and new mining development is expected to occur in surrounding areas with which the study area now trades, thus encouraging maintenance of its existing trade patterns.

With continued economic development, considerable increase is expected in the diversity and scale of Indian industry. India's transport capacity is expected to undergo major expansion accompanied by decreasing transportation costs. Given these long-term developments, study-area activities should become larger and more specialized along current lines. The Area should receive a smaller proportion of heavy raw materials in its total mix of inflows and engage in a larger proportion of interregional trade with the expanding national market. Although planned development of metallurgical industries and new power sources in India's other regions may alter some of the Area's interregional exchanges, these changes are expected to be slow in coming and general economic expansion in these other regions should encourage expansion of the Area's interregional trade. Thus, in the long run considerable reduction is expected in Bengal-Bihar Industrial Area dependence on both the Calcutta metropolitan area and other areas of the surrounding region.

---

[1] Development of such a corridor is now clearly being supported as evidenced in the plans for Siliguri, Asansol-Durgapur and Calcutta cited earlier.

SELECTED BIBLIOGRAPHY

Spatial Organization

Alampiyev, P. M. "Tendencies in the Development of Major Economic Geographic Regions," Soviet Geography: Review and Translation, I, No. 4 (1960), 43-51.

Anderson, Theodore. "Intermetropolitan Migration: A Comparison of the Hypotheses of Zipf and Stouffer," American Sociological Review, XX (1955), 287-291.

Berry, Brian J. L. and Thomas D. Hankins. A Bibliographic Guide to the Economic Regions of the United States. Chicago: University of Chicago, Department of Geography Research Paper No. 87, 1963.

Carrothers, Gerald A. P. "Historical Review of the Gravity and Potential Concepts in Human Interactance," Journal of the American Institute of Planners, XXII, No. 2 (1956), 94-102.

Chinitz, Benjamin. Freight and the Metropolis: The Impact of America's Transport Revolution on the New York Region. Cambridge: Harvard University Press, 1960.

Cooper, Richard N. "Growth and Trade: Some Hypotheses About Long-Term Trends," The Journal of Economic History, XXIV, No. 4 (1964), 609-628.

Dickinson, Robert E. City and Region: A Geographical Interpretation. London: Routledge and Kegan Paul, 1964.

Duncan, Otis Dudley, et al. Metropolis and Region. Baltimore: The Johns Hopkins Press, 1960.

Dunn, Edgar S. "The Market Potential Concept and the Analysis of Location," Papers and Proceedings of the Regional Science Association, II (1956), 183-194.

Friedmann, John, and William Alonso (eds.). Regional Development and Planning. Cambridge: Massachusetts Institute of Technology Press, 1964.

Fulton, Maurice, and Clurton Hoch. "Transportation Factors Affecting Location Decisions," Economic Geography, XXXV (1959), 51-59.

Greenhut, Melvin L. "Space and Economic Theory," Papers and Proceedings of the Regional Science Association, V (1959), 267-280.

Hartshorne, Richard. Perspectives on the Nature of Geography. Chicago: For the Association of American Geographers by Rand McNally, 1959.

Harris, Chauncy D. "The Market as a Factor in the Location of Industry in the United States," Annals of the Association of American Geographers, XLIV, No. 4 (1954), 315-48.

Hoover, Edgar M. The Location of Economic Activity. New York: McGraw-Hill, 1948.

Isard, Walter. Location and Space-Economy. New York and Cambridge: John Wiley and Sons and Massachusetts Institute of Technology Press, 1956.

_____. Methods of Regional Analysis: An Introduction to Regional Science. Cambridge: Massachusetts Institute of Technology Press, 1960.

Komar, I. V. "The Major Economic-Geographic Regions of the U. S. S. R.," Soviet Geography: Review and Translation, I, No. 4 (1960), 31-42.

Kolosovskiy, N. N. "The Territorial-Production Combination (Complex) in Soviet Economic Geography," Journal of Regional Science, III, No. 1 (1961), 1-25.

Linder, Staffan B. An Essay on Trade and Transformation. New York and Stockholm: John Wiley and Sons and Almqvist and Wilesell, 1961.

Linnemann, Hans. An Econometric Study of International Trade Flows. Amsterdam: North-Holland Publishing Co., 1966.

Posner, M. V. "International Trade and Technical Change," Oxford Economic Papers, XIII (1961), 323-341.

Pred, Allan. "Toward a Typology of Manufacturing Flows," The Geographic Review, LIV, No. 1 (1964), 65-73.

Probst, A. Ye. "Territorial-Production Complexes in the U. S. S. R.," Soviet Geography: Review and Translation, VII, No. 7 (1966), 47-55.

Ray, D. Michael. Market Potential and Economic Shadow: A Quantative Analysis of Industrial Location in Southern Ontario. Chicago: University of Chicago, Department of Geography Research Paper No. 101, 1965.

Resources for the Future. Design for a Worldwide Study of Regional Development: A Report to the United Nations on a Proposed Research-Training Program. Baltimore: The Johns Hopkins Press, 1966.

Saushkin, Yu. G. "The Construction of Economic Models of Regional and Local Territorial-Production Complexes," Soviet Geography: Review and Translation, II, No. 4 (1961), 60-66.

_____. "On the Objective and Subjective Character of Economic Regionalization," Soviet Geography: Review and Translation, II, No. 8 (1961), 75-80.

Smith, Adam. The Wealth of Nations. New York: The Modern Library, 1937.

Smith, Robert H. T. "Toward a Measure of Complementarity," Economic Geography, XL, No. 1 (1964), 1-8.

Stewart, Charles T. "Migration as a Function of Population and Distance," American Sociological Review, XXV (1960), 347-356.

Stewart, John Q. "Empirical Mathematical Rules Governing the Distribution and Equilibrium of Population," Geographical Review, XXXVII (1947), 473-475.

Stouffer, Samuel A. "Intervening Opportunities: A Theory Relating Mobility and Distance," American Socialogical Review, V (1940), 845-867.

_____. "Intervening Opportunities and Competing Migrants," Journal of Regional Regional Science, II (1960), 1-26.

Vernon, Raymond. "International Investment and International Trade in the Product Cycle," The Quarterly Journal of Economics, Vol. LXXX, No. 2 (1966).

Warntz, William. Toward a Geography of Price: A Study in Geo-Econometrics. Philadelphia: University of Pennsylvania Press, 1959.

_____. "A New Map of the Surface of Population Potentials for the United States, 1960," Geographical Review, LIV, No. 1 (1964), 170-184.

Weber, Alfred. The Theory of Location of Industry. Translation by Carl J. Friedrich. Chicago: University of Chicago Press, 1929.

Whittlesey, Derwent. "The Regional Concept and the Regional Method," American Geography: Inventory and Prospect. Edited by Preston E. James and Clarence F. Jones. Syracuse: Syracuse University Press, 1954.

Ullman, Edward L. "The Role of Transportation and the Bases of Interaction," Man's Role in Changing the Face of the Earth. Edited by William L. Thomas. Chicago: University of Chicago Press, 1956.

Commodity Flow Studies

Becht, J. Edwin. Commodity Origins, Traffic and Markets Accessible to Chicago Via the Illinois Waterway. Chicago: The Illinois River Carriers Association of Chicago, Illinois, 1952.

Duncombe, Bruce F. Upper Midwest Commodity Flows, 1958. Minneapolis: University of Minnesota, Upper Midwest Economic Study Technical Paper No. 4, 1962.

Gould, Peter R. The Development of the Transport Pattern in Ghana. Evanston: Northwestern University, Department of Geography Studies in Geography No. 5, 1960.

Patton, Donald J. "General Cargo Hinterlands of New York, Philadelphia, Baltimore, and New Orleans," Annals of the Association of American Geographers, XLVIII, No. 4 (1958), 436-455.

Pfouts, Ralph W. "Patterns of Economic Interaction in the Crescent," Urban Growth Dynamics in a Regional Cluster of Cities. Edited by. F. Stuart Chapin and Shirley F. Weiss. New York: John Wiley and Sons, 1962.

Rodgers, Allan L. "The Port of Genova: External and Internal Relations," Annals of the Association of American Geographers, XLVIII, No. 4 (1958), 319-351.

Smith, Robert H. T. Commodity Movements in Southern New South Wales. Canberra: Australian National University, Department of Geography, 1962.

Spiegelglas, Stephen. "Some Aspects of State to State Commodity Flows in the United States," Journal of Regional Science, II, No. 2 (1960), 71-80.

Ullman, Edward L. American Commodity Flow, A Geographical Interpretation of Rail and Water Traffic Based on Principles of Spatial Interchange. Seattle: University of Washington Press, 1957.

Studies of Indian Economic Regions

Ahmad, Qazi. Indian Cities: Characteristics and Correlates. Chicago: University of Chicago, Department of Geography Research Paper No. 102, 1965.

Anstey, Vera. The Economic Development of India. 4th ed. London: Longmans, Green and Co., 1952.

Berry, Brian J. L. Essays on Commodity Flows and the Spatial Structure of the Indian Economy. Chicago: Department of Geography, University of Chicago, Research Paper No. 111, 1966.

Bhat, L. S. "Aspects of Regional Planning in India," Geographers and the Tropics: Liverpool Essays. Edited by Robert W. Steel and R. Mansell Prothero. London: Longmans, Green and Co., 1964.

Brush, John E. "The Iron and Steel Industry of India," Geographical Review, XLII, No. 1 (1952), 37-55.

Das Gupta, Arunendu. Economic Geography of India: Including Pakistan, Burma and Ceylon. 6th ed. Calcutta: A. Mukherjee, 1963.

Gadgil, D. R. The Industrial Evolution of India in Recent Times. London: Oxford University, 1924.

Ginsburg, Norton S. "Urban Geography and Non-Western 'Areas'," The Study of Urbanization. Edited by Philip M. Hauser and Leo F. Schnore. New York: John Wiley and Sons, 1965.

Hoselitz, Bert F. "A Survey of the Literature on Urbanization in India," India's Urban Future. Edited by Roy Turner. Berkeley: University of California Press, 1962.

India (Republic) Directorate of Economics and Statistics. Indian Agricultural Atlas. 2d ed. New Delhi: Directorate of Economics and Statistics, 1958.

India (Republic) Planning Commission. Third Five Year Plan. Delhi: Manager of Publications, 1961.

Kar, N. R. "Economic Character of Metropolitan Sphere of Influence of Calcutta," Geographical Review of India, XXV (1963), 108-137.

Komar, I. V., and K. M. Popov. "Problems in the Economic Regionalization of India," Soviet Geography: Review and Translation, III, No. 5 (1962), 30-40.

Koti, Bhanu. "Inter-State or Inter-Regional Balance of Trade, Methodological and Practical Problems with Special Reference to India," Papers on National Income and Allied Topics, Vol. III. Edited by V. K. R. V. Rao, A. K. Ghosh, M. V. Divatia and Uma Dutta. New York: Asia Publishing House, 1962.

Kuchhal, S. C. The Industrial Economy of India. Allahabad: Chaitanya Publishing House, 1963.

Learmonth, A. T. A. , and L. S. Bhat (eds.). Mysore State: Volume I-An Atlas of Resources. (Indian Statistical Institute, Indian Statistical Series No. 13). Calcutta: Asia Publishing House, 1961.

Learmonth, A. T. A. Mysore State: Volume II-A Regional Synthesis. (Indian Statistical Institute, Indian Statistical Series No. 16). Calcutta: Asia Publishing House, 1962.

MacDougall, John. Ancillary Industries in Asansol-Durgapur: A Preliminary Study. Calcutta: Asia Publishing House, 1964.

Nahai, L. India's Iron and Steel Industry. Washington: United States Department of the Interior, 1961.

National Council of Applied Economic Research. Economic Atlas of Madras State. New Delhi: National Council of Applied Economic Research, 1962.

_____. Techno-Economic Survey of Assam. New Delhi: National Council of Applied Economic Research, 1962.

_____. Techno-Economic Survey of Bihar, Volume I. Bombay: Asia Publishing House, 1960.

_____. Techno-Economic Survey of Madhya Pradesh. Bombay: Asia Publishing House, 1960.

_____. Techno-Economic Survey of Orissa. New Delhi: National Council of Applied Economic Research, 1962.

_____. Techno-Economic Survey of Uttar Pradesh. New Delhi: National Council of Applied Economic Research, 1965.

_____. Techno-Economic Survey of West Bengal. New Delhi: National Council of Applied Economic Research, 1962.

_____. Transport Requirements of the Iron and Steel Belt. New Delhi: National Council of Applied Economic Research, 1964.

Oskolkova, O. B. "Conference on Economic Regionalization of India," Soviet Geography: Review and Translation, III, No. 5 (1962), 41-45.

Prakasa Rao, V. L. S. Towns of Mysore State. (Indian Statistical Institute, Indian Statistical Series No. 22). New York: Asia Publishing House, 1964.

Prasad, Amba. Indian Railways. New York: Asia Publishing House, 1960.

Sahni, J. N. Indian Railways: One Hundred Years. New Delhi: Ministry of Railways (Railway Board), 1953.

Singh, R. L. Banaras: A Study in Urban Geography. Banaras: Nand Kishore and Bros. 1955.

Sharma, Tulsi Ram, and S. D. Singh Chauhan. Indian Industries. Delhi: Shiva Lal Agarwala and Co. , 1962.

Spate, Oskar, H. K. India and Pakistan: A General and Regional Geography. London: Methuen and Co. , 1957.

Tiwari, R. D. , and C. N. Vakil. Railway Rates in Relation to Trade and Industry in India. Calcutta: Longmans, Green and Co. , 1937.

West Bengal. Asansol Planning Organization. Interim Development Plan: Asansol-Durgapur. Howrah: Calcutta Metropolitan Planning Organization, 1966.

_____. Calcutta Metropolitan Planning Organization. Basic Development Plan for for The Calcutta Metropolitan District, 1966-1986. Calcutta: Calcutta Metropolitan Planning Organization, 1966.

_____. Calcutta Metropolitan Planning Organization. Regional Planning for West Bengal. Calcutta: Calcutta Metropolitan Planning Organization, 1965.

_____. Siliguri Planning Organization. Interim Development Plan for Siliguri. Howrah: Calcutta Metropolitan Planning Organization, 1965.

Sources of Indian Data

Hindustan Steel Limited (Statistics Division). Statistics for Iron and Steel in India. Ranchi: Hindustan Steel Limited, 1964.

India (Republic) Indian Bureau of Mines, Nagpur. Indian Minerals Yearbook, 1962. Delhi: Manager of Publications, 1965.

_____. Mineral Production in India, 1958. Nagpur: Bureau of Mines, 1960.

India (Republic) Department of Commercial Intelligence and Statistics, Calcutta. Statistics of the Coasting Trade of India for the Twelve Months Ending March, 1962. Calcutta: Government of India Press, 1963.

_____. Accounts Relating to the Inland (Rail and Water-Borne) Trade of India for Twelve Months Ending March, 1960. Calcutta: Government of India Press, 1960.

_____. Accounts Relating to the Inland (Rail and Water-Borne) Trade of India for Twelve Months Ending March, 1961. Calcutta: Department of Commercial Intelligence and Statistics, 1962.

India (Republic) Directorate of Economics and Statistics. Estimates of Area and Production of Principle Crops in India, 1955-56. Vol. II. Delhi: Directorate of Economics and Statistics, 1961.

THE UNIVERSITY OF CHICAGO
DEPARTMENT OF GEOGRAPHY
RESEARCH PAPERS (Lithographed, 6 × 9 Inches)

(Available from Department of Geography, Rosenwald Hall, The University of Chicago, Chicago, Illinois, 60637. Price: four dollars each; by series subscription, three dollars each.)

*1. GROSS, HERBERT HENRY. *Educational Land Use in the River Forest–Oak Park Community (Illinois)*

*2. EISEN, EDNA E. *Educational Land Use in Lake County, Ohio*

*3. WEIGEND, GUIDO GUSTAV. *The Cultural Pattern of South Tyrol (Italy)*

*4. NELSON, HOWARD JOSEPH, *The Livelihood Structure of Des Moines, Iowa*

*5. MATTHEWS, JAMES SWINTON. *Expressions of Urbanism in the Sequent Occupance of Northeastern Ohio*

*6. GINSBURG, NORTON SYDNEY. *Japanese Prewar Trade and Shipping in the Oriental Triangle*

*7. KEMLER, JOHN H. *The Struggle for Wolfram in the Iberian Peninsula, June, 1942—June, 1944: A Study in Political and Economic Geography in Wartime*

*8. PHILBRICK, ALLEN K. *The Geography of Education in the Winnetka and Bridgeport Communities of Metropolitan Chicago*

*9. BRADLEY, VIRGINIA. *Functional Patterns in the Guadalupe Counties of the Edwards Plateau*

*10. HARRIS, CHAUNCY D., and FELLMANN, JEROME DONALD. *A Union List of Geographical Serials*

*11. DE MEIRLEIR, MARCEL J. *Manufactural Occupance in the West Central Area of Chicago*

*12. FELLMANN, JEROME DONALD. *Truck Transportation Patterns of Chicago*

*13. HOTCHKISS, WESLEY AKIN. *Areal Pattern of Religious Institutions in Cincinnati*

*14. HARPER, ROBERT ALEXANDER. *Recreational Occupance of the Moraine Lake Region of Northeastern Illinois and Southeastern Wisconsin*

*15. WHEELER, JESSE HARRISON, JR. *Land Use in Greenbrier County, West Virginia*

*16. MCGAUGH, MAURICE EDRON. *The Settlement of the Saginaw Basin*

*17. WATTERSON, ARTHUR WELDON. *Economy and Land Use Patterns of McLean County, Illinois*

*18. HORBALY, WILLIAM. *Agricultural Conditions in Czechoslovakia, 1950*

*19. GUEST, BUDDY ROSS. *Resource Use and Associated Problems in the Upper Cimarron Area*

*20. SORENSEN, CLARENCE WOODROW. *The Internal Structure of the Springfield, Illinois, Urbanized Area*

*21. MUNGER, EDWIN S. *Relational Patterns of Kampala, Uganda*

*22. KHALAF, JASSIM M. *The Water Resources of the Lower Colorado River Basin*

*23. GULICK, LUTHER H. *Rural Occupance in Utuado and Jayuya Municipios, Puerto Rico*

*24. TAAFFE, EDWARD JAMES. *The Air Passenger Hinterland of Chicago*

*25. KRAUSE, ANNEMARIE ELISABETH. *Mennonite Settlement in the Paraguayan Chaco*

*26. HAMMING, EDWARD. *The Port of Milwaukee*

*27. CRAMER, ROBERT ELI. *Manufacturing Structure of the Cicero District, Metropolitan Chicago*

*28. PIERSON, WILLIAM H. *The Geography of the Bellingham Lowland, Washington*

*29. WHITE, GILBERT F. *Human Adjustment to Floods: A Geographical Approach to the Flood Problem in the United States*

30. OSBORN, DAVID G. *Geographical Features of the Automation of Industry* 1953. 120 pp.

*31. THOMAN, RICHARD S. *The Changing Occupance Pattern of the Tri-State Area, Missouri, Kansas, and Oklahoma*

*32. ERICKSEN, SHELDON D. *Occupance in the Upper Deschutes Basin, Oregon*

*33. KENYON, JAMES B. *The Industrialization of the Skokie Area*

*34. PHILLIPS, PAUL GROUNDS. *The Hashemite Kingdom of Jordan: Prolegomena to a Technical Assistance Program*

*35. CARMIN, ROBERT LEIGHTON. *Anápolis, Brazil: Regional Capital of an Agricultural Frontier*

*36. GOLD, ROBERT N. *Manufacturing Structure and Pattern of the South Bend–Mishawaka Area* 1954. 224 pp. 6 folded inserts. 2 maps in pocket.

*37. SISCO, PAUL HARDEMAN. *The Retail Function of Memphis*

*38. VAN DONGEN, IRENE S. *The British East African Transport Complex*

*39. FRIEDMANN, JOHN R. P. *The Spatial Structure of Economic Development in the Tennessee Valley*

*40. GROTEWOLD, ANDREAS. *Regional Changes in Corn Production in the United States from 1909 to 1949*

*41. BJORKLUND, E. M. *Focus on Adelaide—Functional Organization of the Adelaide Region, Australia*

*42. FORD, ROBERT N. *A Resource Use Analysis and Evaluation of the Everglades Agricultural Area*

*43. CHRISTENSEN, DAVID E. *Rural Occupance in Transition: Sumter and Lee Counties, Georgia*

*44. GUZMÁN, LOUIS E. *Farming and Farmlands in Panama*

* Out of print.

*45. ZADROZNY, MITCHELL G. *Water Utilization in the Middle Mississippi Valley*

*46. AHMED, G. MUNIR. *Manufacturing Structure and Pattern of Waukegan–North Chicago*

*47. RANDALL, DARRELL. *Factors of Economic Development and the Okovango Delta*
1956. 282 pp. (Research Paper No. 3, Program of Education and Research in Planning, The University of Chicago.)

48. BOXER, BARUCH. *Israeli Shipping and Foreign Trade* 1957. 176 pp.

49. MAYER, HAROLD M. *The Port of Chicago and the St. Lawrence Seaway*

*50. PATTISON, WILLIAM D. *Beginnings of the American Rectangular Land Survey System, 1784–1800*
1957. 2d printing 1963. 260 pp. Available from Ohio Historical Society.

*51. BROWN, ROBERT HAROLD. *Political Areal-Functional Organization: With Special Reference to St. Cloud, Minnesota.*

*52. BEYER, JACQUELYN. *Integration of Grazing and Crop Agriculture: Resources Management Problems in the Uncompahgre Valley Irrigation Project.* 1957. 131 pp.

53. ACKERMAN, EDWARD A. *Geography as a Fundamental Research Discipline* 1958. 40 pp. $1.00.

*54. AL-KHASHAB, WAFIQ HUSSAIN. *The Water Budget of the Tigris and Euphrates Basin*

*55. LARIMORE, ANN EVANS. *The Alien Town: Patterns of Settlement in Busoga, Uganda* 1958. 210 pp.

56. MURPHY, FRANCIS C. *Regulating Flood-Plain Development* 1958. 216 pp.

*57. WHITE, GILBERT F., *et al.* *Changes in Urban Occupance of Flood Plains in the United States*

*58. COLBY, MARY MC RAE. *The Geographic Structure of Southeastern North Carolina* 1958. 242 pp.

*59. MEGEE, MARY CATHERINE. *Monterrey, Mexico: Internal Patterns and External Relations*

60. WEBER, DICKINSON. *A Comparison of Two Oil City Business Centers (Odessa-Midland, Texas)*
1958. 256 pp.

61. PLATT, ROBERT S. *Field Study in American Geography* 1959. 408 pp.

62. GINSBURG, NORTON, editor. *Essays on Geography and Economic Development* 1960. 196 pp.

63. HARRIS, CHAUNCY D., and FELLMANN, JEROME D. *International List of Geographical Serials*
1960. 247 pp.

*64. TAAFEE, ROBERT N. *Rail Transportation and the Economic Development of Soviet Central Asia*
1960. 186 pp.

*65. SHEAFFER, JOHN R. *Flood Proofing: An Element in a Flood Damage Reduction Program*
1960. 190 pp.

66. RODGERS, ALLAN L. *The Industrial Geography of the Port of Genova* 1960. 150 pp.

67. KENYON, JAMES B. *Industrial Localization and Metropolitan Growth: The Paterson-Passaic District.* 1960. 250 pp.

68. GINSBURG, NORTON. *An Atlas of Economic Development*
1961. 119 pp. 14 × 8½". Cloth $7.50. University of Chicago Press.

69. CHURCH, MARTHA. *Spatial Organization of Electric Power Territories in Massachusetts*
1960. 200 pp.

70. WHITE, GILBERT F., *et al.* *Papers on Flood Problems* 1961. 234 pp.

71. GILBERT, E. W. *The University Town in England and West Germany*
1961. 79 pp. 4 plates. 30 maps and diagrams.

72. BOXER, BARUCH. *Ocean Shipping in the Evolution of Hong Kong* 1961. 108 pp.

73. ROBINSON, IRA M. *New Industrial Towns of Canada's Resource Frontier*
1962. (Research Paper No. 4, Program of Education and Research in Planning, The University of Chicago.) 192 pp.

74. TROTTER, JOHN E. *State Park System in Illinois* 1962. 152 pp.

75. BURTON, IAN. *Types of Agricultural Occupance of Flood Plains in the United States*
1962. 167 pp.

76. PRED, ALLAN. *The External Relations of Cities during 'Industrial Revolution'* 1962. 124 pp.

77. BARROWS, HARLAN H. *Lectures on the Historical Geography of the United States as Given in 1933*
Edited by WILLIAM A. KOELSCH. 1962. 248 pp.

78. KATES, ROBERT WILLIAM. *Hazard and Choice Perception in Flood Plain Management*
1962. 157 pp.

79. HUDSON, JAMES. *Irrigation Water Use in the Utah Valley, Utah* 1962. 249 pp.

80. ZELINSKY, WILBUR. *A Bibliographic Guide to Population Geography* 1962. 257 pp.

*81. DRAINE, EDWIN H. *Import Traffic of Chicago and Its Hinterland*

*82. KOLARS, JOHN F. *Tradition, Season, and Change in a Turkish Village*
NAS-NRC Foreign Field Research Program Report No. 15. 1963. 205 pp.

83. WIKKRAMATILEKE, RUDOLPH. *Southeast Ceylon: Trends and Problems in Agricultural Settlement*
1963. 163 pp.

84. KANSKY, K. J. *Structure of Transportation Networks: Relationships between Network Geometry and Regional Characteristics* 1963. 155 pp.

85. BERRY, BRIAN J. L. *Commercial Structure and Commercial Blight* 1963. 254 pp.

86. BERRY, BRIAN J. L., and TENNANT, ROBERT J. *Chicago Commercial Reference Handbook*
1963. 178 pp.

87. BERRY, BRIAN J. L., and HANKINS, THOMAS D. *A Bibliographic Guide to the Economic Regions of the United States* 1963. 128 pp.

88. MARCUS, MELVIN G. *Climate-Glacier Studies in the Juneau Ice Field Region, Alaska* 1964. 128 pp.

89. SMOLE, WILLIAM J. *Owner-Cultivatorship in Middle Chile* 1964. 176 pp.

*90. HELVIG, MAGNE. *Chicago's External Truck Movements: Spatial Interaction between the Chicago Area and Its Hinterland* 1964. 132 pp.

*91. HILL, A. DAVID. *The Changing Landscape of a Mexican Municipio, Villa Las Rosas, Chiapas* NAS-NRC Foreign Field Research Program Report No. 26. 1964. 121 pp.

92. SIMMONS, JAMES W. *The Changing Pattern of Retail Location* 1964. 202 pp.

93. WHITE, GILBERT F. *Choice of Adjustment to Floods* 1964. 150 pp.

94. MCMANIS, DOUGLAS R. *The Initial Evaluation and Utilization of the Illinois Prairies, 1815–1840* 1964. 109 pp.

95. PERLE, EUGENE D. *The Demand for Transportation: Regional and Commodity Studies in the United States* 1964. 130 pp.

96. HARRIS, CHAUNCY D. *Annotated World List of Selected Current Geographical Serials in English* 1964. 32 pp. $1.00

97. BOWDEN, LEONARD W. *Diffusion of the Decision To Irrigate: Simulation of the Spread of a New Resource Management Practice in the Colorado Northern High Plains* 1965. 146 pp.

98. KATES, ROBERT W. *Industrial Flood Losses: Damage Estimation in the Lehigh Valley* 1965. 76 pp.

99. RODER, WOLF. *The Sabi Valley Irrigation Projects* 1965. 213 pp.

100. SEWELL, W. R. DERRICK. *Water Management and Floods in the Fraser River Basin* 1965. 163 pp.

101. RAY, D. MICHAEL. *Market Potential and Economic Shadow: A Quantitative Analysis of Industrial Location in Southern Ontario* 1965. 164 pp.

102. AHMAD, QAZI. *Indian Cities: Characteristics and Correlates* 1965. 184 pp.

103. BARNUM, H. GARDINER. *Market Centers and Hinterlands in Baden-Württemberg* 1966. 172 pp.

104. SIMMONS, JAMES W. *Toronto's Changing Retail Complex* 1966. 126 pp.

105. SEWELL, W. R. DERRICK, et al. *Human Dimensions of Weather Modification* 1966. 423 pp.

106. SAARINEN, THOMAS FREDERICK. *Perception of the Drought Hazard on the Great Plains.* 1966. 183 pp.

107. SOLZMAN, DAVID M. *Waterway Industrial Sites: A Chicago Case Study.* 1967. 138 pp.

108. KASPERSON, ROGER E. *The Dodecanese: Diversity and Unity in Island Politics.* 1967

109. LOWENTHAL, DAVID, editor, *Environmental Perception and Behavior.* 1967

110. REED, WALLACE E., *Areal Interaction in India: Commodity Flows of the Bengal-Bihar Industrial Area* 1967

111. BERRY, BRIAN J. L. *Essays on Commodity Flows and the Spatial Structure of the Indian Economy.* 1966. 334 pp.

112. BOURNE, LARRY S. *Private Redevelopment of the Central City, Spatial Processes of Structural Change in the City of Toronto.* 1967. 199 pp.

113. BRUSH, JOHN E., and GAUTHIER, HOWARD L., JR., *Service Centers and Consumer Interaction: Studies in the Philadelphia Metropolitan Fringe* 1967

114. CLARKSON, JAMES D., *The Cultural Ecology of a Chinese Village, Cameron Highlands, Malaysia* 1967

Date D-